Penguin Education

Education Specials
General Editor: Willem van der Eyken

Television and the People
A Programme for Democratic Participation

Brian Groombridge

Television and the People
A Programme for Democratic Participation

Brian Groombridge

Penguin Books

Penguin Books Ltd, Harmondsworth,
Middlesex, England
Penguin Books Inc, 7110 Ambassador Road,
Baltimore, Md 21207, USA
Penguin Books Australia Ltd,
Ringwood, Victoria, Australia

First published 1972
Made and printed in Great Britain by
Hazell Watson & Viney Ltd, Aylesbury, Bucks
Set in Linotype Plantin

Contents

Foreword 7

Acknowledgements 9

Part One **Television and Participation** 11

1 A Mission for the Medium 13
2 Protest and Participation 27
3 Planning for Participation 48
4 Participants or Voyeurs? 67
5 Agenda for Social Action 78

Part Two **Information for Democracy** 85

6 Home and abroad 87
7 Information as Spectacle 105
8 Knowledge is Power 123
9 New Goals and New Values 138

Part Three **Programmes for Participation** 159

10 Alternatives and Precursors 161
11 Foreign Experience 187
12 Mobilizing British Resources for Democracy 219

Notes 242

Index 251

Foreword
Why an Education Special?

My chief subject is obviously television; my theme is television's present and potential role in the creation or frustration of a participatory democracy. Furthermore, a great deal of the book is not about education, and very little of it is about education in any of its most familiar forms. But my publisher has not made some curious category mistake in putting this work out as an Education Special. Television is a major educational force in our society, perhaps the chief one, even though most people do not think of it in that way; the criteria by which I criticize its present performance are, fundamentally, educational criteria, though much of my critique is shared by professional broadcasters who do not think of themselves as educators; and finally my main prescription is for a development of a new kind of educational television, which I believe would have a benign influence on the medium as a whole and would certainly reduce the gap between those who make programmes and those who receive them.

Provisional and eminently corrigible though my answers will be, I know that the questions I ask are of interest not only to educationists, but also to people actively or theoretically concerned – as citizens, politicians, social scientists, or social workers – with the state of British democracy; to broadcasters, especially those working in news and current affairs; to professionals in, and consumers of, other media of communication. Revolutionary readers will distrust my reformism, especially my belief that change must start from where we are and with our present resources; conservatives may see in my modest reforms a threat to their hegemony and privilege. They at least will not be wrong. Participatory democracy is not expected to make life comfortable and untroubled for an elite or smooth for administrators. I hope there is enough substance in my ideas to make them worth improving, and some of them worth trying in practice; and that there is enough energy in the book, whatever its obvious imperfections, to help stimulate the collective effort which is required.

Acknowledgements

I am grateful to the Independent Television Authority for encouraging me to publish this book, even though they cannot be expected to endorse it – not only because it says things with which they might disagree, but also because it raises issues on which the Authority is not even meant to have a view.

The book as a whole owes a great deal to the active interest of four people: Dr Jay Blumler, Director of the Centre for Television Research at the University of Leeds, who helped me to clarify my ideas at the most difficult levels of concept and structure; Jennifer Rogers, who showed the same sensitivity in her reading of the MS. as she conveys, and the same capacity for encouragement as she recommends, in her own *Adults Learning*; Dr Rex Cathcart, the ITA's Regional Officer in Northern Ireland, whose reflections on his experiences there provided a standard against which to test the cogency of some of my arguments; and my wife, Joy Groombridge, to whose insight, support and editorial help I am once again indebted. There are many others, chiefly educationists and broadcasters, here, in Sweden, and elsewhere, whom I would like to thank for help with particular parts of the book, especially Mary Adams, Paul Barnes, Dr Fred Bayliss, Hal Bethel, J. H. Embling, John Gale, Tony Gibson, David Glencross, Pat Hawker, Keith Jackson, Bob Jones, Ken Jones, Rosemary Kavanova, Justin Keating, John King, Keity Klynne, Peter Lewis, Tom Lovett, Rolf Lundgren, Richard Mabey, Arne Okkenhaug, Dr Hans Palmstierna, Bent Pihl, Barbra Salaj and Geoffrey Stuttard. I have had valuable discussions on aspects of the book with participants in seminars at Wansfell College, Dartington Hall, the Television Research Centre, Leeds, and the European Broadcasting Union annual seminar in Basle.

In writing a book of this kind, which attempts to synthesize so many different ideas, one is conscious of the contribution of formative influences over the years. In this respect I would wish to thank or to recall especially six friends – N. B. C. Lucas, a remarkable headmaster who practised democracy at my grammar school thirty years ago; Forrest Alter, the chief librarian from Flint, Michigan, who first fostered my interest in the relevant American traditions; Dr Henry Cassirer, at whose UNESCO conferences some of the seeds were sown; Professor Edward Hutchinson, the chief advocate and theoretician of comprehensive adult education, the late Joe Trenaman, whose research and concern helped provide the essential perceptions on which all subsequent progress in this field has depended; and the late Frank Milligan, who believed in respecting popular culture and popular pleasures as vehicles for popular education.

The librarians at the National Institute of Adult Education and Linda Coles, Librarian of the ITA, have given indispensable help, and I am particularly grateful to my secretary Kate Booth and my friend Viv Morris for spending hours of their spare time in typing the MS.

Part One
Television and Participation

1 A Mission for the Medium

'You might just as well say,' added the March Hare, 'that "I like what I get" is the same thing as "I get what I like".'

Alice in Wonderland

What is television for?

No doubt if Bernard Shaw were still alive he would be stirring up the current debates about television with infuriating brilliance. He would almost certainly adapt one of his old aphorisms for the purpose, the one based on the March Hare's useful distinction, and remind us that if we do not actively try to get what we like, we shall end up liking what we get. Despite the frequency with which worries about television are voiced in Parliament and the press, the public does like what it gets. Their conditioned satisfaction shows in the familiar but amazing fact that watching television continues to hold its place after sleep and work as what most people spend most time doing. It shows also in the research. Only a small minority of the audience displays any anxiety over, for example, the widely publicized problems of sex, violence and bad language on the medium; and when viewers are asked what kinds of programme they would like to see, their preferences always reflect currently popular programmes.[1,2]

There are however significant minorities which do not go along with this general acquiescence, three groups which are more energetically trying to get what they would like. First, there is a section of conscientious and vigilant viewers, notably but not exclusively those connected with the National Viewers and Listeners Association. They are apprehensive about the violent iconography of television and the subversive effects of the values – permissive, anti-family, anti-authority – which they believe the programmes are disseminating, especially through plays and programmes for schools.[3] Secondly, there are politicians: those aware of the wide range of public policy matters due for review when the BBC Charter and the Television Act expire; and those aggrieved by what they take to be the bias and disrespect which infect too many programmes dealing with politics and politicians. And last, there are broadcasters, dissatisfied in different ways with the present constitution, structure or management of the industry, some simply wanting more air time or another channel, others protesting against the weight of bureaucracy which they say stifles their creative talent. Even broadcasters who are not chafing with radicalized discontent are worried that the medium though young, has settled prematurely for routine. These groups are not pushing in the same direction, though there are points of agreement between NVLA and some of the politicians – in that both tend to accuse broadcasters of social irresponsibility, and want them reined. But to satisfy those inside who yearn for more freedom of expression on television would intensify the worries of those outside who want it cleaned up, or tamed, or both.

The organized viewers have an ethical perspective. They want programmes which promote their somewhat theocratic version of Christianity and do not outrage their standards of decency. Broadcasters have a commercial and professional perspective. Some, especially those at management level in the independent companies, want more time; creative personnel want more scope, more freedom. Some at least of the politicians want television to be kinder to politicians. Underlying these positions, thus crudely delineated, are four philosophical tendencies – in turn: neo-calvinist, expansionist, syndicalist, *étatist*.

These are so far the main ingredients in a public debate about television and its future, but none provides an adequate base for that debate and some elements in it are potentially dangerous. The terms of reference of the discussion need expanding and deepening. They can be opened up by posing the simple but complex question: what do we want television for? The development of television needs to be viewed in the light of a multiplicity of personal, social, cultural and political needs which can be diagnosed in late twentieth-century Britain. (The articulate groups which are trying to get what they like seem to have been less concerned with such fundamentals than certain individual critics of the medium, such as Anthony Wedgwood Benn and Raymond Williams.)

Television is the chief means of communication in a society desperate for effective communication. We are not likely to devise constitutions for broadcasting that are apt for our needs, unless we have thought more about what those needs are. And thinking about needs will provide a framework which in turn will prompt creative innovation in the contents of the medium. We are back, really, with Ruskin's wise question. On hearing that a cable had been laid at great expense and with enormous engineering skill, from here to India, he was not impressed. 'And what', he asked, 'do you have to say to India?'

Asking what television is for is to put an elusive and somewhat puzzlingly abstract question. In this book I attempt to make it more concrete and intelligible by providing an answer to it in relation to just one set of needs, a politically basic set. I shall explore the interaction between the future of British television and the future of British democracy, and suggest ways in which the medium might contribute to the improvement of that democracy, by helping it to become more participatory.

Such a concentrated consideration of the relationship between the medium and political participation may seem to produce a distorted model for television, like a figment from some obsessively Fabian imagination, so let me stress that possibilities for the fruitful progress of television can also be discerned from the standpoint of many other ranges of needs.

I have chosen to talk about television in relation to 'external' needs – the social nexus and political framework within which we live out our lives; but it would be just as productive (in answering the 'What is TV for?' question), to look at the medium in relation to 'interior' needs. For example, given that it is part of the essence of our humanity that we lead alternative lives inside our heads, that we inhabit our own imaginations, what does/could television do to nourish or stultify that inner spiritual domain? Such a book would have a good deal more to say about art and entertainment than this one. (It might in some ways turn out to be a parallel book. If it is true, as I shall argue, that too much television journalism is a distraction from the development of social being and action, it could also be true that too much television entertainment is a distraction from the development of an authentic inner being and imaginative life.) Some of the argument in the third part of this chapter (p. 21) is meant to offset the inevitable one-sidedness of my subsequent treatment of the medium.

In transplanting Ruskin's question to the television epoch, we need to think of the analogy of what we have to say to India in relation to the cost of laying the cable. The Conservative Government has decided at least to broach the large political issues of 1976 through an investigation of the technical prospects for broadcasting. The political questions will have to be faced sooner or later – unless engineering convenience is to be the sole criterion – because it will be necessary to choose between the range of technical possibilities in the public interest and to argue about where that interest lies.

But starting at the technical end may at least sober us up by reminding everyone that television is an enormously expensive resource. There is more to it than the notorious cost of the programmes themselves (e.g. one episode of *Callan* costs £25,000, if on tape, or £35,000 if on film; one episode of *The Persuaders* takes £100,000 etc., etc.). These above-the-line sums need to be set against the £59m in which the BBC spent on its entire domestic operation in 1969–70, or against the £16m which the Independent Television Authority had spent since its inception up to 1970 in discharging its statutory responsibility for building a transmitting system (the Authority expects to incur another £25–£30m in the following ten to fifteen years, in addition to the cost of staffing, running and maintaining the system). By mid-1971, the Authority and the companies had invested £30m in converting to colour. It is clear that, as a society, we should be keen to get social and personal value for money.

There is also the social and economic cost of using the airwaves for television. This can be measured quantitatively in terms of hertz or megahertz (one million hertz). To send a telegram, a communications channel occupies only 200 Hz; a telephone circuit requires 3000 Hz; but to send out a high quality television picture with sound takes up eight million hertz (8 MHz). There is only one spectrum with a physical limit to the range of suitable frequencies. A society which invests in one television channel transmitting sound and vision in one direction, may have to do without a thousand two-way telephone links or 40,000 teleprinters. Just as earth and water have to be conserved and their uses properly considered, so do radio waves.

Hence the debates about broadcasting are really important – do we want more of it? How should it be controlled (managed, or made more accountable)? What purposes should it serve? How should its programming be developed?

But it is anomalous not to relate these debates to the still larger debate about the future of democracy, as one way of facing the question of purposes for the medium. The functioning of all modern states depends upon their communications resources and modalities. States which purport to be democracies need to be specially sensitive to the connection between their viability and their use of the media. The position I adopt and elaborate in the rest of this book can be summarized in five bare propositions:

1. Representative democracy is unlikely to persist for long in its present instability: it must move forward into participatory democracy, lest it degenerate into some kind of autocracy, which could be bland and manipulative, but might well be brutish and tyrannical.

2. The fundamental questions about television are therefore not about bandwidth, nor even about management; they are – how can television help usher in and give expression to participatory democracy?; to what extent will television as we know it in Britain today ease or hamper the transition?

3. It will be necessary to devise new kinds of programmes, in new relations with the audience and other institutions including other media of communication.

4. Fortunately relevant experience is already being accumulated throughout the world in a species of broadcasting regarded by many professional broadcasters as an aberrant, almost treasonous, form – educational television.

5. By helping to create a participatory democracy, television

itself – constitution and control as well as programmes – will change and develop, finding a release from premature middle age.

As will appear, many doubts and problems are raised by this proposed new mission for the medium, but there are two which need facing at the outset, since they concern the two major terms in the relationship – television and participatory democracy. As to television, is it not intrinsically too lightweight, superficial, ephemeral, fly-by-night a medium to sustain the earnest burden of social responsibility which even these five bare propositions seem to lay upon it? I shall sketch an answer to that question in the rest of this chapter and, in more specific detail, in Parts Two and Three (chapters 6–12). As to participatory democracy: is not the phrase itself a transitory enthusiasm of the media, of dubious value as a serious political concept? In effect the rest of Part One is devoted to this question and to a justification of the concept. The answer to the large doubt about television is provided by the way it is evolving and by its positive achievement to date.

Television's capacity for its new mission

Most people think of television as a fun medium – for entertainment and relaxation, a more convenient alternative to the old social custom of going out to the cinema, a form of vicarious sociability. 'After a hard day's work', people say, 'I just want to put my feet up. I don't want to be educated. So I watch television.' This popular view is shared by many of those whose professional business it is to watch television and write about it. The *Daily Mail* critic Peter Black, for example, though he treats it seriously enough in his reviews does not regard it fundamentally as a serious medium. In a reflective piece in the *Listener* he concluded: 'The trouble is that television is basically a frivolous medium.'[4] For Milton Shulman, this frivolity is not intrinsic: it is the result of conscious decisions, even though those ultimately responsible are not always pleased by the results:

Politicians have insisted that TV be primarily an entertainment medium. The methods by which it is financed makes it impossible for it to be anything else.

Politicians, catering to the entertainment medium they have created, insist on being popular bit-part actors in this electronic spectacular.

They turn up on chat shows, giggle away with comics and starlets, run election campaigns that belittle the issues, produce Party political programmes modelled on quiz shows and detergent commercials.

Having created an undignified medium they should not be surprised if from time to time they cut an undignified picture when they appear on it. If they insist on being part of the showbiz scene, they must not be surprised if they receive an occasional custard pie in the face.[5]

In later chapters I shall elaborate some of those very same criticisms. At this point, however, they need putting into perspective. Out of a better proportioned judgement on television arises a confidence that it is capable of assuming the demanding political responsibilities which a more participatory democracy would impose on it.

Television was not set up merely to be a fun medium, nor is that an adequate summary of its present role and performance. The BBC Charter and the Television Act both require broadcasters to educate and inform the public as well as entertain it. Two assessments are valid: that to a remarkable degree the broadcasters successfully carry out this threefold requirement (often simultaneously in the same programmes); and that as the medium and its public mature, there is a change in emphasis within those three global objectives. This evolution was remarked on by Sir Robert Fraser, the first Director-General of the ITA, when he retired. Surveying fifteen years' development of British television, Sir Robert pointed up the contrast between television in 1955 and in 1970, the year of his retirement. In 1955,

Television ... was a medium of entertainment, almost pure and simple. That was true of BBC television as it was of us. I am not now speaking of the cultural level of the entertainment provided. It might have been at the level of Covent Garden or the Festival Hall or the Old Vic, or it might have been at the cultural level of the Palladium or the chain cinema or Wembley. Whichever it was, concert hall or music hall, opera house or race course, it was entertainment. ... News and current affairs and other forms of information were embryonic. ...

Now the interesting thing to notice is that in the world in general the media of entertainment and of information are quite separately and independently organized. On the one side are the theatres and cinemas and music and concert halls and sports grounds, and that's where you go if it is entertainment you are seeking. On the other side are the newspapers and the periodicals and the lecture halls and even the universities and schools: all kinds of information, not just political information, current affairs and world affairs.

The most striking and absorbing change in television in the last ten years, or even in less, is that it has grown into a great medium of information; that it is now two things in one; that there has grown up within it this second medium, and more than that: it is not only the largest medium of popular entertainment, it is also the largest medium of popular information. It is theatre and newspaper in one.[6]

Since a medium of information has, as Fraser puts it, grown up within the first medium of entertainment, without at all alienating or losing touch with its better educated, increasingly sophisticated audience, there is no reason to suppose that a third medium of education will not mature within the first two.

To an extraordinary degree it has already done so. Television, through its general output (not just through its capital E Educational programmes), is now the chief agency of adult education in this country and a principal educational influence on the entire population. From this point of view, television passes the severest test that educational philosophy can devise – it is not merely an educator, it is also in large measure a liberal educator. This is not the place to penetrate the semantic mists which swirl round the distinctions between, say, instructing, training, informing, educating and liberally educating, but most educationists would recognize that liberal education represents the apex of educational goals. Education may imply merely the transmission of a body of knowledge or socially useful skills; liberal education lays emphasis on the fullest possible development of the individual, stressing the importance of imaginative experience as against the cognitive, and of the realm of values as against intellectual contents and practical techniques. Educationists prone to adopt a stance of prophylactic resistance to television might consider the case that follows, and even to wonder which – at this liberal level – does more educational *harm* – the frivolous fun medium or the arid activities of conventional secondary schools, technical colleges, and most institutions of higher education.

Television the liberal educator

Television's power as an educator is best demonstrated by one crucial comparison: between what most children know now before they go to primary school and what they knew at the same age before there was television.

Towards the end of the nineteenth century, the boy Stephen Dedalus wrote in the fly leaf of his geography book:

Stephen Dedalus
Class of Elements
Clongowes Wood College
Sallins
County Kildare
Ireland
Europe
The World
The Universe

Half a century later I was doing the same as James Joyce's hero; and today small children still play the cosmological address game. It was a game then which enabled a child to express and enjoy his mastery of information acquired gradually, perhaps with difficulty, and his wonder of being an inhabitant of such an unimaginably vast geographical complex. Children today absorb this information and perspective almost without noticing it. The address game helps them marshal their awareness.

The reception class in the infant school will have been part of that audience of 600 million people all over the world that watched Aldrin and Armstrong set foot for the first time on the moon. A child of four or five may still have some difficulty knowing whether or not England is part of his home town, but without effort, he knows that England is in some way a distinct entity from Western Germany, Italy and Brazil – just from watching the World Cup on television. So for all of us, television has destroyed most of those monopolies in experience which are based on location (one of the few happening to be in the right place) or on privilege, or both. Shulman, in a more enthusiastic mood, caught the spirit when writing a few days after the successful moon-landing of Apollo 11:

There were no privileged guests or spectators at this unique moment in man's existence. It was shared at exactly the same moment by monarchs, dictators, heads of state and tycoons – no matter how rich or powerful – with the humble mechanic in Tokyo and the poorest Mexican grape-picker in California.[7]

As we watch – small children and adults alike – a man long-jump twenty-nine feet in the Olympic Games; as we watch tennis at Wimbledon; or American troops withdraw from Cambodia; or babies die in Biafra and Bihar; or Klemperer conduct the Eroica symphony, we either know the kind of matters that previous generations did not know at all, or only *knew about*, through reading descriptions of events. Small children used to be ignorant; they are ignorant no longer.

Creating this admittedly diffuse awareness is a function of liberal education, because liberal education has to do with providing frames of reference, making people aware of what lies beyond their own milieu, outside their own knowledge, their own specialism; with making us all conscious of possibilities, conscious of possible choices and options either for ourselves personally, our society or the human species as a whole.

Television liberally educates because it is an ecumenical medium – not that it makes us love one another nor necessarily that we even understand one another better, but in the sense that it presents us to each other with a greater disposition to treat us all as of equal worth than any other medium. Thus through television we are faced by alternative life-styles, cultures and mores, based on differences of class, race, generation and sub-culture. (One reason why some viewers find television disturbing may be precisely because it brings people into the sitting room, with their dirty habits and foul mouths, whom it used to be possible to ignore when they were safely herded away at a distance from 'better-class' districts.)

Television liberally educates because it provides a rich diet of imaginative experience, most successfully and consistently through drama. For most people theatres were and are geographically inaccessible, socially alien. Cinema and radio began to democratize experience of drama; television has provided universal access to it and at an astonishingly high level. (Before the post-war revival promoted by such dissimilar institutions as the

Mercury Theatre and the Royal Court, the West End theatre was effete and most British drama artistically worthless.) The audience even for slot-filling series and serials (*Z Cars*; *Softly Softly*; *Manhunt*) is an audience for well written, well acted, well produced plays. (What routine pre-war West End play would have accommodated a character as complex, in acting and writing, as Robert Hardy's Sergeant Graz from *Manhunt*?) Television has raised the standards of drama as a whole and brought a huge comprehensive audience with it, making obsolete the former divisions which stratified the public into high-, middle- and low-brows.[8] The paperback sales of *The Forsyte Saga*, the endless queues at the Victoria and Albert and other museums to see the costumes for *The Six Wives of Henry VIII* showed that viewers are caught, held and moved.

People habitually say that television is a visual medium. This truism may however distract attention from the status which television has given to the spoken word. Before television showed it the way, the spoken word on radio was scripted; it was prose of a special kind written to be read aloud. Television has established the public use of oral speech. In drawing its material – actual and imaginative – 'ecumenically' from a variety of cultures, television has done something of immense social and educational significance: it has asserted the validity and acceptability of a wide range of accents, dialects and idioms. It has almost entirely subverted the idea that authority, authoritativeness, 'correctness' go with standard English or received pronunciation. The change which this represents in the media may be gauged by looking back a mere fourteen years or so, to the publication of Lindsay Anderson's angry denunciation of the class-ridden and puny British cinema of the day, in which he wrote:

A young actor with a regional or a Cockney accent had better lose it quick – for with it he will never be able to wear gold braid round his sleeve – and then where are his chances of stardom?[9]

The artistic revolution which makes that observation so incredibly dated was accomplished by the theatre – recruiting writers from a wider range of social backgrounds, and by the cinema – the unexpected success of Karel Reisz's *Saturday Night and Sunday Morning* in 1960 was a watershed. That revolution was established as a universal feature of our cultural life by television, the first medium which could not afford to be snobbish. Television's use and acceptance of varieties of English as they are spoken is of enormous educational importance. Insistence on 'correct' speech has been one of the most insidious ways in which the education system has hitherto accomplished its repressive task of social segregation. It has been a chief function of schools to cream off an elite to run the country and its institutions and to discourage the majority destined for subjugation. Television has countered that systematic demoralization by treating the way people actually speak with respect. Meanwhile, academic linguists have undermined the old dominative rationale, substituting for it a socially neutral analysis of language in terms of effective communication, in which different 'registers' and vocabularies are used according to task and milieu. Their work is at last percolating through to the schools. Academic theory and the practice of the schools will now consciously begin to reinforce the profound change in attitudes and self-attitudes to public speech unconsciously brought about by television. It is arguably one of the most important educational by-products of the rapport which the medium has had to establish with its audience.

The significance of television as a liberal educator is by no means exhausted by these examples of its influence. There is at least one other which ought to be mentioned: its ability to help us distinguish the sin from the sinner. Ability to make this theological differentiation is one of the objectives of liberal education. Through television there is a widespread awareness that a man can be sincere but mistaken; he can voice our own view yet be unpleasant; he can be an opponent and nevertheless a man of integrity. It is on awareness of such distinctions that the democratic virtues of tolerance and understanding are founded.

The point of evaluating television in these terms, considering it not merely as an instrument of entertainment and information, but also as a vehicle for some of the values rated most highly in the canon of educational philosophy, is to appraise its viability for a role of major social importance. I conclude that television is fully capable, though not yet ready, for such a role. Some of the weaknesses that need to be overcome will be treated in detail in later sections, but they may be prepared for by acknowledging that, judged as a liberal educator, television has some major failings. One of the most important functions of liberal education is to enable men and women to consider critically the dogmas by which they live their lives, to discover what their values are, to test their adequacy and measure them against alternatives. It seems to me doubtful whether television is particularly effective at this level.

It may be unreasonable to expect more. It may be pointed out, first, that the socially necessary work of maintaining an ongoing critique of values, the licensed subversion needed to prevent moral as well as intellectual and technical stagnation, is so difficult and demanding that it is a specialized task (albeit an often neglected one) of institutions of higher and adult education. It is a task which requires dedication, concentration and specialization, and hence it is quite unreasonable to expect much of a contribution towards it from a medium which is also meant to excel at journalism and entertainment.

It may be pointed out, secondly, that the broadcasting media are in this respect unusual and that by comparison, most newspapers and magazines are hardly ever liberal educators – they must cater continuously to the prejudices of their readers if they are to survive.

Nevertheless, I shall argue that television is nowhere near the limit of its effectiveness, even in this area, since some of its deficiencies are due not to inherent characteristics, but to conventions, at policy level (especially the convention of neutrality) or at programme level (trivializing formats, for example), which are patently remediable.

In discussing a new mission for television, we are not talking about car stickers or posters in the underground. We are talking about a dominant and polymorphous means of communication, already possessing the cultural weight or specific gravity to be considered as candidate for a major part in the civilizing of our arid communal existence and in the improvement and enlivenment of our democracy, such that more people may have the opportunity, the aptitude, the incentive and the desire, to play an active personal part in what is with unconscious irony called 'public life'.

I must now turn to the second term in the relationship between television and participatory democracy. Having found that
prima facie television may be taken seriously as an instrument of
social and cultural significance, what of 'participatory democracy'? Is it merely a catch phrase? Or, more sinisterly, a
'Catch-22' phrase, disguising more sophisticated oligarchic
manipulation? Or a concept urgently needing implementation
for the sake of democracy's future and the happiness of the
people?

2 Protest and Participation

Perceptions of change

At three in the morning on 12 July 1971, a Welsh Congrega-
tionalist minister and a student from Cardiff started to climb up
the BBC's 520-foot-high television mast at Blaenplwyf, near
Aberystwyth. They climbed to about half way up, not high
enough to be burned or killed by radiation from the aerials, but
high enough, they thought, to prevent the BBC switching on.
They sang to each other for hours so that they should not fall
asleep and drop off the mast. They were members of the Welsh
Language Society. At the same time, seven other members of the
Society had climbed five more television masts (BBC and
ITA) in Wales (or tried to – the police frustrated the attempt at
Nebo in Caernarvonshire). Their aim was to disrupt broadcast-
ing for the day as a protest against the further Anglicization of
Wales which they feared the dominance of English-language
programmes was causing.

At half past one in the afternoon on 12 July the police persuaded the Rev. Elfed Lewis and Philip Wyn Davies to come off
the Blaenplwyf mast. They were unhurt. No doubt they would
have dared more. There are always some prepared to risk everything for a great cause in which they passionately believe. When,
many years before, Emily Wilding Davies had employed a similarly dramatic tactic of protest, she was killed. She had decided
to risk her life and to spoil the Derby by throwing herself in the
path of the King's horse. The year was 1913. Other members of
her protest group had squatted on the doorsteps of cabinet ministers, slashed pictures in public galleries, cut telegraph wires, and,
as everyone knows – taught by archive film on television rather
than by history books – chained themselves to the railings of
Downing Street. Two had themselves delivered to politicians as

postal packets. Others set fire to empty houses, poured acid into pillar boxes and planted home-made bombs.

The militant suffragettes knew what they wanted from society: the vote, the right to participate through enfranchisement and representation in the public business of the society from which they were excluded.

The Welsh Language Society knew what it wanted from television: more programmes in Welsh, fewer in English. The Society acted as a pressure group using constitutional methods and illegal ones. (Only a short time before the assault on the masts and a subsequent attempt to break into the BBC's Bristol studios, the Society had sent a not unpersuasive deputation to the ITA's Welsh Committee.)

The Welsh Language Society is obviously only one of many militant protest groups, and television itself only one of the many 'target' institutions, which could have been chosen to illustrate an important phenomenon of the 1960s and 1970s – the tactics used by the suffragettes, reformist and militant, to secure an extension of representative democracy are now being used because of a widespread discontent with and lack of confidence in representative democracy, which is felt not just to be inadequate but often irrelevant or even in itself a source of frustration and repression. Women's Lib. is one of many symptomatic examples, highly significant even though it does not command the active support of most women any more than the militant suffragettes did. The fundamental issue was seen, among others, by E. M. Forster. Writing between 1908–10, he created this conversation at a luncheon party thrown by Margaret Schlegel, the heroine of *Howards End*, for Mrs Wilcox, coming from an older generation. Mrs Wilcox speaks first:

'I sometimes think that it is wiser to leave action and discussion to men.'

There was a little silence.

'One admits that the arguments against the suffrage *are* extraordinarily strong,' said a girl opposite, leaning forward and crumbling her bread.

'Are they? I never follow any arguments. I am only too thankful not to have a vote myself.'

'We didn't mean the vote, though, did we?' supplied Margaret.

'Aren't we differing on something much wider, Mrs Wilcox? Whether women are to remain what they have been since the dawn of history; or whether, since men have moved forward so far, they too may move forward a little now. I say they may. I would even admit a biological change.' [1]

At the level of society as a whole, and on an international scale, women, blacks, even the young, are seeking ways to 'move forward', the historical pace having been set for too long by aggressive, white, adult males; they often want to break through the integument of the existing structures of social organization, of which representative democracy is a part. At the level of the institutions within each society, an increasing number of people are disposed to resist being oppressed in their relations with any particular institution – town council, school, hospital board, factory. This also calls into question the adequacy of representative democracy and promotes the clamour for 'participation'. Men and women of all sorts of different political persuasions assent to the Young Fabian verdict that 'The battle for democracy in the nineteenth century was over the franchise. Today it should extend to every centre of power in society.' [2]

In this chapter I shall indicate some of the sources of disenchantment and the origins of the push towards greater participation. Against that background, the chapter that follows will attempt a definition and a rationale of participatory democracy. These two chapters taken together will in turn provide the background for an assessment of television's role in relation to the historical shift described (Part Two) and for recommendations about the way it should be used in the future (Parts Two and Three).

The story starts just after the Second World War, but before embarking on it, there is one further point of contemporary relevance which comes out of the suffragette reference, a theoretical clarification of considerable practical significance: the suffragettes sought representation as a *means* of participation, which implies that representation and participation must not be conceived antithetically. It is unhistorical to see them so. 'Representative democracy' describes existing constitutional structures. 'Participatory democracy' prescribes changes that are needed to protect the spirit and the reality of democracy when it is in danger of settling for the mere letter and ritual of its constitution. To talk of participation is to press for regeneration, to want to revitalize and extend the reach of processes which are becoming ossified through outward forms which are no longer adequate or appropriate. Today's 'participators' are tomorrow's 'representatives', and it was always so. Today's representative structure includes the Labour Party and the trade unions, but when these bodies were being created, their founders were fighting to make Parliamentary democracy and an authoritarian economy more participatory.

One has to look at the concepts of 'representation' and 'participation' more concretely and dynamically. We are not dealing here with acts in a well-made play, the chaos of Act II yielding tidily to the denouement of Act III; we are in the midst of a *process*, and a laminated process at that, with society carrying the different layers of its past and present unevenly into a perpetually unresolved future.

Looking back over the past fifteen to twenty years of that process there seem to be at least six major reasons why doubts about representative democracy have arisen, accompanied by demands for greater participation – 'a climatic change in our society' in which 'The "deferential" society may be giving way to an "assertive" society'.[3] These reasons may be summed up as so many 'experiences', 'awarenesses', 'perceptions', not all unanimously shared by the public; on the contrary, many of them comprising highly controversial specifics, but all contributing to this climatic change:

1. A primitive perception of continuing oligarchy.
2. A perception of the oligarchy's stupidity and dangerousness.
3. A perception of a more sophisticated model of the oligarchy's composition.
4. An awareness of the complexity and remoteness of contemporary decision making.
5. A heightened awareness of the individual-versus-society dichotomy intrinsic to urban life and a highly industrialized economy.
6. Experience both of demonstration and of constructive participatory action, leading in turn to more confidence in and demand for participation.

Looking back to anger

Nobody ever supposed that British democracy was a perfect thing, even while it was being defended against Hitler's Germany. Compared with Nazism, however, which had quite obliterated freedom, abnegated the Rule of Law, and harnessed technology for a reign of genocidal terror, it was in fact a way of life manifestly worth defending. But when the euphoria of wartime national unity had quite evaporated (morale weakened by the inevitable persistence of material austerity and sacrifice after the justification for it had disappeared, alarm and despondency spread by the obscene risks implied by the cold war), a surge of impatience arose in Britain.

'Anger' became a symbolic word for the new mood. It was largely a negative mood, expressing hostility towards the discovery that the old oligarchy seemed to sit as securely as ever, at the apex of our democracy. There was a strong revival of anti-ruling class feeling. It was in 1955 that Henry Fairlie first used the word 'Establishment' as a shorthand for ruling class – the word is active still.[4]

In 1956, John Osborne's most negative anti-hero Jimmy Porter captured the imagination of the young by being virtually a dropout (graduate turned market stallholder) and by venting his eloquent spleen against the upper classes:

Have you even seen her brother? Brother Nigel? The straight-backed chinless wonder from Sandhurst? ... Well, you've never heard so many well-bred commonplaces come from beneath the same bowler hat. The platitude from outer space – that's brother Nigel. He'll end up in the Cabinet one day, make no mistake. But somewhere at the back of his mind is the vague knowledge that he and his pals have been plundering and fooling everybody for generations.[5]

A year later, in a collection of anti-Establishment essays called *Declaration*, Osborne spoke in his own name:

I can't go on laughing at the idiocies of the people who rule our lives. We have been laughing at their gay little madnesses, my dear, at their point-to-points, at the postural slump of the well off and mentally under-privileged, at their stooping shoulders and strained accents, at their waffling cant, for too long. They are no longer funny, because they are not merely dangerous, they are murderous.[6]

John Osborne was writing a few days after the Christmas Island explosion which led the *Daily Express* to cheer: 'It's our H-Bomb'.

The fact that the commercially successful *Daily Express* could cheer is a reminder that, as I have said, the attitudes whose course I am indicating, were never, in the large, or in detail, universal. Nevertheless, dangerously stupid though the country's rulers did seem to be, with their Palmerstonian excursions to Suez, for example, Britain kept on laughing at them even if John Osborne could not. In a sense we could afford to, since the culpability award had clearly passed to the rulers of two other countries. Britain giggled partly because an imperial burden of responsibility and guilt had been shed. The Goon Show purged and exorcized the past – transmuting patriotic symbols, stiff-upper-lip heroics, even the dread noises of explosions, into the elements of the craziest fantasy world ever conjured up on radio. The Union Jack became a decoration for cheap tin trays in Carnaby Street. The spirit of the decade has been admirably captured by Antony Jay, whose name began at the end of the period he describes to appear in the credits for new kinds of television journalism and satire:

As the thaw came in the middle fifties, we gradually found that authority could be questioned and challenged, and the harder we looked, the more suspicious it all became. Authority in the Ministry of Defence couldn't keep its military secrets; authority in industry was losing ground rapidly to the Germans and the Japanese; authority in the law was sending innocent men to the gallows; authority in the police was beating up peaceful demonstrators; authority in morals was prosecuting *Lady Chatterley*; authority in domestic politics was building Blue Streak and authority in foreign affairs conducted that smash-and-grab raid at Suez which was all smash and no grab. For about six years authority took an almighty beating. It was forced into retreat on every front until finally with *That Was The Week* in 1962 and the Profumo scandal in 1963, it even stopped believing in itself.[7]

Authority remained authority, none the less, but with its aura diminished and not subsequently restored (those who took Tories seriously found plenty to knock when Labour was in power—no administration has proved competent in the management of the economy). More important, for the health and maturity of democracy, the self-confidence of the people, though still at a low level and still unevenly distributed, began to establish itself and to increase. The extent to which people are both assertive and constructive is a consequence of this shift of confidence power. The necessary demolition work on the attitudes and taboos which sustained the old order, like dusty caryatids propping up a Victorian museum, was done by writers and their iconoclasm was widely backed up by irreverent talents on the radio and television.

These artists who, from a wide variety of viewpoints, complained of the sterility of English life, and especially those who, like Osborne, raised the cry of Down the Ruling Classes might have accomplished even more, but they suffered from ordeal by journalistic stereotype. This is one way in which the media frequently, as a by-product of pursuing their own commercial ends, inoculate the body politic against any virus which seems likely to do much harm to privilege and the *status quo*. These highly dissimilar writers were glibly labelled Angry Young Men. There were at the time many who feared that such journalistic packaging would emasculate what these writers were about. Tom Maschler was one:

The phrase 'Angry Young Men' . . . has been employed to group, without so much as an attempt at understanding, all those sharing a certain indignation against the apathy, the complacency, the idealistic bankruptcy of their environment. Thus the writers who have set themselves the task of waking us up have been rendered harmless in the AYM cage.[8]

There was something in the fear. The writers mellowed; the ruling classes widened their ranks to let in a handful of ex-grammar school boys; younger siblings of Alison and Nigel helped make Britain a gayer, if more escapist place, by opening boutiques in the King's Road, and many others of their generation from all classes felt the whole business of class was a boring irrelevance.

Crude though their diagnoses might have been – and Jimmy Porter's attitude is, after all, little more than inverted snobbery and class hatred rendered particularly splenetic by hypergamy; and crude though the AYM label undoubtedly was (indiscriminately lumping Amis and Osborne together with, say, Colin Wilson) – these writers had done something of great social importance.

They had made talk possible again. After the war Britain seemed to pass through a period like that Victorian England evoked by Virginia Woolf in *Orlando*. The country was as though confined and muffled within a clamp filled with soot. But now, actors could speak like people, and people could say what they meant and felt in public. Malcolm Muggeridge could dare to ask in the *New Statesman* whether it was necessary to render to the Queen homage of a kind which was indistinguishable from that paid to God himself. Nothing was taken for granted. They railed against stuffiness, and England went gay; they thundered against apathy, and young England marched; they attacked oligarchy, and in ten years the Establishment itself or a section of it, began to use the emollient jargon of 'participation'. By shouting rude words at the snow, they started an avalanche. The world is now teeming with angry young men, and their anxious elders are either liberalizing constitutions or getting out the tear gas and the truncheons.

Politics in the streets

Nevertheless, the best publicized writers and artists at this stage were not doing much more than clearing the ideological air. There were others, contributors to *Universities and Left Review* (which also started in 1957 the year of *Declaration*), and to the follow-up volume to *Declaration* (*Conviction*, 1958), who were rethinking Marxism and Fabianism in an attempt to improve social policies and the political theories on which they should be based. Their work later had its influence on the propaganda and to some extent the policies of Labour administration. The Bow Group had started even earlier, in 1951, with similar objectives but related to right-wing philosophies, but the group became more public in 1957, with the publication of *Crossbow*. The concept of a Conservative intellectual had ceased to be a contradiction in terms.

The attack on authority, the beginnings of popular self-confidence, were psychological path-clearing operations, preparing the way for attempts at using action to offset the ossification of representative democracy, flawed as that was by the persistence of oligarchy. In general, the action was to take two forms – militant or at least extra-Parliamentary protest and the constructive creation of new institutions as channels of political pressure.

Osborne's Jimmy Porter, in the most famous of his diatribes, had complained:

There aren't any good, brave causes left. If the big bang does come, and we all get killed off, it won't be in aid of the old-fashioned, grand design. It'll just be for the Brave-New-nothing-very-much-thank-you.[9]

The good cause was under his nose; why not try to stop the big bang happening at all? The first Aldermaston march took place in 1958.

The Aldermaston Marches advanced the process of redefining democracy. Historians will continue to argue about what effect they had, if any, on governments, but as a contribution to the gradual articulation of the participatory ideal, they were important in at least two ways.

1. Popular influence over foreign policy has always presented severe problems for democratic theory and practice. The intrinsic secrecy and secretiveness affecting this area of government makes it the least susceptible to democratic control. The marchers were using a crude weapon against the most impregnable citadel, but it soon became apparent that the method, though chancelleries may seem impervious to it, works more convincingly against lesser ministries and local authorities.

2. The marches were not only demonstrations against the Bomb. They were also demonstrations of demonstration, as a political technique, and one peculiarly suited to the television age. Petitions and letters to MPs, however numerous and passionate, compare poorly, from the camera's point of view, with a long line of colourful protesters, waving their banners, singing their songs, and pushing their prams. The marchers were teaching everyone to say to those with power: we the governed are affected by everything you do and decide. We are not remote correlates to your statistics, we are people, and these are our children. We are here and we will not go away until you listen to us.

Despite the disappointments and disillusionments that followed the Aldermaston marches, in terms of their effect on policy, the impatient protesters who went on them did add to the repertoire of democratic instrumentalities. This was not at the time an obvious and predictable outcome, as may be seen by referring back to the last section of Raymond Williams's major work on the development of democracy, *The Long Revolution,* which was first published in 1961 [10] Williams speculates about 'Britain in the 1960s', and says this, in a passage which describes the consensus of feeling at the time (though it clearly does not at all reflect his own personal judgement of the political situation):

As we enter the 1960s, the effective historical patterns of British Society seem reasonably clear. . . . It is generally assumed that the democratic process has been essentially completed, with parliamentary and local government solidly established on universal suffrage, and with the class system apparently breaking up.

Yet the decade following the publication of *The Long Revolution* was a decade in which that revolution was confusedly continued, a decade of impatience with the inadequacies of representative democracy – when farmers marched as well as students; when the demonstration, often violent, became a normal form of political action; when those in charge of schools and hospitals, found that parents and patients could be militant, insisting on explanation, demanding a say.

Constructive participation

It would be quite one-sided, however, to identify the continuous growth in pressure for participation solely with militant political and economic behaviour. The right to participate is not only won by forcing those with power to listen, pressing for more sensitive policies or for constitutional changes in institutions *which already exist*. It is also exercised by creating new institutions, new channels through which to achieve results outside the established structures. 1957 was not only the year of *Declaration* and *Universities and Left Review*, the year before Aldermaston 1. It was also the year when Michael Young started Consumers' Association. Although the success of this organization depends in large degree on the determination of relatively affluent consumers not to be sold short by shopkeepers, this apparently egocentric, materialistic concern unexpectedly turned out to be just as significant for the growth of participatory democracy as the marches and demos. Consequently there are three reasons why it is also featured here:

1. It was an attempt to make a major sector of our economy as good as its word. The theory is summed up in the best-known statement in Adam Smith's otherwise unread classic *The Wealth of Nations*:

Consumption is the sole end and purpose of all production; and the interest of the producer ought to be attended to only so far as it may be necessary for promoting that of the consumer.

It was not anything like the naïve proposition then (1775) that it seems now. To us it rings as hollowly as that old retail cant about the customer being always right or the more recent adman's cant about the consumer as king. But 1775 was also a year when industrialist Mathew Boulton went into partnership with scientist James Watt; Britain was all set to become the workshop of the world and increases in productive capacity could hardly help but make life better for consumers. No one's goodwill had to be involved. As Smith said: 'It is not from the benevolence of the butcher, the brewer or the baker, that we expect our dinner, but from their regard to their own interest.'

The system (mutual benefit shaped by Smith's 'invisible hand' out of the unregulated self-interest of one and all) did not work out so idyllically. It had been found necessary in the Middle Ages to deal harshly with delinquent brewers and bakers –

If a Baker or a Brewer be convict, because he hath not observed the Assize of Bread and Ale, ... if the offence be grievous and often, and will not be corrected, then he shall suffer Punishment of the Body, that is to wit, a Baker to the Pillory and a Brewer to the Tumbrel.

Through the last century, new and more appropriate laws were created to protect us all from the disastrous effects of uncontrolled trading, culminating in the Sale of Goods Act 1893.

And of course the process continues still. It is astonishing to realize that it was as recently as 1932 that the House of Lords decided by a narrow majority that manufacturers of products owe 'a duty to the consumer to take ... reasonable care'. The Law does not permit manufacturers to harm us. It now prevents them, and retailers, from misleading us. It can hardly be expected to see that they do us good. It is not illegal to make a handsome profit by the successful marketing of inferior goods. And the law unavoidably drags behind technological and social change. Today the manufacturer may persist in profitable business not because the consumers are satisfied, but because enough consumers are indifferent; the consumer, on whose godlike percipience Smith's self-regulating economy would now depend, is baffled by the technological complexity of many products, increasingly isolated from advice through super-marketing and the ignorance of retail sales staff, and hence increasingly dependent for guidance on advertising agents and other partisans. David Ogilvy's father spoke for most of us when he said: 'They speak well of it in the advertisements.[11]

The successful establishment of Consumers' Association and its direct aftermath (local consumer groups, the albeit short-lived Consumer Council, major improvements in legislation, a new form of outspoken brand-naming consumer journalism) are the expression of a consumer militancy exerting pressure on the system to bring the facts more in line with the ideology of consumer supremacy.

The movement differs in purpose from most market research. Market research looks democratic in that it involves consulting representative samples of consumers about their tastes, wants and lifestyle, so that producers may gear their efforts more closely to consumer needs. But market research, like advertising, is an aspect of the management of demand, ideally the control and manipulation of demand, on which contemporary consumer capitalism depends. Setting up the Consumers' Association, to represent consumers in opposition to producers (who include trade unionists *and* manufacturers), was similar in principle to founding trade unions in opposition to manufacturers. The successful challenge to the law of libel, which was dared in the first issue of *Which?* and the subsequent continuous vigilance both of Consumers' Association and of independent consumer journalists have led manufacturers not to reach for their writs but to improve their quality control. The movement which, after nearly fifteen years is still best typified by Consumers' Association, stands for a genuinely democratic principle of accountability and in a sense supervision by the consumers on whose behalf the economic enterprise is in the end supposed to be organized.

2. The example of Consumers' Association helped encourage a range of analogous organizations working in other fields. If the products of privately owned consumer industries could be publicly scrutinized, then *a fortiori* it was legitimate to organize critical pressure groups exercising public vigilance over public services. Hospitals and schools, for example, are already subject to democratic control through elected representatives of the people. In practice, the social services have become bureaucratized in the pejorative sense as well as in the sociologists'. Their administration has often seemed inadequate, even indifferent to the needs of the very people for whom they are designed. Consequently, organizations have been set up to achieve reform in the state schools, in hospitals, in housing and environmental planning and other aspects of social life in which the conventional forms of representative democracy have proved wholly inadequate. People will not be reconciled to a 'take it or leave it' attitude by bureaucracy. They demand a more direct say in what is done in their name and on their behalf.

One of the most successful exemplars of these new agencies of participation are the Associations for the Advancement of State Education, which, together with the Advisory Centre for Education, the National Federation of Parent–Teachers' Associations and other bodies, have organized the voice of parents in the debate on the educational system and even in its day to day running, all this at the very time when educational psychologists have identified the home–school interface as crucial to child development. These new voluntary institutions are characteristically specialist in their aims, professional in the level of their work, and, most significant of all, they promote political change outside one of the principal components of representative democracy – the competition between political parties for electoral support.

3. The Council of Consumers' Association has always sought to overcome one of the movement's main weaknesses: those who benefit most directly from its activities (especially the magazines *Which?* and *Money Which?*) are the most prosperous and the best educated. The experimental consumer clinic in the working-class high street of Kentish Town is the latest in a series of efforts to democratize by sharing the power and the findings of CA. It is to be followed by a television series, in collaboration with ATV, designed to reach and help those who are too poor to find *Money Which?* appropriate. It is undoubtedly sound for CA's conscience to be troubled over the upper-middle-class bias of its supporters. In a society in which severe poverty persists, it is at best trivial, at worst obscene, to hear members of consumer groups agonizing about which deep freeze to buy.

On the other hand, from the perspective of a developing participatory society and the devolution of political power, it is of considerable significance that the new wave of voluntary organizations is dominated by well-educated people. Apart from the fact that from their socially concerned activities, the whole population benefits, these movements are important because they demonstrate that reforms in the provision of education have now narrowed the education gap between government and governed. It is no longer true, and people know that it is no longer true, that all the best brains are to be found in government and the civil service. The new middle classes are conscious of an equality with those who run the political apparatus. The spread of higher education is notoriously a factor – variously assessed – in the rise of student militancy. It is less often remarked that it is already a factor in the rise and success of new forms of participatory voluntarism. Consumers' Association matches the expertise of industry with an equal expertise, highly technical and professional, on behalf of consumers. Shelter speaks on housing with an authority which challenges and equals that of the government.

The individual versus society

Members of all classes in society now have experience of demonstrations and protest activity, but, as I have said, constructive participation, through the devising of new instruments of pressure and persuasion, and even for the devising of policies and plans, remains at present a mainly middle-class development. Working-class organizations loom large in the establishment of representative democracy – Cooperative societies, trades unions, the Labour Party – but these organizations are not notably more sensitive to the wishes of their members than other major political and economic enterprises. For most working-class people, as for most people of the time, participation in the making, shaping, or at least modest influencing of public policy, is not within their experience. Life consists of making sure you don't get unduly screwed by the system.

Thus the vast majority of the population still find themselves in the condition described as long ago as 1950 by the American social scientist, Gordon W. Allport. When he was Professor of Social Psychology at Harvard University he wrote a portrait of a day in the life of Citizen Sam, which is worth referring to because from such origins many ideas about participation, now in currency, were derived.

Long before it moved into respectable parlance and into the mass media from the journals of the New Left, the language of participation inhabited the writings of social scientists studying and anxious about the workings of industrialized democracy and the mental health of its citizens. Participation is what a growing number of people feel they want. If Allport and others who anticipated the concern of most political activists by several years were right, then it is profoundly what most of us need, whether we perceive it yet or not.

Citizen Sam appeared in a paper which was actually called *The Psychology of Participation*.[12] Most of the diagnosis and prescription still apply. Allport's allusions, naturally, have dated, and evidence that some progress has been made in the past decade or so is perhaps provided by the unacceptability now of his tone and style.

Citizen Sam ... moves and has his being in the great activity wheel of New York City. ... He spends his hours of unconsciousness somewhere in the badlands of the Bronx. He wakens to grab the morning's milk left at the door by an agent of a vast dairy and distribution system whose corporate maneuvers, so vital to his health, never consciously concern him. After paying hasty respects to his landlady, he dashes into the transportation system whose mechanical and civic mysteries he does not comprehend. At the factory he becomes a cog for the day in a set of systems far beyond his ken. To him (as to everybody else) the company he works for is an abstraction; he plays an unwitting part in the 'creation of surpluses' (whatever they are), and though he doesn't know it his furious activity at his machine is regulated by 'the law of supply and demand', and by the 'availability of raw materials' and by 'prevailing interest rates'.

A good deal of that is probably still true for Sams in the States and in Britain. 'Unknown to himself he is headed next week for the "surplus labour market".'
     Alarmingly true.

A union official collects his dues; just why he doesn't know. . . . After more activity in the afternoon, he seeks out a standardized daydream manufactured in Hollywood, to rest his tense, but NOT efficient, mind. At the end of his day he sinks into a tavern, and unknownly victimized by the advertising cycle orders in rapid succession Four Roses, Three Feathers, Golden Wedding and Calvert's which 'men of distinction' like to drink.

For 'Hollywood' read 'television', up at least to ten o'clock most evenings. For brand names substitute others from television commercials as appropriate. The parable is condescendingly over-stated (Sam is more probably indirectly victimized by mergers between breweries than gulled into buying a drink he does not really like), but it carries at least an important part of the truth, and it prompts Allport to ask a searching question:

Sam has been active all day, immensely active, playing a part in dozens of impersonal cycles of behaviour. He has brushed scores of 'corporate personalities', but has entered into intimate relations with no single human being. . . . Throughout the day Sam is on the go, implicated in this task and that – but does he, in a psychological sense, *participate* in what he is doing? Although constantly task-involved, is he ever really ego-involved?

Allport's paper anticipated much subsequent writing by seeing that solving this problem of complex, industrialized societies would contribute simultaneously to the progress of democracy and to the psychic health and development of the individual. He wrote:

The answer to growing complexity in the social sphere is renewed efforts at participation by each one of us, or else a progressive decline of inert and unquestioning masses, submitting to government by an elite which will have little regard for the ultimate interest of the common man.

It is easy to be over-earnest about participation, so it is perhaps worth briefly interpolating here that in advocating it, I am not suggesting that the psychic health of each one of us depends on our being card-carrying members of a political party, out on the knocker four nights a week, at meetings two nights and collecting dues on the seventh. That would hardly be a recipe for mental health – and such enthusiasts notoriously neglect their families and their own private and inner selves. There are many ways, and many un-political ways, in which we can contribute to the active fabric of social life.

It is also easy to be vague, romantic and imprecise about participation, but Allport was perfectly aware that it is wholly unrealistic to imply, as some advocates seem to do, that everyone will or could be equally involved in every aspect of social life. In participation, as in production or scholarship, a division of labour is obviously necessary, but it should be asked:

Do we find Citizen Sam truly participating in some *one* political undertaking; in some *one* of his economic contracts (preferably, of course, in his job where he spends most of his time); is he really involved in some religious, educational, recreational pursuits, and in family affairs? . . .

It is neither possible nor desirable that all of our activities and contacts in our complex social order should penetrate below the surface of our personalities. But unless we try deliberately and persistently to affect our destinies at certain points, especially where broad policies are concerned . . . we are not democratic personalities, we have no balance or wholeness, and society undergoes proportionate stultification.

As I have said, Allport's tone and some of his allusions are dated. It is no longer tenable to adopt an Olympian stance, observing the problems of 'the common man' and Citizen Sam as though being an academic and an intellectual conferred immunity from the forces affecting 'ordinary people'. Apart from the social pressures which have since made it abundantly plain that relatively protected intellectuals are as much alienated as Allport's somewhat patronizingly observed Citizen Sam, this progress in insight owes a good deal to the critique of industrial civilization by sociologists. C. Wright Mills, for instance, devoted his short, passionate academic life to the diffusion of 'the sociological imagination', and the opening sentences of his book of that name concentrate on a major aspect of Sam's condition which Allport overlooked:

Nowadays men often feel that their private lives are a series of traps. They sense that within their everyday worlds, they cannot overcome their troubles, and in this feeling, they are often quite correct: what ordinary men are directly aware of and what they try to do are bounded by the private orbits in which they live; their visions, and their powers are limited to the close-up scenes of job, family, neighbourhood; in other milieux, they move vicariously and remain spectators. And the more aware they become, however vaguely, of ambitions and of threats which transcend their immediate locales, the more trapped they seem to feel.[13]

In this book, Wright Mills argues the necessity to enable people today to increase their power over their destinies by helping them to transform *private troubles* into which they have little insight and over which they have no control, into *public issues,* which they might begin to understand and master.

Allport (among others) had seen that a participatory society was necessary because the complexity of industrial and bureaucratized life, in which most men are persistently at the receiving end of initiatives taken remotely, in which they are rarely expected to commit themselves wholeheartedly, was undermining the psychological health of the people. (Or does the high incidence of mental illness in women, especially socially isolated women, and the almost equally high rate among men, derive wholly from other causes?) This would lead in time to a decline in the viability of that society as a whole. Furthermore, extending Allport now rather than paraphrasing, the processes and rituals of representative democracy provided no more than yet another superficial brush with another set of corporate personalities.

C. Wright Mills (again among others) saw the important new ingredient in the psychology of the alienated citizen: the sense of being in a trap. For many the trap has been comfortable, furlined, well equipped with gadgets, but a trap it remains, and over the past decade or so men and women have started fighting their way out.

The new militancy, the development of 'assertiveness', as Radice calls it, may be due to two major changes which have occurred since Citizen Sam's day. I have already referred to the most obvious – although access to anything but the most rudimentary grounding in education is still limited by social class, more people are better educated than in any previous generation.

Poor downtrodden, brainwashed Citizen Sam had a better educated son, who was an anarchistically inclined student with no respect for deans of faculty. And, as we have seen, he also had a much more prosperous cousin who, affluent though he was, cared unusually about value for money and joined the Consumers' Union.

Secondly, the system which the citizen has to negotiate has become much more complex, even in the last twenty years. Radice sums up the changes in a century under three heads: [14]

Over the last hundred years, there have been three revolutionary changes in the nature of decision making. The expanded resources of decision makers cause their decisions to affect more people more drastically; the information on which their decisions are based has become more complex; and decisions are so interdependent that it is increasingly difficult to apportion responsibility for them.

The decision makers include not only government, which is formally controlled by representative democracy, but also large-scale private industries, whose operations are constrained by law but whose administrative structures and decisions are neither democratic nor democratically arrived at. Their influence is enormous. A faulty demand forecast can throw thousands out of work. Radice continues:

If the power of the decision makers has grown, the complexity of the decision-making process makes it more difficult for the people to exert influence. It is hard to challenge decisions which are based on a highly technical analysis of the factors involved. Unless the citizen has access to the information and the techniques to evaluate that information, he is at an almost insurmountable disadvantage. The findings of a computer can sometimes be challenged only by another computer.

We have become a good deal more sophisticated since the sharecropper bulldozed off his land in Steinbeck's *Grapes of Wrath*, asked his futile question, 'Who do I shoot?' only to find that the enemy was the system, an abstraction, not even a banker, but banking. But it seems doubtful whether, faced by a more complicated environment, many of us are better able to cope with that environment or to locate responsibility for its assaults upon us – when the path of the motorway results in our being bulldozed out of our homes, for instance – than Steinbeck's sharecropper.

This increased complexity of the social system is what makes John Osborne's diatribes against Nigel from Sandhurst seem so old-fashioned now. Oligarchy persists. There are still rulers who make decisions from the commanding heights of the economy who are not elected and who are not accountable: there are others who, though elected, have to depend on a huge corps of experts who are contracted or appointed and whom hardly anyone understands. Even those who are elected, as Members of Parliament say, often find themselves tantalizingly remote from the levers of power. There still isn't anyone to shoot. Radice again:

The interdependence of decisions makes it difficult to locate the persons responsible. Who is responsible when a management sacks some of its employees during a recession? The firm, because of its unintelligent demand forecasting and inadequate manpower planning, or the government because its economic measures have brought about the recession? Is it the politician or the civil servant who should be blamed for the inadequacy of a social service? And how is one to answer President Kennedy's question – 'Who took the command decision?' – when actions at home are influenced by others abroad? A decision to put up council-house rents in Wiltshire may be determined by a decision about the relative advantages and disadvantages of holding sterling by a small number of business men abroad.

The complexity, interdependence and remoteness of twentieth-century decision making increase the difficulty of answering the old democratic question, 'Who watches over the rulers?'. Yet the far greater power of decision makers means that they need more surveillance. Even if we are forced to accept that we cannot change the nature of modern decision making, and that modern decisions are usually more rational and better informed than those of previous centuries, we cannot take the benevolence or the wisdom of the decision makers for granted.

And in the confusion which prevails, privilege continues to flourish, hard-core poverty persists. Some surf-ride the system; many drown; the rest of us struggle, splutter and come up for air at intervals. How then is British democracy to be seen? Will government and authority in other dominating institutions recognize that a high degree of participation is what people, the society as a whole, and government itself, need and must achieve?

3 Planning for Participation

Let the people in, or how to govern successfully

Representative democracy cannot be swept aside; though in the passionate centre of a campus teach-in or a spontaneous community happening, when leadership seems an anachronism, when representatives seem redundant because the group is so articulate and mutually sensitive, when all seems possible and indeed a great deal actually is possible that was not before, it is tempting to believe that it could be swept aside; that Athens could come again (without its substructure of slaves); that a network of moots could replace Parliament, local government, hospital boards, political parties, agents. . . .

It cannot be done, and if it could be done, the inevitable pre-revolutionary questions would have to be faced: how to get there? how to unpick the inherited structures of the past? how to get rid of the garbage without also throwing out some of the glory? Fifty-five million people cannot, in practice, run Britain, and if the population forecasts turn out to be accurate, seventy million people in the year 2000 will find it no easier. Even if, in some way, it were administratively practicable to replace representation by some more radical, anarchistic form of democracy, it is a dubious prospect. I doubt whether many people would find a society tolerable in which no major decisions were taken until after a prolonged teach-in of a kind that is only possible at moments of crisis, when a great many protagonists are prepared to drop their normal work, indeed to suspend their normal daily lives altogether, in order to take part.

All this will seem obvious to most of my readers, but wrong and perfunctory to a few. It is important to go on to the next proposition: It may not be possible or desirable to jettison representative democracy in favour of some more humane and amiable tribalism, but representative democracy will not do, not as we have it at present.

Democracy is a system of government which enables the people to have an active say in and control over the formulation and implementation of policies which affect their personal and social destinies. Much of this, necessarily, has to be conducted through representatives who are elected and accountable, to whom responsibility for much of the policy detail has to be delegated and who must, in turn, delegate responsibility for executive action to experts and functionaries. Formally speaking, we have such a system in Britain. Frequently it works; but the growth of protest and the push for participation described in the previous chapter is happening because the system does not work well enough. Society is felt to be something by which we are dominated and frustrated, not something that we belong to and through which we live. Representatives get out of touch; experts never were in touch. Representatives do not control everything; they are themselves controlled. Politics are dominated by economics and the economic world is authoritarian, not democratic. There are two connected mitigating features. The oligarchy is not monolithic; vested interest clashes with vested interest; error and evil are not transmitted inexorably into every corner of the system, as in totalitarian countries. And, further, the social system is now so complex that power inevitably devolves. It has, without irony, been described as a centrifugal society.

One consoling fact for the people: government was never so difficult as it is today. In *The Long Revolution*, Raymond Williams wrote (and his unaffected first person plural signals an advance in understanding since Gordon Allport wrote about Citizen Sam. The academic is now alongside the rest of chivvied humanity):

There is a deep-felt discontinuity, for most of us, between what we as individuals desire to do, and what, by some mysterious process, actually happens 'out there' in society. . . . Individuals feel radically insecure when their lives are changed by forces which they cannot easily see or name, and as societies become larger and more complicated . . . this insecurity has certainly increased.[1]

No doubt a shipyard worker wondering where to get a job, or a Notting Hill Gate tenant puzzled how to get the rats out of the basement, feel a more distinct sense of insecurity than most, but it is perhaps worth remembering that there must be moments when the Prime Minister, or the President of the United States, when even the President of IBM and the Chairman of Shell-BP are aware of a 'discontinuity' between what they do and what actually happens out there. The difficulty of government is one of the most encouraging features of the current political landscape.

But it does not of itself guarantee progress. Britain could stagger on, an uncomfortable emulsion of attenuated democracy and plutocracy, occasionally stirred by eruptions of popular discontent. The other alternatives (especially since the governments of Western Europe, not all noticeably more competent than our own, are determined to compound both the opportunities and the problems created by the Treaty of Rome), seem to be a kind of bland fascism, an affluent corporatist state, in which the people are discreetly manipulated; or a barbarous, highly unstable capitalism, in which governments are capriciously rough and smooth.

These alternatives are real threats. As we have seen, the profound individual–society problem has grown no easier in the past twenty years. Alongside the patient growth of new, inadequately acknowledged, channels of participation and the impatient growth of protests, vividly publicized, against ossified channels of representation, the world has seen a counter-revolutionary spread of disciplinary government. The world is full of restless, populist anarchy; but it is also full of autocratic governments, some of them clutching a few remaining veils in hypocritical tribute to democracy. Britain cannot expect to remain immune to these trends – the symptoms are already present, but neither does it have to succumb to them. Conscious thought and decision about the evolution of society have become urgent. It may be that representative democracy must become more of a participatory democracy if it is to survive as a democracy at all.

That would certainly seem to be the most promising way forward if society is to change without degenerating into anarchy or provoking a backlash of autocracy. In many advanced countries, including Britain, frustrated causes are recruiting urban guerillas, using techniques that make better sense in Latin-American autocracies, putting such democracy as we have at risk; and frustrated governments are taking powers to permit them to get on with the business of governing, without the people in whose name it is all for getting in the way. The alternatives, though possible, are hardly viable. No doubt a modern state can survive, can stagger on, after a fashion, under any of these modes, but if it is to surmount the internal contradictions set up by the exponential changes in its technology and the unforeseen consequences of its actions, a modern state must be able to command unprecedented reserves of critical intelligence, political imagination, commitment and action in its people.

It is now a necessity of successful government that the people should be involved and not merely told, however democratically those doing the telling might have been chosen. Although the temptation exists throughout the world to strengthen the hold of central government, it is now questionable whether, in the even not so long run, tyrannical, autocratic government can be effective or efficient government, especially in small countries which do not have enough people or material resources to be wastefully exploited. Franco's Spain shows signs of realizing that more freedom and better education may do more for the country's future than money from tourists. Novotny's Czechoslovakia went bankrupt; even Husak's has to contain its illiberalism.

A democratic socialist country cannot function properly, let alone live up to its own ideology, unless it works out ways in which the people can participate in their own government. The Yugoslavs are trying. A democratic capitalist country will strangle itself in its own contradictions unless the people achieve the Jeffersonian ideal in practice. Perceptive Americans are recognizing it. Thus the American futurologist Hermann Kahn is thinking for all of us when he identifies certain features which will be forced on the organization of American business-life if it is to adapt and survive. I know that Kahn is a somewhat risky witness to cite. He may not appeal to readers who recall his thermonuclear *sangfroid* or who agree with Theodore Roszak's condemnation of him as an archtechnocrat. My view is that the things one wishes would happen conceivably might when the angels and the Kahns of this world agree for once. Long spoon in hand, I'm ready to sup. In his comments on the Hudson Study of the Corporation and its Environment 1975–85, he predicts this as a dominant trend: 'Greater dependence on consensual techniques' and 'even "participatory democracy" rather than classical use of rules, orders, directives and "top-down" command and control'. Kahn expects that these decentralizing, consensual tendencies will affect not only the corporation, but also the political scene and hence government as a whole, because of another development which he predicts: the initial emergence of what he calls 'quaternary (i.e. services to services) economics and the erosion of the production-oriented (primary, secondary, tertiary) economics'. There will be a 'diminishing emphasis on narrow economic efficiency – greater emphasis on social, cultural, environmental and life-style values'.[2]

This development has already begun. It is illustrated by the intervention of CA and other user pressure groups in economic and public affairs described in the previous chapter. In so far as governments and, increasingly, publics are taking seriously and not just ephemerally, the fundamental message of European Conservation Year, for example, they are moving into this new area of politics. (The Swedes especially are beginning to accept that preserving the environment and eliminating waste has to become a cost of production.) When politicians speak, however vaguely, about 'the quality of life', they are dimly recognizing what has been obvious to ordinary people for a long time and now finds sophisticated advocates – namely, that the pursuit of GNP is an instrumental economic goal of politics, not the transcendental target. Governments cannot do it all on their own, try as they inevitably will, by legislation, taxation, exhortation and manipulating the bank rate. They cannot even do it by compromising between the claims of the strongest pressure groups. And furthermore (to reiterate in order to bring these strands of the rationale together) the people seem disinclined to let them. People are, as noted above, increasingly reluctant to be pushed around in the name of progress or posterity ('what did posterity ever do for me?' is the cry of indignation in a secular society putting a higher value than ever before in history on happiness-for-me-*now*), whether it be for their own good, or, often as not, someone else's profit.

We will make our altruistic gestures, plant the avenue of trees for later generations to enjoy, if we see the point of it; we will even do what has to be done in our own interests, providing the data are shared with us, the diagnosis worked out with us and the remedies devised or improved by us. That arch-conservative Edmund Burke had the radical temper for today when he wrote (in *Reflections on the Revolution in France*):

I have never yet seen any plan which has not been amended by the observations of those who were much inferior in understanding to the person who took the lead in the business.

The tactics of militant students may be maddening (it is a tautological privilege of the young to be jejeune), but they find it easier to face in the right historical direction than wise Vice Chancellors. And there is nothing jejeune about CA, AASE, or the many amenity societies talking with professional assurance to professional planners.

Effective democratic government must become more participatory because the public must not only know what policies are proposed: they must also understand them, even enthuse about them, if they are to work. People cannot be coerced into making a prices and incomes policy work, or into increasing productivity, but their passivity can and has undermined both of these. Just talking about pollution will not stop them dumping bedsteads in the pond in the middle of the night.

Official backing

In this situation, it is more a matter for satisfaction than for cynicism that participation has found advocates in official reports and among cabinet ministers. Well, perhaps a touch of cynicism may be permitted. There could certainly be a danger that participation might be encouraged as a low level, diversionary tactic. As one MP has warned.

All sorts of worthy and high-minded people want to extend popular participation in the micro-politics of the factory, the housing estate or the local school. Few of them have reckoned with the disagreeable fact that decisions taken at the micro-political level are ultimately determined by what happens at a macro-political level of Whitehall and Westminster.[3]

It would be wrong to dismiss the importance of participatory democratic processes at humbler levels, for two reasons: many decisions affecting people's lives are in fact taken locally. Representative democracy is a better means of taking them than any authoritarian procedure; but if the people concerned can also be involved in discussion and enactment of those decisions, that would be better still. Secondly, for a democracy to work, people must have direct experience of making it work; they must learn what applying their wills, minds, energies and emotions to self-determining social action means. Democrats are better trained in schools with student councils (with power and a budget) than in schools where civics is taught from a teacher's rostrum to passive rows of desks.

But a touch of cynicism about 'worthy and high-minded people' is valuable not merely because some of them may not have reckoned with the overriding significance of macro-political decisions, but precisely because they have. Active democracy could be a side-show permitted or encouraged at parish level to allow the oligarchy to get on, undistracted by too much popular interest, with the serious business of government at the national level (an example of what Marcuse calls 'repressive tolerance'). Participation is meant to be an intrinsic component at every level of social and political life, not a Sunday afternoon ball game on the village green.

That said, however, it is quite remarkable that an idea, derived from the writings of academic social scientists (suspect), which became an eccentricity of the New Left (highly suspect), should in only a few years have become a regular conclusion arrived at by the kind of responsible mainstream experts and others who find themselves serving on official committees of inquiry, even by cabinet ministers. Participation is, for example, the central theme, the desired goal of the Skeffington Report *People and Planning*;[3] it is the inspiring impulse behind *Youth and Community Work in the 1970s*;[4] it was the subject of the Seventh British National Conference on Social Welfare (Swansea, April

1970). The National Council of Social Service, which sponsored that conference, is a notoriously cautious body, anxious that all its constituent organizations should do good and improve society without actually upsetting governments or getting on the wrong side of senior civil servants. Welcoming the conference, the Rt Hon. George Thomas said: 'citizen participation ... is the core of democracy, necessary in all fields, at local and national level'. In the keynote speech, Sir Goronwy David, Principal of the University College of Wales (Aberystwyth), declared, 'I must say at once that I am in favour of participation.' And the Rt Hon. Richard Crossman made a speech answering the question: 'How can the Government encourage citizen participation in Community Life?'

'Participation' is, then, becoming a received idea. Indeed, it has sometimes seemed that it was a merely modish idea. It is certainly an occupational perversity of journalism that an important idea which might take years to be shaped, take a hold on men's minds, and begin in turn to shape reality, seems to become old hat in a few months. And it is certainly true that 'Participation' is at risk as such a word. On New Year's Day, 1970, *The Times* Diary, called 'Participation' 'the biggest see-through gimmick of 1969' (the metaphor itself significantly drawn from fashion). A few months earlier David Marquand had felt it necessary to open the article from which I quoted above with the bright, defensive and, as we have seen, quite untrue statement: 'We are all participators nowadays.'

The health of the words wants watching, but it should be remembered that they have not simply flashed in and out of the popular media. Nor are the events and processes that prompt the words transitory either. The pressure for participation is certainly not a fashion or a momentary spasm. Demonstrations are not mere epiphenomena struck from the surface of society by the greedy eye of sensational television cameras: they are phenomena symptomatic of deep-seated defects in the structure of our society, and in the ability of its constituent parts to communicate with each other. It is important that the momentum of those who are trying to work out the best ways of achieving participation in different spheres should be sustained by a commitment to it from above, as well as by a demand for it from below. There are signs that such a commitment may be emerging even though it obviously runs counter to all the conditioned reflexes of those in authority. I will give a number of examples, the first two being the official reports: *People and Planning* and *Youth and Community Work in the 1970s* to which I have referred. It does not matter that the 'Skeffington Report' and *Youth and Community* were commissioned by the Labour Government. It does not even matter that the Conservative Government has taken advantage of a certain vacuousness in *Youth and Community* to ignore it altogether, which it does not deserve. Attitudes towards participation do not run neatly along party lines and in any case the government of the day is only a changing part of a much more durable structure of authority. What does matter is that people in local government are still trying out the ideas in Skeffington, and that others in youth work are drawing on *Youth and Community* for some guidance in an unusually directionless sector of the education service.

Youth and Community recognizes the key weaknesses of conventional democracy and points out that its failures are less tolerable now that rapid change is endemic:

In the past, our society, in common with others, has responded to the interests of some of its members and, as a result of their pressures, made changes which reflect their values.

This responsiveness to the influential privileged has never been without its risks of provoking reaction from the underprivileged. In a situation like the present, where change is not merely an occasional event but a characteristic condition, the exclusion of individuals from decision making in public affairs, or lack of encouragement for them to be engaged, is much more likely now to create a sense of the individual's powerlessness to influence social policy, so that at best he becomes apathetic and indifferent, and at worst cynical, nihilistic or anarchic. We seek 'the active society' in which all are encouraged and enabled to find the public expression of their values, avoiding the extremes of indifference and alienation.

The eloquent chapter in which they describe their vision is in fact called 'The Active Society', a title derived from an important but difficult study by the American sociologist Etzioni. The two committees whose work is synthesized in *Youth and Com-*

munity found they were unable to answer the question 'What kind of youth service do we want?' in the abstract, just as I do not think it possible to say what kind of television we want, until it is clearer what kind of society we want. The writers of *Youth and Community* are not immune to the unhistorical abstraction which locates the participatory democracy in the future, but they provide an outline of the constitutional relationships towards which we need to aim concretely here and now:

The sort of society we describe may be a long way off, perhaps unattainable in full ... [but] in a country such as ours, subject to the changes consequent upon a rapidly changing technology, society needs to engage in an intensive and perpetual transformation of itself, unless it is to respond to tomorrow's world with yesterday's activities and modes of organization. Our commitment is to a society in which every member can be publicly active; for only in this way can society become positively responsive to them, and, in the constant renewal of itself, reflect their values.

Like Allport, the authors base their case for the active society on twin grounds – the mental health of its citizens and the viability of the society itself. Allport might almost have been at hand when they drafted this paragraph:

It is not only the community which benefits from the active society: there is in it profit for all in their individual capacities. The development of human maturity has many continua, but we would take one of them to be the increasing acceptance of and seeking for responsibility towards oneself and others. In the public sector of our society this growth of responsibility is often either frustrated or 'bred out' of the human organism. For many their only political decision is a quinquennial or triennial one: to hand over the political decision making to others. In industrial settings mass-productive efficiency is too often happiest with controlled robots deciding nothing for themselves except the decision to be acquiescent – both on and off the production lines. Our consumption-dominated society is happiest with those who respond to stimuli, and sink their individual differences in similarity with the mass; where the only decisions are to buy, and, in buying, to be fashionable.

Our call then for people to be democratically involved in decision making is the outward and audible expression of the other strand of our underlying principles: that all individuals should grow towards maturity; and that a society in which all can make more and more decisions about more and more things is a more mature society than one in which this exercise of responsibility is reserved for the chosen few (no matter how democratically chosen they may be).

The Skeffington Report naturally deals with participation more fully, analytically and practically in relation to the large but specific issue of planning. Nevertheless, the Committee was fully aware of the climate of changed political expectations which had led to its being set up and hoped that its practical recommendations might have wider application. 'It may be', says the report,

that the evolution of the structures of representative government . . . is now entering a new phase. There is a growing demand by many groups for more opportunity to communicate and for more say in the working out of policies which affect people not merely at election time, but continuously as proposals are being hammered out and, certainly, as they are being implemented. Life, so the argument runs, is becoming more and more complex, and one cannot leave all the problems to one's representatives. They need some help in reaching the right decision, and opportunity should be provided for discussions with all those involved. . . . Planning is a prime example of the need for this participation, for it affects everyone.

The Committee defined participation as

the act of sharing in the formation of policies and proposals. Clearly, the giving of information by the local planning authority and of an opportunity to comment on that information is a major part in the process of participation, but it is not the whole story. Participation involves doing as well as talking and there will be full participation only where the public are able to take an active part throughout the plan-making process (p.1).

Two major advances in attitude are expressed in those passages from the Skeffington Report. It has long been acknowledged that one's representatives need help in reaching right decisions but it has usually been assumed that experts, town clerks, borough surveyors and the like were there to supply it, not that it might also be useful to tap the experience of the public affected. Secondly, the Report stresses that action, as well as receiving and commenting on information, is intrinsic to participation – a substantial step forward from the old civics-class notion that citizenship means being well enough informed to choose men and women to do one's thinking and acting on one's behalf, at widely spaced intervals in time.

In the field of planning there is already ample experience to justify the complete feasibility of the Skeffington objectives. The Birmingham City Council asked the Sparkbrook Association for 'your local knowledge in relation to the quality of life in your area and the tangible and intangible improvement which could be brought into it'. The Association subsequently produced a document called *Community Plan*, which contained reports from study groups on housing, education, consumer provision and recreation, and a series of planning proposals dealing with traffic, industry and other issues, all clearly illustrated with maps and diagrams. The report was quasi-professional in standard and owed much to the help of the staff and students of the Birmingham School of Planning, who interviewed 1250 households in the area and analysed the data. By this fruitful relationship with the School of Planning, the Association was able to meet the problem described by Radice and others – the imbalance between the information and knowledge possessed by authority and by the public affected by that authority's decisions. The brief which was given to the School of Planning was formulated by the study groups of the Sparkbrook Association and the student planners presented the Association with three possible plans, which were discussed at joint meetings before the final report was approved.

Similarly the Richmond Society produced a plan for the development of the town centre of Richmond-upon-Thames. The Council, though pigheaded in its dealings with knowledgeable pressure groups of parents over education, was generous enough to admit publicly that the Society's plan was superior to that devised by its own staff. Naturally, mistakes are made. The procedure is new, both to planning authorities and to the public. Some local authorities, whose members and staff are used to attending meetings and living their lives by diaries, think that all they have to do is to call a public meeting; they then interpret the poor attendance as evidence of the public's indifference to the fate being prepared for it. Other authorities are more patient, using slower, more explanatory, more organic methods, door to door. There is much to be learned. It must be learned.

One of the major tasks for our society during the next decade is to overcome the obstacles – out-of-date institutions, the attitudes of men reared in oligarchic presuppositions, inertia and other negative factors – which incontestably still inhibit the very idea of participation in many spheres. Meanwhile, the reason reiterated by the Skeffington Committee for believing that their approach to planning should be extended to other spheres of social and political life is a beacon:

The Committee feel that this broader aspect of their work is important in a large, complex and socially advanced industrial nation like ours where the principle of public participation can *improve the quality of decisions by public authorities* and give personal satisfaction to those affected by the decisions (Introduction, my italics).

The Abingdon gasholder should become a symbol of this new approach to democracy, relating the needs of people and society to the provision of competent government. In 1966–7, a regional gas board decided that it would plant a huge gasholder in the middle of the beautiful Berkshire town of Abingdon. The plan leaked out; there was a short public inquiry, and, as a result, it transpired that the gasholder did not actually have to be in the middle of the town; and nor did it have to be huge, since a new, unobtrusive type of holder in which gas is compressed, was now available.

It makes for progress when authority prudently involves the public affected by new policies and developments, lest they prove still more tiresome by turning into the disaffected public, with all the usual irksome consequences, including keeping the media at bay. But it is a major advance when authority recognizes that it really has something to learn from the public or from specialist pressure groups set up not to 'represent' the public but to represent a receiving-end point of view which needs advocating and considering before decisions are taken. Thus the Ministry of Social Security, when it was newly established, was not sure what new measures it needed to introduce. In addition to initiating several research projects, the Ministry was willing to listen to the Child Poverty Action Group. When the Campaign Against Racial Discrimination offered information about and contact with racial minorities, the Government responded by giving individual members of CARD, a voluntary pressure group, seats on the National Committee for Commonwealth Immigrants.

Government has in fact gone further still, under Labour and Conservative Administrations alike. As an aspect of the Urban Programme, directed by the Home Office, numerous community development projects have been set up in 'areas of multiple deprivation', often associated with designated Educational Priority Areas intended to practice the positive discrimination recommended by the Plowden Report. One aim of the Home Office 'CDP' is to help the present providers of organized public and voluntary services become 'more responsive to the needs of a community as they are perceived by the Community itself'. This requires 'more sympathetic understanding than is often shown at present at the value of the contributions that can be made by individual citizens'. Through CDP, people in some of the most demoralizing downtown environments are being encouraged to develop the self-confidence to stand up for themselves and are currently being *taught how to participate*.

These hopeful signs of a new relationship between authority and the people are still atypical, but they must be treated as pioneering a new mainstream style, not as eccentricities, tolerated because they tend to operate in the welfare field, so enabling an uncouth society to enjoy inexpensively a modest exercise of conscience.

Efficient democracy

The positive developments mentioned in the previous section imply that it is now urgently necessary to rethink the relationship between democracy and efficiency. There is a traditional aristocratic, entrepreneurial, administrative suspicion of democracy which is thought to be 'all every well in theory' but in practice clogs up the means of effective action. This suspicion is normally disguised since, after all, democracy provides the official ideology and rhetoric of our society, but occasionally it reveals itself. It showed for example in the Tyzack Report on the administrative structure of Warwick University. This report was unusual for its candour of expression, not for its point of view:

We have been told that democracy has a special place in university life, and that there is constant political pressure from the rank and file of the academic staff claiming the right, not only to be consulted more, but to 'have a hand in decision making'. The result in practice is already an amorphous and time-wasting system which has led to needlessly protracted argument, dilatoriness in the taking of decisions, uncertainty regarding the effective centres of power and action, and at times to conflicts of policy. . . . Sooner or later the University of Warwick will have to come to terms with the age-old conflict between democratic principles and effective government.[6]

I am not concerned here with the rights and wrongs of the Warwick University controversy. I am simply concerned to point out the easy antithesis in that quotation between democracy and efficiency, since it is a point of view that is still widely held. It only has to be etched in such imprecise sentences as these to evoke the wordly smile of the realist, rendering cogent analysis unnecessary. He takes for granted the old contrast between, on the one hand, the idealists with their touching faith in democracy, and on the other, men of affairs who actually get things done. Such men regard committees, for example, as a necessary evil, fit only for manipulation (and of course a self-fulfilling prophecy begins to work – manipulated committees degenerate into uselessness or into providing PR smoke screens).

No doubt any undergraduate in his first year at Warwick or any other university could shoot the necessary holes in that passage from the Tyzack Report. Why no distinction between democracy as such and the specific, patently remediable, procedures and pieces of machinery which happen to be in operation for the time being? What criteria of 'effectiveness' lurk behind the phrase 'effective government'? Do not protracted arguments sometimes produce less shakeable conclusions? Are not decisions sometimes wiser for prolonging the time spent in arriving at them? (The Swedes, for example, spent far more years than the English in debating and deciding on comprehensive education.

Now they have a better system, much more swiftly and efficiently put into operation, than we have.) And finally, what is so intrinsically distressing about conflicts of policy – providing the machinery exists for resolution and action?

The lurking criterion of 'effectiveness' behind this standard contra-distinction between democracy and efficiency is plain: those who make it are really asking for unimpeded opportunities to implement their own prevailing ideas. And this is politically simply not on. Not any more. It is they who are living in cloud cuckoo land, not the idealists.

The world has moved on and it is now desperately old fashioned to speak in such terms as the 'age-old conflict between democratic principles and effective government'. The swift movement of the world is responsible, for example, for making almost the entire institutional inheritance of representative democracy maladapted to contemporary needs. It is this disjunction between the available institutions and the actual political tasks to be performed (and not the mere idiosyncrasies of individual prime ministers, some liking small cabinets, some liking large, for instance) which underlies the frequent changes in ministerial structure, terms of reference and nomenclature. The Ministry of Labour becomes the Department of Employment and Productivity, then, simply of Employment. The Department of Economic Affairs, Ministry of Technology, Prices and Incomes Board, Consumer Council and others, come and go. The Ministry of Education evolves into the Department of Education and Science, but governmental responsibility for education as a whole is discharged also through the Home Office, the Ministry of Defence, the Overseas Development Administration, the Ministry of Health, the Department of Agriculture etc., etc. (and all those names could be out of date by the time this goes to press). Under the circumstances, those in authority may well find themselves asking the historically unprecedented and unthinkable question: what the hell are we supposed to do? The answers come by a patient examination of what is needed and this may usually involve finding out more about the circumstances, experiences and wishes of parties likely to be affected. That was precisely the significance of the openness to outside suggestion of the new Ministry of Social Security. Efficient government could not proceed without democracy of a participatory kind.

There is another equally basic reason why democracy must be strengthened if government is to be effective. There is now a growing area where government, as such, simply will not know what policies to advocate because moving away from GNP as an obsessive end of politics involves us in having to make choices of a fundamental kind. This is an area where Parliament itself needs reforming. The capacity of our representatives to represent us needs to be increased, involving a change in the committee procedure of the House, which would in turn provide a basis for closer participation by the public in the deliberations of Parliament about choice (once again indicating the falsity of setting 'representation' and 'participation' up against each other). This is the chief significance of the recommendations of a House of Commons procedure committee on the *Scrutiny of Public Expenditure and Administration*. A member of that committee has appraised it in these terms:

What the procedure committee propose, in effect, is a much more powerful and renamed estimates committee, with a series of functional sub-committees covering the main fields of expenditure. These would examine the estimates of the government departments in their fields, and report on the efficiency with which they are administered. The report also proposes that the form of the estimates should be changed wherever possible to make it much clearer than it is at present what the money is actually being spent on; and that they should eventually be supplemented by output budgets, expressed in terms of the purposes for which the expenditure is made rather than of the resources being used.

It sounds prosaic, but if it is carried out it will mean that parliament has a coherent committee system for the first time in its history – and that the public will have an opportunity to discuss the choices made in its name, not only between the broad categories of expenditure discussed in the Green Paper, but within them as well.[7]

Marquand expressly relates 'a coherent committee system' for Parliament with discussion by the public of 'the choices made in its name'. The specimen choices he uses ('not only between the broad categories of expenditure . . . but within them as well') show that this reform of representative government must, as the

Skeffington Committee envisaged, be complemented with an enlargement of the debate presupposed by participation:

Roads or environmental pollution? Nursery schools or universities? Cash grants or tax concessions? Embassy buildings or the British Council? Health centres or kidney machines? Choices like these are and must always be political. They involve fundamental questions of value, and the vital interests of masses of people. They have to be taken by someone, and they ought to be taken in the light of discussion and debate. The question now is whether a reforming government has the courage to make this more possible than it has ever been in this country so far.

These reforms, or something like them, seem likely to come about. It would clearly be a great advance if 'parliament and the people' were actually 'given an opportunity to feed their preferences into the decision-making process'. But there are even more difficult choices ahead of us which most of us are not remotely qualified to make.

These choices are posed by the development of science and technology, and relate to the possible range of directions that could be taken by scientific research and the applications of technology which are now feasible, but not necessarily desirable.

Until quite recently most scientists believed that more science, more research, more applications in technology, would be a boon to mankind, providing politicians and the public made wise decisions about how to use and develop their discoveries. This was to perpetuate Adam Smith's economic fallacy into this specialized but fundamental field of social effort. It may be significant that another voluntary organization has come into being which is no more prepared to accept passively what is done in the name of science and technological progress than Consumers' Association is prepared to take what the market offers without scrutiny of the products for safety, soundness and fitness for purpose. This is the British Society for Social Responsibility in Science. Two of its members (Dr Shiraji Lal and David Dickson) have pointed out that although, as everyone knows, 'modern society is too complex to be fully understood by any one individual', nevertheless 'we are still geared to the assumption that there can exist a specially trained and selected body of decision makers'.

They argue, on the contrary, that:

One of the crucial factors leading to a seemingly uncontrollable environment is the lack of any truly democratic decision-making procedure that can be followed as a matter of course in the formulation of community policy. This is due partly to the isolation of the community from the effective levers of power, and partly to the decreasing importance of the individual's own social experience in an advanced technological society. The ability to exercise control over 'expert' decision-makers lies increasingly beyond the powers of either individuals or social groups. At the same time, the very factors of remoteness and lack of knowledge that created this alienating situation are still allowed to reinforce its basic undesirable trends, and thus help extend its influence to all spheres of life.[8]

The editor of *New Scientist* has observed that 'greater involvement of the citizen in scientific policy-making' (essential for the sake of both of science and society) '. . . requires a greater degree of scientific literacy than we have today'.[9]

In stressing the same need, Shiraji Lal and David Dickson indicate how such issues of policy depend on participation which, in its turn, depends on education, communication and improved political mechanisms:

To find solutions for this type of problem, we must look toward the development of an educated and informed public, a Socratic public inclined to critical discussion of [issues of this kind]. . . . This will require changes in both education and *communication procedures* [my italics] if it is to happen soon enough to be of value.

Further, mechanisms must be devised by which rational decisions can be taken on these issues in the widest possible social context. An adequate planning system must also be developed which can anticipate and meet social demands, and cope effectively with problems as they arise; this system, too, should be able to exploit the opportunities created by scientific innovation in a manner consistent with accepted democratic ideals. Finally the development of a set of indicators would be desirable if value judgements on the quality of life and the way in which it is affected by social trends, are to have any form of rational basis. These suggestions are, of course, widely generalized. To develop them into a coherent plan for legislative action will require intellectual resources of a major order. Yet the problems which now face us are ones which we must solve if advanced societies are to survive the onslaught of science with traditional human values intact.[10]

4 Participants or Voyeurs?

Before attempting to show how television might contribute to the growth of participation, there are two other views about the connection of these two terms which must be considered right away, because if either of them is true, then the argument stops here and the hero gets tantalizingly killed in the first reel. The first view is not to be taken seriously, but paradoxically its author is, which is why it must get a mention. The second view deserves to be taken very seriously on any terms, though it is commonly regarded as good for a laugh.

On my right then, McLuhan: Pangloss of the media, mistaking one of tomorrow's possible extrapolations for today's reality; relishing what appalls; finding that whatever is, is right. On my left: Alexander Cockburn, Daniel Cohn-Bendit, Jerry Rubin and others, for whom television is part of the distracting spectacle laid on to divert people's eyes from the iniquities of capitalism.

If McLuhan is right, my case – a new mission for the medium – is otiose, for according to him the connections I am advocating already exist. If the revolutionary critics and activists are right, my case is foolish, and I might as well hope to use the stock exchange for the founding of kibbutzim in the City of London.

According to Marshal McLuhan, television and the other electronic extensions of our central nervous system have actually obliterated the distinction between actor and audience, agent and viewer. According to this 'insight', the world is converted from an alien matrix into a 'global village'. According to him, we are all participants now. McLuhan reworked this well-known image in a characteristically pyrotechnic talk on the radio programme, *The World at One* (in itself a McLuhanesque pun of a programme title):

Perhaps politics and entertainment have now become one thing. . . .
Since the satellites have gone round the planet, the planet has become
a theatre, not figuratively but literally; the whole planet is now a single
stage and everybody is enrolled.[1]

or again:

When the whole world becomes a stage, the whole world becomes
entertainment. Everybody is engaged in the entertainment business
now.

McLuhan is a kind of intellectual magician – the ideas pass
before your eyes and you think them solid. Try to grasp them
and they vanish; yet he seems to have created illumination, and
indeed in a way he has; the illumination is akin to poetry, working in paradox and in associated ideas, simultaneously sharp and
vague, as the multifaceted ball of his mind flashes. Some commentators would feel that there is more to it, however, than
prestidigitation. Kenneth Richmond, for example, in *The
Education Industry*,[2] finds that McLuhan provides an answer
to this question, which is highly relevant to my main theme:
'Did young people feel strongly and passionately about the
horrors of warfare, say, until film, radio and television news
coverage "brought it home to them", strongly and passionately
enough to organize protest marches and demonstration?' He
answers with this quotation from McLuhan's *Understanding
Media*:

The young people who have experienced a decade of TV have
naturally imbibed an urge toward involvement in depth that makes
all the remote visualized goals of usual culture seem not only unreal
but irrelevant, and not only irrelevant but anaemic. It is the total
involvement in all-inclusive *nowness* that occurs in young lives via
TV's mosaic image . . . It is, of course, our job not only to understand
this change, but to exploit its pedagogical richness. The TV child
expects involvement and doesn't want a specialist *job* in the future.
He does want a *role* and deep commitment in his society.[3]

By writing here about 'an urge toward involvement in depth',
'role and a deep commitment in his society' McLuhan is indeed
drawing attention to changes in sensibility and awareness for
which television should take some credit and which could and
sometimes do facilitate or provoke participation, and this is an
aspect I shall return to. But an 'urge toward involvement' is by

no means the same as actual involvement. It may be its tantalizing converse. The quotation certainly throws some light on television's effect on the young, but it is not authentic McLuhan: it is doctored McLuhan. For some reason, Richmond has left out two sentences which show that McLuhan is apparently not talking about the lavishness of television's information on the here-and-now-and-everywhere, nor about its news coverage which 'brings events home to us'.

The missing sentences read (and the italics are mine):

This change of attitude has *nothing to do with programming in any way*, and would be the same if the programme consisted entirely of the highest cultural content. The change of attitude by means of relating themselves to the mosaic TV image *would occur in any event*.

Elsewhere in the same chapter, McLuhan writes:

Political scientists have been quite unaware of the effects of the media anywhere at any time, simply because nobody has been willing to study the personal and social effects of media apart from their 'content'.

And a page later he refers expressly to 'the power of the TV mosaic to transform American innocence into depth sophistication, independent of "content".' This approach to television is after all what the most famous of all McLuhanisms, 'the medium is the message', is meant to sum up.

Kenneth Richmond makes McLuhan more or less intelligible, and certainly relevant to his subject and mine, but only by omitting key sentences. Restore these sentences and the meaning is at once lost in obscurity; and not only in obscurity – also in triviality. When McLuhan says and defends his view that 'TV is a cool, participant medium', he is, to be fair, partly attempting something intrinsically difficult – trying to evoke in us an awareness of a new kind of awareness, indicating the medium's influence on our sensibility, on our modes of apprehension, especially in those young enough not to have known a world without it. Yet his undoubtedly provocative commentary on this theme largely derives from the curiously trivial observation that television is a 'low-definition' medium, that is, compared with the cinema, you don't get a very good picture. From the base of this transitory technical deficiency of the medium, McLuhan ruminates on the way it 'involves' viewers and uses that to explain a profound 'psychic and social disturbance', with such diverse effects as the American passion for skin diving, the disappearance of the assembly line from industry and of the pencil line from the backs of nylons.

McLuhan is a pop artist. His paradoxes work in a remarkably similar way to Claes Oldenburg's objects – a huge soft baggy typewriter does something to the way you feel about typewriters, but no one would mistake it for a clear or clarifying statement about the hardware of communication. McLuhanisms are part of a superb tutorial technique, excellent devices in the hands of a seminar chairman, but, considered as ideas they are as lacking in definition as the television image itself.

Jerry Rubin is even more of a humourist than McLuhan. McLuhan uses intellectual wit to force a reconsideration of old print-bound modes of perception and categorization; Rubin uses the practical joke as a way of making capitalism look ridiculous. His appearance on British television was not up to his best comic standard, but nevertheless, it should ensure that the Frost show on Saturday 7 November 1970, will rate a mention in the history of television and the history of protest. David Frost had intended to interview the Chicago trial defendant, whose book *Do It* had just been published, but the show was invaded, taken over and all but demolished by a party of Hippies and Yippies mustered by the London underground press. In principle it could be described as a spontaneous act of participatory television; in practice many viewers felt that the programme had been appropriated by a crowd of childish hooligans with ideological pretensions. The cause of democracy may have been marginally advanced; depending on the backlash which might have been stimulated, the cause of freedom, in whose name the happening was engineered, may conceivably have suffered. Before the rostrum was conquered by the gang, firing water pistols and uttering into the mircrophone language of a more everyday kind than is yet thought suitable for the medium, Rubin had managed to tell Frost that he stood for the destruction of Western culture. 'Like this', he said, looking round the studio: 'narcotic television'.

Alexander Cockburn, using a more serious style of rhetoric, makes this charge:

Late bourgeois society can offer the underlying population neither security nor adventure. Bourgeois politics with its soporific consensus tries to provide a substitute for the former while the spectacle provides a substitute for the latter .... Britain, the most stagnant capitalist country, has naturally become a centre of spectacular production. Within the electronic space created by the new media the consumer is drenched in the pseudo-dramas and myths of the spectacle; and the ethos and mode of the spectacle penetrate the entire culture.

The quotation is from Alexander Cockburn's introduction to *Student Power*.[4]

It is worth noting, in passing, that Christopher Booker's tract against the times, *The Neophiliacs*,[5] written from the point of view of a conservative Christian, repelled by the hold of neurotic fantasy on British public life during the 1950s and 1960s, provides a minutely detailed description of what the left-wing revolutionary Alexander Cockburn calls 'the spectacle'.

Daniel Cohn-Bendit applies the same charge expressly to television. Instead of using 'the new media so as to gain greater mastery over the environment ... people today simply watch television as a surrogate for the lives they have ceased to live'.[6] In such terms, revolutionary critics of capitalist (and equally of bureaucratic communist) societies castigate television for providing a seductive distraction from action and participation, substituting a spectacle to be enjoyed for a world to be remade. According to McLuhan, we are all participants now; according to the revolutionaries we are all voyeurs now. Here is Cockburn again, listing television as part of the diversionary spectacle:

Our waning imperial system needs its combination of bread and circuses to retain the support of the population. In late capitalist society the fetished commodity and the spectacle conveniently answer this need. In helping alleviate the curse of over-production the spectacle brings into existence a motley retinue of its own: television producers, fashion consultants, show business personalities, gossip columnists, public relations officers, press departments, etc. The very essence of the spectacle is that the spectator should remain passively receptive towards the whole design, however frenzied he is in the pursuit of a particular spectacular myth or fashion.[7]

Daniel Cohn-Bendit allows that the television producers would have their part in a society that was communicating with itself, not merely being mesmerized by the spectacle:

While people today simply watch television as a surrogate for the lives they have ceased to live, in the new society they will use it as a means of widening their experience, of mastering the environment and of keeping in touch with the real lives of other people. If television programmes were to be put on for their social value and not solely because they induce the maximum hypnosis in the greatest numbers, they would enable it to extend the real democracy to the entire population.[8]

Something very like this critique would be accepted, and indeed has been advanced, by writers who would absolutely part company with student revolutionaries on political fundamentals. Jerry Rubin's very phrase 'narcotic television' can in fact be traced back to a hideous piece of jargon in the writings of two social scientists, the leading American communications theorists Paul F. Lazarsfeld and Robert K. Merton. They coined the term 'narcoticizing dysfunction' to describe what they hypo-sized was one of the main social consequences of the mass media. In an essay published in 1948 they explained[9]:

With distinct variations in different regions and among different social strata, the outpourings of the media presumably enable the twentieth-century American to 'keep abreast of the world'. Yet ... this vast supply of communications may elicit only a superficial concern with the problems of society, and this superficiality often cloaks mass apathy.

Their perceptive fears are worth quoting in full:

Exposure to this flood of information may serve to narcotize rather than to energize the average reader or listener. As an increasing meed of time is devoted to reading and listening, a decreasing share is available for organized action. The individual reads accounts of issues and problems and may even discuss alternative lines of action. But this rather intellectualized, rather remote connection with organized social action is not activated. The interested and informed citizen can congratulate himself on his lofty state of interest and information and neglect to see that he has abstained from decision and action. In short, he takes his secondary contact with the world of political reality, his reading and listening and thinking, as a vicarious performance. He comes to mistake *knowing* about problems of the day for *doing* something about them. His social conscience remains spotlessly clean. He *is* concerned. He *is* informed. And he has all sorts of ideas as to what should be done. But, after he has gotten through his dinner and after he has listened to his favored radio programmes and after he has read his second paper of the day, it is really time for bed.

In this peculiar respect, mass communications may be included among the most respectable and efficient of social narcotics. They may be so fully effective as to keep the addict from recognizing his own malady.

That the mass media have lifted the level of information of large populations is evident. Yet, quite apart from intent, increasing dosages of mass communications may be inadvertently transforming the energies of men from active participation into passive knowledge.

Two decades of research and conceptual refinement later, we can see there was a touch of the Golden-Age fallacy about the way they then framed this hypothesis. It is highly unlikely that people were reading and listening in time and with energy that would otherwise have been used 'for organized action'. Nevertheless, the narcotizing-dysfunction hypothesis still has value. When Dr William Belson, for example, at a time when only 35 per cent of the British population had television sets, studied the effects of television on viewers' interests and power of initiative, he found that on the whole (there were many exceptions), viewers' interests, even when featured in television programmes, were diminished, and so was their active behaviour. Politics was one of the areas in which their interest and initiative was reduced.[10]

A further twist to this critique, even providing ammunition for anyone disposed to a conspiracy theory about such matters, was unexpectedly provided by a highly experienced political journalist, the late Leonard Beaton. Beaton's subject was certain weaknesses of television's treatment of current affairs due to its dependence on visuals:[11]

A great sector of public affairs is concerned with money: with the management of the government's very important part in the economy, with the financing of the social services, with defence procurement and the nationalized industries. Putting this on television is very difficult, though many valiant efforts have been made. In Britain at present the greatest issue is undoubtedly the kind of political and economic relationship the country should make with her European neighbours. How can this be put on film? What can American public affairs programmes do about the great issues raised by the Strategic Arms Limitation Talks? The public has had to put up with those boring graphics with the bombers and rockets on each side over and over again: the public is bored and so are the producers.

But it was not a Yippie, crying 'narcotic television', or a Marxist cursing television's power to distract attention from what is really happening on the commanding heights of politics, but Beaton himself who went on to make this observation:

This situation is viewed by many responsible people with equanimity. There has been little resistance to the rule of television public affairs by impact men trained in film whose grasp of what is important is rudimentary. Occasionally we hear rumbles from politicians: but this is usually because they resent (with good reason) editing for impact which can sharply distort; or because they feel their opponents are having the better of the television time. It is seldom, however, that powerful voices show concern at the great issues which are not being converted into public debate. The reason, I suspect, is that there is relief that the system is being left to get on with these matters undisturbed.

Which at least serves to put us on our guard when evaluating television's contribution to participatory democracy in later chapters. The same fear, that television may be playing a similar diversionary role, but by distraction rather than selection, underlay one of Milton Shulman's liveliest essays. Shulman is well known as a constant critic of television (in the negative sense). He is often carping, he usually overstates, but he is frequently perceptive. The title of this particular essay carried on the addiction motif. It was called *The Big Fix* and sub-titled 'Why has TV tried to get us hooked on sport?'.[12] He wrote it soon after the 1970 General Election. Shulman shared the view of 'some serious foreign observers' (there were others in Britain who shared it too), that a

considerable proportion of the British electorate only realized there was an election taking place after England lost the quarter-final round of the World Cup to West Germany on 14 June. . . . For the first two weeks of the election campaign a large slice of the electorate was living in a fantasy world in which the winning of the World Cup was far, far more important than entry into the Common Market, the balance of payments, lower taxes, the future of trade unions and comprehensive schools, the choice of the rulers of their country.

No one expects Mr Shulman to be fair to the broadcasters, and it is not surprising that this article shows no appreciation that the expensive, technically complicated arrangements to transmit the World Cup via satellite from Mexico were negotiated long before Mr Wilson, unexpectedly and at short notice, chose that very time in which to hold an election. But that may not be a sufficient explanation for the relative air-time made available for the World Cup and the Election or for the difference in World Cup coverage between Britain and West Germany. According to Shulman:

In the week of the election itself – both Sundays inclusive – BBC-1 gave us no fewer than thirty-one hours of football. Its rival channel, ITV, produced nineteen hours of the same stuff. Most of that time England wasn't even in the competition. Frank Bough, the BBC commentator, accurately reflected the Corporation's present sense of proportion by claiming that England's defeat was a 'national disaster' ... I would estimate that the overtime session between Italy and West Germany was repeated no fewer than twenty-five times that frantic week.... West Germany, who beat us and took part in that hectic extra-time game with Italy and was not involved in a General Election, thought that the World Cup on its two channels merited a total of sixteen hours. We goggled at these kicking foreigners just three times as much.

General Elections usually occur every five years; World Cups every four. This particular World Cup was followed immediately by Wimbledon and other regular events. There were consequently six consecutive weeks of major sporting events and the BBC made a feature of this sequence in its publicity and promotion ('Six Glorious Weeks of Sport'). Milton Shulman's comment was typical of his distrust of the broadcasting authorities –

six neurotic weeks in which the BBC had acted like some sort of giant dope pedlar doing its best to fix the nation in some kind of psychedelic illusion about strength through sport.

His view is a shade puritanical. Although there were no doubt imperfections in the World Cup as a sporting event, on balance it seemed to add to the gaiety of nations and it is hardly necessary to lament television's part in that. On the other hand the unfortunate coincidence of six glorious weeks of sport with one of those rare quinquennial moments when the people as a whole may actually have some effect on the government did point up the power of the medium to distract when it is needed for more consequential purposes.

Whatever may be said about McLuhan's view, if it is his view, that we are all participants now, there is evidently more substance in the left-wing revolutionary charge that we are all voyeurs now, if only because substantial witnesses who are not left-wing revolutionaries, but are on the contrary prominent social scientists and journalists, agree with so much of it. The essence of the revolutionary case is, however, unconvincing. It is that television under capitalism is inevitably a surrogate and a diversionary spectacle, and that there is no point in tinkering about, trying to improve the medium, when what matters is the overthrow of the social structure in which it is embedded and whose values it inevitably embodies. This is obviously not the place to discuss the large political issue, but to justify the feasibility of my thesis, I would point to three factors to which neo-Marxist, anarchist and other revolutionary critics give insufficient weight – the complex and changing nature of British capitalism, the status of broadcasting in Britain, and the part which television has already played in fostering aspects of a participatory society.

It is obviously true that the constitution and programme content (including the unspoken assumptions of that content) of any television service are in some ways a direct reflection of the dominant political structure. In the United States, television is primarily a selling medium, and still earns Alistair Cooke's description, 'The Bartered Bride'; in the Soviet Union, it diffuses its master's voice. In both countries it is a chief instrument of indoctrination with the values of the ruling oligarchy. In the Netherlands, television reflects the ideological divisions of the country; in Scandinavia, it is the contemporary voice of the Scandinavian social conscience and respect for freedom.

British capitalist democracy contains within itself a great many conflicting tendencies, and such is the confusion of pressures and voices that there are many alternative routes which the society might take. When there was a clear distinction between the government, supervising a vast empire, and the governed; when Britain was run by a confident ruling class which read *The Times*, then its broadcasting was cast in a proconsular and missionary mould. When Britain lost its empire and had to live more by its commercial wits than by its ownership of other people's land; when those who ruled lost their magic with the governed, then the BBC became more of a forum for the society, and ceased acting as its mentor. Moreover, it found itself faced with a competitor, wholly financed out of advertising revenue.

These large changes in British broadcasting have nevertheless taken place *within* the tradition that broadcasting is a public resource to be used in the public interest (as chiefly demonstrated by the Television Act 1964, the prohibition on sponsored programmes and the rigorous system of advertising control). This is a profoundly valuable tradition on which to build. The task of reform would be appallingly difficult if broadcasting were the property of limited interests within society or if it were an agency of government. In Britain we have neither of these obstacles to overcome. Reform should be much easier here than it would be in, say, France or the United States. One must not be discouraged from working towards it by any *a priori* suspicion of rigidity which our society does not in fact show.

I have said nothing about the part which television has already played in furthering aspects of a participatory society, since that is a recurrent topic in subsequent chapters, but by overlooking the complexity of an evolving capitalism and the strength of the British tradition of independence in broadcasting, revolutionary critics may underestimate the extent to which the 'social-value' approach (as Cohn-Bendit called it) may be adopted and promoted now, without waiting for a 'new society' on the other side of the barricades. As a result of which they may ignore the democratic role that television might play in helping people decide what kind of new society they actually want.

5 Agenda for Social Action

Revolutionaries share a fatal flaw with conservative autocrats: both want to limit democracy, to cast it in a mould which they personally find acceptable. The point of democracy, on the contrary, is to contain within one society a dynamic struggle between alternative and often antagonistic life styles, policies and interests, without that society falling apart. Adopting a practical, rather than a utopian stance, it follows that progress can and will be achieved through working on two processes of reform, the larger of which contains the other but which could be in turn strongly influenced by it: on the basis of the positive beginnings already noted in chapters 2 and 3, our society should, as a matter of some urgency, embark on a programme for the development of a more fully participatory democracy. As part of this programme it will be necessary to appraise our communications resources, and as part of that to make television, the chief communications resource, adapt its own ways to serving the larger purpose of revivifying democracy, helping to create a community of discourse capable of sustaining and containing argument and tension.

This is not at all an impossible enterprise, not one of those situations in which chickens endlessly await eggs which perpetually yearn for transformation into chickenhood. Such situations are frequently construed in terms which inevitably produce an immobolizing pessimism: institution X or situation Y cries out for reform; but X and Y are seen to have their roots in P and their intimate connections with Q, which also seem therefore to need reform. In no time it is apparent that, as someone will certainly say: 'It is not X that needs reform, it is society itself!' This pervasive and paralysing fallacy rests on the failure to recognize that whereas institution X is concrete, 'society' itself is an abstraction. No wonder the task of reforming it seems daunting.

The enlargement of the participatory mode in democracy is labour for many hands, different people working in and on different institutions, hopefully seeing from time to time the actual interconnectedness of things and engaging in sufficient crosstalk for a strategy of priorities to appear. Certain features of this agenda for social consideration and action can already be discerned:

1. It would be useful (though not indispensable, since participation can be forced from below as well as encouraged from above) if all political parties were to endorse the Skeffington approach across the political board. It would not be sufficient to mouth the jargon of participation without making changes in the structure and operation of the numerous arms of government.

2. Social, political and economic institutions of many kinds need either to introduce for the first time democratic procedures or to enlarge existing procedures by providing channels of consultation to facilitate participatory action by those affected, and to promote dialogue between authority and the public. For many industrial and commercial enterprises this could amount to a revolution in itself. Suggestion boxes would not count as an adequate instrument of participation. For institutions which are already part of the democratic structure it would mean positively welcoming the intervention of such bodies as AASE, Release, Shelter and the like. Consulting popular pressure groups should be as legitimate a part of the democratic process as consulting the CBI and the TUC. Town councillors who resent such pressure groups and feel that it can 'all be left to them, since it is their job to represent the people', are deceiving themselves.

Since the pattern to be adopted may now be found even in North Kensington, it can be adopted anywhere. The Borough Council there used to give every appearance of callous indifference to the welfare of the inhabitants of Notting Hill. After a period of hostilities between the Council and voluntary groups agitating about housing, the Council ultimately realized that its own work would prosper if it brought bodies such as the Golborne Social Rights Committee into its confidence and into the pre-planning process. The Department of the Environment inspector had been more impressed by the housing statistics collected by this Committee than by those of the council.

3. There will need to be new institutions to encourage the articulation of hitherto unvoiced needs and viewpoints. Radice and his colleagues advocate a network of consumer shops, extensions of the Citizens Advice Bureaux, which might provide supportive secretarial and other services for popular pressure groups.[1] The Association of Neighbourhood Councils is pressing for a new tier in local government to offset the large scale and remoteness of new organs of local government. The successful, voluntary community councils in Liverpool exemplify another approach. They complement the work of city councillors without over-riding it and improve understanding between 'the Corpy' and the population it governs. Some of these new institutions need to be formally set up; others will arise spontaneously, as voluntary bodies; the growth and maintenance of yet other voluntary organizations could be deliberately stimulated.

4. The post-Seebohm reorganization of the social services provides one framework for such official stimulation of unofficial endeavour. The Home Office Urban Programme shows one way in which it can be done. It is right to concentrate the limited resources of the Urban Programme in areas of severe and multiple deprivation, but quite wrong that the resources should be so limited and more fundamentally wrong to assume that community development is appropriate only to backward countries and seedy city centres. The experiences and methods being acquired and devised could profitably be applied to all areas of the country, modified to reflect varieties of milieux, population composition, and the presence within populations of appropriate professional talents, leadership skills, and so on.

5. This extension of community development would need to be accompanied by the provision of a comprehensive service of adult education. Representative democracy pays lip service to adult education, but governments have always treated this part

of the education system with indifference or contempt bordering sometimes on hostility. A participatory democracy cannot afford such negligence, and no doubt the Russell Committee of inquiry into the future of adult education will advocate a more central role for it.

6. The growth of community service as a feature of school life and of such activities as Community Service Volunteers and Task Force need also to be used, not merely for their value as a character-forming influence or even for their objective contribution to welfare, but also to implant in young people the notion that it is *their* society and participating in its workings is a right, a duty and even a source of satisfaction. Apart from apathy and indifference towards social life and its impact on individuals, two major attitudes are often manifest. The more common expresses itself as discontent that some part of the social machinery is failing, and leads to an indignant: 'something ought to be done about it'. The other attitude, less common but growing, says in effect: 'these are our organizations and we must pitch in, as necessary, to help work them properly'. This is the attitude which the schools need to inculcate and which other social institutions must respond to.

7. This brief summary of the kinds of social action by which participatory democracy could develop must conclude with an explicit reference to the organs of communication. The scientists quoted at the end of chapter 3 saw the necessity for action at three levels – political, educational, and at the level of communications procedures. This item on the agenda provides a bridge to the chief concern of all that follows: the role of television in the social transformation envisaged.

The people are active in an Active Society, says Etzioni, when they are 'aware, committed and potent', and clearly the growth of these three attributes depends on more than 'communication procedures'.[2] The constitutional, political structure within which these procedures operate is of fundamental importance. But equally clearly the development of a participatory society depends even more on the range, variety and openness of its communication procedures than does merely representative democracy. All societies now need to appraise their communication resources: are they capable of bearing the loads that will be laid upon them? In what ways do they need adapting? In which of a multiplicity of new forms of communication which are technologically feasible should each society decide to invest? How should these modes of communication be used? For what kind of messages? What do we need to wish to say to each other through them? These large questions break down into a battery of specifics, some of which refer to broadcasting in general and television in particular.

Does television already make us 'aware, committed and potent', as some allege? Could it be used more than it is at present to foster awareness, commitment and potency? Will it help us talk to each other or drift into being an escapist adjunct to repression? What sort of programmes would facilitate public participation in deciding the destinies of society? Since – and this much has been conceded – all mass media are permeated by the values and practices of the larger society of which they are a part, is our liberal democracy in effect too oligarchic and hierarchical to take full advantage of television's capacity? Remembering the metaphor which McLuhan borrowed and popularized to put the supposedly powerful medium of television in its place, is the giant just too irredeemably timid, or, in using it for the promotion of a participatory democracy, shall we find a mission for the medium?

The development of a more fully participatory democracy requires then the appraisal and adaptation of all institutions – evaluating them through such questions as, do they provide proper channels of communication with their users and other affected sectors of the public? Are they sufficiently accountable? and so forth; and as part of this process it specifically requires an appraisal of communications resources.

In one sense, television is already unofficially under this kind of review, with pressure mounting as I write to create a Broadcasting Council and a fairly widely voiced feeling that broadcasters have power without responsibility. The same has been said of press journalists in the past, but more abusively – press critics used to make much of the point that power without responsibility was 'the privilege of the harlot through the ages'.

The obvious danger, when strong criticisms of broadcasting begin to develop a political head of steam, is that its generators may be more eager to restrain the medium than to make it genuinely more accountable; to reduce 'being responsible' to 'avoiding giving offence'. They may intend democracy, but achieve only emasculation.

The reforms proposed so far suffer from assuming that the broadcasting to be more adequately supervised is the same that we have today. The approach is administrative, not creative. In Part Three I shall explore ways in which television programmes may positively encourage participation in the running of society and show that, as a result, it is even possible, unthinkable though it may seem in terms of current practice, for 'ordinary' members of the public to become involved in programme planning, that is, participate in the running of television. Such a development would really be of democratic significance, much more profound in its reality and its effects than setting up for broadcasting either something remote and ineffectual, like a Consumers Consultative Committee for a nationalized industry, or something much more effective, in which case freedom of communication could be at risk.

To determine what participatory needs television will be expected to service is not easy, because the extent and nature of participation cannot be judged. It was acknowledged earlier (in chapter 2) that keenness and readiness to participate would partly be a function of temperament and personality, and that the areas of social life in which given individuals would choose to participate would likewise vary. On the other hand, a society in which most people's lives are perpetually and comprehensively shaped by the decisions of a relatively small group of other people, is clearly failing to afford its members the fullness of stature to which as human beings they are entitled. Furthermore, there is much evidence, some of which I have quoted, that increasing numbers of people no longer find such a society tolerable. A programme for the deliberate enlargement of participation will increase the demand, for feasibility strengthens the motivation of those who want the prospect of effective action and not just those pleasures of the fight which are sometimes enough to sustain more militant minorities. This is not a real problem; the evolution of television will proceed *pari passu* with the implementation of the larger process.

Making due allowance for varieties of temperament, talent and concern, it is clear that all people all the time need a clear and accurate picture of the world in which they live, not in order to participate in all its doings at all levels – international, national, regional and local – but in order to keep it under surveillance; most people most of the time will need information to keep them vigilant over specialized aspects of that total scene, so that they may actively intervene either over long periods (because it happens to be a sector of political, social or cultural life in which they are particularly interested) or in an emergency (because a contemplated change of policy seems to threaten them, for example). At these different levels and for these different purposes, there are at least three essentials – basic, ongoing information – about the main features of political life; knowledge of where further or more specialized information may be obtained; and access to effective channels of action and communication as necessary. Since many of the actors and voices will be in conflict in any situation, it is also important that these channels should facilitate dialogue through which conflict, compromise or reconciliation may be expressed. These are difficult matters to generalize about, but not so difficult to understand in practice. They provide pointers at least to what needs television must serve.

Part Two
Information for Democracy

6 Home and Abroad

Information in abundance

In August 1968, television enabled us to witness the Soviet invasion of Czechoslovakia and to be part of a large audience of witnesses all over the world. Thirty years previously Neville Chamberlain, taking advantage of the public's vast pre-television ignorance, treacherously dismissed Czechoslovakia as 'a small country a long way away of which we know little'. It is inconceivable that a politician should use such a rationalization today.

First, then, we look to television to provide us with information to keep us, as national and world citizens, 'in the picture', so that we can maintain a watch on all those developments which we need to take account of in running our own lives, or to engage our sympathies for and enrich understanding of the lives of others. It is obvious that television already meets this requirement to a remarkable degree. The high rating of television as a major educational force in the very first chapter largely rests on this lavish provision of information of many kinds – not only about politics and current affairs, but about a shifting range of subjects which in total take in almost every aspect of life. The BBC's Charter and the Television Act oblige the broadcasters to inform, and inform they do. One week's topics on three channels evoke a situation which we take for granted: in the first week of July 1970 the BBC and ITV provided information about the weather, sport, gardening, a curate's life, stained-glass windows, farming, life in Norway, Louis Armstrong, insects, current movies, the cosmetics industry, Victorian architecture, zoos, the Peak District, life in Borstal, painters (Giacometti and Charles Russell), the Spanish Riding School, the International Musical Eisteddfod, decimalization, house repairs, safer driving, clay-pigeon shooting, the New Forest, the Great Abbai Expedition, organized crime, George Robey, Sammy Davis Jr, and the reception of the musical *Hair* in Tel Aviv. Most of this information satisfies curiosity, gives pleasure, does no harm.

The amount of political information in this profusion is enormous. News and news magazines represent about 30 per cent of the productive effort of Independent Television as a whole. The amount available to viewers varies in different ITV regions from about 7 to 14 per cent of total transmission time. In the four weeks ending 15 March 1970, the average number of homes watching the *News at Ten* was 8·7 million, representing about half the population. This huge audience should be compared with that for the most consistently popular show on television: during the same four weeks 8·85 million homes were tuned in to *Coronation Street*. The audience for *Manhunt*, the serial about the French Resistance, was 6·95 million homes. Nearly as many (6·9 million) watched *World in Action*'s current affairs documentaries and *This Week*'s review of politics and current questions (6·75 million).[1] BBC news and current affairs output also reveals massive audiences tuning to the medium. An audience of ten million for the 8·50 p.m. news bulletin on BBC–1 'is not exceptional' and *Panorama* continued to attract audiences of about seven million in 1968–9.[2] (The BBC counts viewers not homes.)

Given such enormous viewing figures, it is hardly surprising that most people now identify television as their chief source of information. If the public is right about what it knows and about how it knows what it knows, then television has moved into first place as the agent of a supposedly well-informed citizenry. This is the finding of several research projects and opinion surveys. As I write, this conclusion has been confirmed by two surveys conducted by Opinion Research Centre. The first was published in the *Sunday Times*, a month before the General Election in June 1970. ORC asked its sample of the public 'Which medium do you think helps you most to know and understand what is going on in Britain?' Fifty-six per cent of the public replied 'television'. Radio was almost a non-starter (7 per cent only, just ahead of the 'Don't Knows'!), and newspapers were a

poor second, at 32 per cent. People were also asked which kinds
of television programme helped them most 'to understand what
is going on in Britain'. News bulletins were picked out by 58
per cent, current-affairs programmes by 34 per cent and party
political broadcasts by 4 per cent.[3] Two days after the General
Election, fieldwork started on the second survey, commissioned
on this occasion by the Independent Television Authority. This
time ORC asked: 'Where do you get most of your ideas about
what is going on in the world today?' To this question, 59 per
cent of the sample replied 'television', and 39 per cent mentioned
newspapers. Television was relatively more important to women
(61 per cent), to men and women over fifty-five years of age (64-5
per cent), to the C2 DE socio-economic groups (63-5 per cent)
and for some reason, to the public in the Yorkshire Television
area (67 per cent).[4]

The enlargement of awareness – geographical, social, cultural
– is television's most indisputable achievement. And increasing
awareness is in itself a major democratizing function – it is the
antithesis of the language which only a particular caste may
understand, or the club tape which conveys information only to
subscribers. But democrats want more from it and they seem to
have got more; they have welcomed it as a potentially unrivalled
creator of a necessary condition of democracy: a well-informed
public. To be well informed is a specific form of awareness. Sir
Robert Fraser was one of many who welcomed television with
these high hopes. In a speech to the Newspaper Society, another
retrospective one delivered shortly before his retirement, he
looked back on some of his earlier expectations:

When Independent Television was less than three years old I find I
committed myself to some views about the influence of television on
the democratic process. ... I was then, in the first place, greatly
struck by the emergence of a vast new political audience. I did the
little sums all of us in television do from time to time. I noticed that,
while the old style political meeting had fallen into decline, television's
political audiences, even in those early days, were so large that a
politician could, in one night, talk to more electors than he could
hope directly to reach if he addressed public meetings, even of a
respectable size, every single night in a creditably long political

career. So much more is that now the case, for the television audience, then half the nation, is now virtually the whole of it.

Through the news bulletin, the party broadcast, the political interview and the political discussion, the electorate could see and hear and to some extent judge the personalities of their leaders as never before in the history of the franchise. Never had there been such a democratic exposure.

I noticed that this new exposure had also a new feature – a singular feature not to be found in exactly the same form in any other of the mass media – namely, that in television programmes no viewer would hear one side of an argument without hearing, usually then and there, and in intended equality, the other. It was not thought strange . . . but robust and proper that newspapers should espouse opinions. Indeed, this was an accepted and indispensable part of the continuing democratic debate. But it was through television that the mass of the electorate was now consistently and as a matter of policy subjected to the process of hearing both sides.[5]

So that television was playing, or was thought to be playing, an educative role as well as an informative one. John Stuart Mill had pointed out in his essay *On Liberty* that a man who only knows his own point of view has an unsure grasp even of that.

Television was now beginning to educate us to take account of differences of opinion, to measure and test our own against those of others, helping us to distinguish the validity of policies from the integrity or sincerity of the politicians advocating them, fostering not only awareness but also perhaps understanding.

As the Skeffington Report points out, the provision of information is a necessary part of the process of participation, even though it is by no means the whole story. Hence the assessment of television's fitness, as it works at present, to help carry us through to a more participatory style of democracy, must start by examining its role as chief source of public information. How should we assess the value of the information television makes available, especially political information in the widest sense? Is it comprehensive enough? is it authentically delivered? is it useful? do we make good use of it? (not the same as, 'is it useful?') are we in fact well-informed citizens distinguished by our insight and understanding?

Television's ability to promote a well-informed democracy depends on three factors – on the information accessible or available to television for diffusion (the rest of this chapter); on the way in which television mediates that information (chapter 7); and finally on the audience – our sets may be switched on, but what about our minds? (chapter 8). Each of these factors is complex, requiring a range of specialisms properly to comprehend and explain them, but they are all germane to my main theme and I must indicate some of their implications for it. The review starts, then, with the issue of what information is available, nationally and internationally, to the people and to television.

Reticence of government

It must be remembered that the world is now so complex, and the business of governments so comprehensive, that legislatures are themselves not particularly well informed. Under the circumstances, it is hardly surprising that the people have only a partial inkling of what is going on and only a superficial acquaintance with the issues and the data relevant to the wise selection and scrutiny of governments.

Members of Parliament, even though they spend all or most of their working time on public affairs, do not consider themselves particularly well-informed about the matters on which they formally decide in the division lobbies. Anthony Barker and Michael Rush, who interviewed 111 backbenchers for their study *The Member of Parliament and his Information*, found that:

Nine MPs in ten ... did not believe that members as a whole felt adequately informed on Government administration; only one of those nine excepted himself from the general feeling of inadequacy which he perceived among his colleagues.[6]

These feelings of inadequacy were not only due to the sheer range and complexity of the issues on which members are expected to deliberate and adjudicate. It was in part due to the way in which Parliament itself worked. Seven members in ten wanted more specialized select committees set up, along the lines described in chapter 3. And part of the blame was attributed to the reticence of governments:

Our survey of backbenchers found little feeling among MPs that ministers were over-indulgent with official information: about half thought that ministers, of any party, positively wished to limit MPs knowledge while only one MP in six denied this. The rest (mostly more experienced members) considered that both ministers and times varied.

Labour members were, of course, responding on their own party's ministers and longer-serving ones tended to distinguish, sometimes by name, Labour ministers who were very open on both information and policy discussion with their backbench colleagues from others who seemed hardly able to blow their noses in Labour backbenchers' company without checking their departments' official view and perhaps asking the Prime Minister's permission as well.

If this complaint by backbench MPs is justified, and even our representatives find their participation hampered, it is not surprising that lack of information among the governed is exacerbated even more by the reluctance, not unique to senior civil servants, but found among men of power everywhere, to tell people what is happening or what is proposed. Modern governments have been forced to overcome this reticence to some extent. It is now customary to consult representatives of vested interests before implementing policies directly affecting those interests and this is not a negligible contribution to democracy. But governments wanting to know how to manoeuvre their way through the conflicting pressures exerted by big business and small shopkeepers, managements and trades unions, the Association of Education Committees and the National Union of Teachers, by the aircraft manufacturers and the naval establishment, are obviously still a long way from knowing what corresponds to the wishes and best interests of the public at large.

During the 1960s, British governments became marginally more information-conscious. White Papers, enunciating government policy prior to Parliamentary debate, were now sometimes preceded by Green Papers, indicating the lines on which the government was thinking. The amount and quality of statistics improved. The Department of Education and Science provided a good example. Since 1961 the Department had published annually volumes of statistics providing essential information about the education service which was not previously available. Traditionally, Her Majesty's Inspectors, who know more about the quality of educational activity in this country than any other body of experts, have acted like a clandestine corps – their survey reports were only available to those reported on and their masters. But in 1966, the Department started publishing *Trends in Education*, through which HMIs were not only allowed to express opinions about educational policy and practice, but even to sign their names to them.

This gradual acceptance by governments of the need to share information is not only important for the people. It also affects the soul of the administration, on which the authenticity of democratic life in part depends. Jay Blumler discerns a 'quite pernicious and corrupting consequence of the existence of steep informational disparities between political leaders and ordinary voters', which he sums up in the phrase 'unfamiliarity breeds contempt'.

The point is that informational inequalities between people who are unavoidably and persistently engaged in communication with each other do seem to breed manipulative forms of political behaviour. In fact a vicious circle with two reinforcing tendencies can be set in motion whenever politicians and citizens think about public affairs on quite different informational and conceptual wavelengths. Politicians who perceive voters as ignoramuses may conclude, not only that a manipulative public relations strategy is necessary in order to achieve certain desirable policy objectives, but also that those individuals who are too apathetic and indifferent to become better informed even *deserve* in a sense to be manipulated.[7]

Such attitudes militate strongly against the growth of informed participation as a right.

The business of government or of administering a major enterprise is so demanding in itself that those responsible for it often find it irksome to have to explain and justify what they are doing as well. Inertia is also reinforced by the inheritance of an aristocratic sense that it is undignified and ought to be unnecessary for *les responsables* to give an account of themselves, and this makes resistance to providing the public (or employees or consumers) with information even stronger. Publicity is felt to be vulgar and potentially dangerous; accountability is merely part of the mythology of public life, to be circumvented in practice as much as possible. The growth of the public relations business is in part a response to this disagreeable situation: employ specialists to tell people as much as it is fit for them to know, enough to pacify them, preferably enough to make them loyal and proud of the system.

Consequently, the pull of tradition causes governments to remain taciturn, and institutions, on whose operations all our fates depend, singularly uninformative. (Take the Bank of England, for instance. What the Bank of England knows and recommends about the British economy is of fundamental importance. One does not expect bankers to be any more loquacious than poker players, of course, and for similar reasons. But the Bank of England could provide a better service to the public than it does at present without putting the economic security of the country in jeopardy.)

In chapters 2 and 3 we saw that there begins to be a pull in the other direction, however. There are signs that governments and leaders of major corporations are slowly accepting that the mythology of accountability might be a guide to practical politics. There are so many areas of life where policies simply will not work unless the people are prepared for them, properly understand them, even have an opportunity to comment on them. This awareness at the top is pricked into a more urgent, responsive state of mind by three forms of pressure from below:

1. *Power has been decentralized* to an increasing extent. In the pamphlet which led The Open Group optimistically to call this 'the centrifugal society', they wrote:

The Government is now ringed by tens of thousands of organizations trying to influence it and each other. Civil rights were won in the eighteenth century, political rights in the nineteenth century and in the twentieth economic rights. But change has throughout depended on exercising the right to free association and combination. It has become more crucial than ever in this century. If parliament was the great exemplar of democracy in the last century, in this it is the Old Chiswick Protection Society, the Post Office Engineering Union and the National Union of Students.[8]

As we have seen, all these pressure groups want to know where they stand. They insist in knowing what government intends. They assert their right to affect what government proposes. As a result of their pressure, a wider public sometimes learns what is going on and provides a climate of approval, acceptance or resistance which to some extent shapes what happens by conditioning the initiatives of the principal protagonists.

2. As we have also noted, *the public is now much more volatile.* If the crossing is dangerous to children, it will be blocked by mothers with banners and prams; if the noise from the motorway is intolerable, the residents will picket the roads until they are rehoused; if families are homeless, they will squat in unoccupied premises; if pay increases too slowly or if managements are cavalier, the workers will strike. The model of industrial action is now reproduced in the wider society. The industrial community, though regulated by law and custom, is an authoritarian system, with strike action as a necessary antiauthoritarian form of protection for those at the bottom of the hierarchy. Militancy in civic and academic life means the people now feel that in effect society, though it has pretensions to democracy, is as authoritarian and hierarchic as industry, to be influenced more effectively by harassing and demonstrating against leaders than by reasoned discussion. Although those in power still tend to oscillate between stubborn obtuseness and precipitate capitulation to pressure, indications were cited in chapter 3 that a growing number recognize that it will pay to inform and consult those at the receiving end of policy decisions.

3. *The media are vigilant.* They magnify the effect of group pressures and popular manifestations by reporting them. Although Cecil King and others have hoped that democracy would prosper through a closer working partnership between governments, the press and broadcasting, democracy continues to benefit profoundly from the tension between the media and the rulers.[10] The media exist to disclose, to publish and be damned. Secrecy in high places is a perpetual challenge to them. In principle, and frequently in practice, the television interview, for example, represents a real advance in the democratic process. Underlying this new form of journalism are three assumptions: the people have a right to know; the people want to know; and the accountability of politicians, captains of nationalized industries, general secretaries of trades unions, means they must

literally and in person give an account of themselves not only when challenged in Parliament and boardroom but in public, on the box.

It is not inconceivable that these forces – pressure groups, popular agitation, amplified by media coverage and reinforced by media vigilance – might begin to act in unison well enough to achieve a legislative advance already made in Scandinavia. For profound historical and geographical reasons, the Scandinavian countries are notoriously more effective as democracies than Britain and it is unwise to expect over-populated, class-divided, half-educated Britain to move easily in their direction. Nevertheless, the momentum behind community action groups (such as the Golborne Social Rights Committee in Notting Hill Gate), could lead to something like the bill introduced in Norway in 1970, which establishes the right of the public to access to information from state and municipal authorities (except on matters affecting security, foreign relations and the like). The Danes are planning similar legislation; in Sweden and Finland they already have it. If the Right to Know were introduced here, at a sweep all these *ad hoc* agitations, nibbling away at a sometimes impervious, sometimes nervous authority, would be rendered anachronistic. Not only does participation depend upon information; the provision of information *as a right* makes an enormous difference to people's sense of whether they are members or subjects. When so much information is secret then *we* seem to be living, often on sufferance, in *their* society. Access to information helps to induce awareness that the society *is* the people who constitute it, both those in power or office, and the public.

In short, by joining with other media in giving status and prominence to protest and participatory action, television may help to improve its own access to information and thus provide in turn a better informational springboard for further popular vigilance and action.

Through a glass darkly

However, Britain is now only in a residual geographical sense, an island. The lives of people in a democracy depend on far more than the decisions of their own elected and partially accountable governments. They also depend on events and forces in the rest of the world. Our futures are being shaped at this moment by the accumulation of changes in Latin America and the Third World. Our economic viability is conditioned by the decisions of trans-national firms. The morality and efficiency of our actions as a nation depends on information, more than most of us have, on say, life in South Africa or the intricacies of the European Economic Community. For all the talk about a global village, how much do we actually know about what is going on in it? To know that there is a war on in Vietnam is like knowing there is a fire blazing on the other side of the village. We are not clear who started it, we are puzzled that some of the firemen seem to be using petrol to extinguish the flames, and we are meanwhile quite unaware that someone is excavating a mine into which another part of the village will shortly subside out of view.

Television is not itself responsible, or mainly responsible, for the way in which international information and news is gathered and distributed. The fact remains that the imbalance in the supply and flow of information is seriously disabling to a world that needs to communicate effectively with itself and to any nation that needs to pick its way with any confidence through to a future in that world. Television has inherited and cannot single-handedly reform a highly distorted set up. It is well described in Wilbur Schramm's *Mass Media and National Development*.[10]

Schramm's sub-title 'The Role of Information in the Developing Countries' indicates his perspective of concern. He looks at the problems created for developing countries by the uneven and distorted flow of information (not only news) between different parts of the world. I am concerned with the complementary problem created for Britain and other relatively more developed countries.

This is the position, as Schramm summarizes it:

the flow of news among nations is thin ... it is unbalanced, with heavy coverage of a few highly developed countries and light coverage of many less-developed ones, and ... it tends to ignore important events and to distort the reality it presents.

It is probably inevitable and to some extent right that the flow should be so heavy from a few highly developed countries. Analyses and surveys quoted by Schramm show that for one month in the spring of 1961, the foreign news in the press of thirteen nations on five continents was dominated throughout by four countries – the United States, the Soviet Union, the United Kingdom and France. In Brazil, the newspapers carried more stories about these four countries than about nearby Argentina; the Indian press had more to say about them than about its neighbour Pakistan. News flows from the highly developed to the less-developed countries, from Europe and North America to the other continents, above all from the USA and the USSR to all other countries. This flow is inevitable because gathering and diffusing news is an expensive business. The richer the country, the more it can afford it. The four dominant countries are the homes of the five world news agencies – AP and UPI, Reuters, *Agence France Presse* and Tass. The flow is also in large part justifiable, at least in respect of the USA and the USSR, because these countries dominate the politics of the whole world.

But as Schramm observes: 'the heaviness of news flow from a *few* countries is less disturbing than the thinness of the flow from *many* countries'. He notes the conclusion of the Latin American editor of the *Miami News*, who analysed the flow of one agency's news from Latin America: if this wire file were the only source of enlightenment for the rest of the world, then Latin America would be considered to consist mainly of Cuba. From several countries there was no news at all during the month of the analysis. Brazil got a mention once, when it was visited by Prince Philip. Peru was notable for producing short items about an aeroplane crash and a bus wreck. Nothing happened, apparently, in Chile except that Billy Graham was evangelizing in Santiago. Thus one of these countries only appeared in the cables because it produced two routine disasters, important to people locally concerned, but, considered as information, totally unilluminating to the rest of the world. Two other countries qualified for attention solely because they were visited by eminent persons from two of the four dominant news-providing countries.

This pattern persists. We know about Mexico City because that is where the World Cup was held. We know that Brazil is where the world's best footballers come from, as well as the nuts. What else do we know about Latin America? Do we understand why it is a continent in which diplomats are kidnapped?

The flow of news through television, as distinct from other media, is beset by peculiar balance problems of its own. Robin Day makes this diagnosis:

one of television's *inherent* limitations is that its coverage contains a built-in bias against free and open societies. Television is far more able to give a critical and unflattering picture of a free society than of any totalitarian one.[11]

This bias is caused by some of the physical and practical characteristics of the medium. To cover a situation in a particular country, television must first get in. And that, as Robin Day points out, 'is a lot less easy for a four-man television team with twenty boxes of equipment, than for a single newspaperman with one air-travel bag and a notebook'. Once in, the team has to move about, rather noticeably, with their truckloads of paraphernalia. Then they have to find people who will talk. And even if the misson succeeds, the team 'still has to get its film *out*, intact and uncensored'.

The result, in Day's words:

On the television screens of the Western world (and, no doubt, of the Communist world also) pictorial reports of violence, injustice and protest in the United States are part of the viewers' daily diet. Much of this coverage is made and marketed throughout the world by America itself. Yet how effectively is television able to cover injustice, oppression and brutality in other parts of the world such as China, Russia, Czechoslovakia, Spain or Rhodesia? By reason of its own operational needs television is inherently incapable of giving fair and balanced reporting of a very large part of the world today.

Television needs to be harnessed to strengthen democracy, actually to make it work better, not merely to make people feel better about it. Yet the result of the bias which Day describes may be to undermine even such confidence in democracy as it exists. This was certainly one of Sir Robert Fraser's fears when he was in charge at the ITA. I have already quoted the optimistic opening of his valedictory speech on this subject. He continues more apprehensively by observing that 'the frontiers of democracy have not expanded, but contracted':

only a very few people for a very brief time have been able to govern themselves, a tiny proportion of the world's population for a tiny proportion of the centuries of history. I see that even today democracy, a word that half the world has stolen and other parts do not even bother to appropriate, is safely and successfully practised by only a small group of nations. . . .

This has deepened my sense that self-government is the happiest of all human achievements, but also my sense that it is a rare flower of man's total accomplishment, and that those of us who tend it had better be conscious not only of its beauty, for human freedom is beautiful, and in danger if we do not feel it to be so, but also, in the long tides of history, of its fragility.

Television provides a distorted critique of this world, leading Fraser to ask:

If people are continuously exposed to a recitation of the troubles of a democratic community . . . if they are so frequently told that this is wrong and that is wrong, and perhaps the other is actually scandalous, is there not some danger that in the end some may conclude that, as a method of reaching political decisions, democracy does not seem to work very well, that maybe there is something wrong with a system that seems so productive of abuse? . . . How much of this constant wear and tear is democracy expected to take?[12]

Robin Day shares the anxiety:

This cannot fail to have a profound effect on public opinion in free countries where television is *the* mass medium of news and information. The public is constantly reminded in the most vivid way of the evils in its own society and in those other countries where television is free to prowl. But the evils of life in closed totalitarian countries cannot be given anything like the same emphasis. All of which tends to lead to a grossly distorted view of the world.[13]

We must not become complacent about this 'grossly distorted view'. But in drawing up the balance sheet it is important to remember that most people in previous generations had no view at all. At the end of the Second World War, Wendell Wilkie wrote an optimistic book entitled *One World*. Even as he wrote,

Stalin, Churchill and Truman were hard at work providing justification for the suspicions mutually entertained by the communist and capitalist allies. Although we are still far from being one world, the widespread awareness of the interdependence of each nation's fate with every other, is much stronger. This is due in part to the knowledge that war could be more literally total than ever before. A planet which can be overseen and obliterated from the moon, must needs begin to think more of its unity at risk than of its division. But it is not only a sense of threat to the planet and the species which is involved. It is also a far greater sense of shared humanity, for which television is mainly responsible. Not so long ago, civil war in Jordan would have been regarded with xenophobic indifference. Few people in Western Europe or North America would have cared all that much about Arabs killing Arabs. When fighting did break out between King Hussein and the PLF guerrillas, the rest of the world was appalled. Great power diplomats were active because local hot wars between nominees of Cold-War powers are not supposed to get out of hand. They had the earnest support of people everywhere because they were so outraged at the slaughter and suffering. It was as though the professional point of view on international affairs maintained by the International Red Cross had suddenly found support from public opinion throughout the world. Remembering for example, the despatches from Keith Hatfield and others and the pictures they brought back from Amman, it is clear that through such coverage television has helped initiate a mass conversion to the ethic of the Red Cross.

Apart from its intrinsic advantages over other media, television has endeavoured to compensate for some of its disadvantages, and to offset the imbalance in news flow, by sharing facilities on some kind of international basis, through Eurovision and the use of satellites. The new link in Spain, for example, may result in an improved flow of messages and pictures via satellite from Latin America, thereby remedying that large gap in present coverage. Apart from such permanent facilities, television commonly sends news teams *ad hoc* to a situation which has reached crisis point, especially if that situation has become visible and therefore filmable. It will occasionally ferret out information for itself, but this is so expensive as to be a limited operation.

Apart from the brilliance with which television frequently shows important events as they are, the television interview is also important in the overseas field. Just as it has added a qualitatively new and important dimension to the practice of democratic accountability, so it has even to some extent altered the framework of international diplomacy. In 1958 Robin Day was the first British reporter to interview President Nasser after the Suez invasion. As a result, Nasser addressed the British people in their own homes, even though diplomatic relations had been broken off. Protocol has not been quite the same since and, as Day observes, 'similar interviews are now commonplace'.

Despite the major advances achieved by television, the severe imbalance in the flow of news regretted by Schramm persists and seems likely to do so since it is a consequence of the more fundamental imbalance in political, economic and technological power between the developed countries and the Third World, and of the political divisions within the world. We know little of the Chinese and they know little of us, though it will clearly be of growing importance that we should not long remain so ignorant and so frightened of each other. The new interest of the Americans and the Chinese in each other will gradually dispel that ignorance: changes in the world balance of power and in relations between states will therefore have more effect on the flow of news than any efforts to reform the situation at the level of the media themselves.

It might still be useful, however, if, through UNESCO and other international agencies, reviews could be undertaken of the supply and demand of news and information throughout the world. Some reforms may turn out to be possible even within the limits set at present by international power relationships.

Such a review would be more practical if individual states had a clearer idea of what news and information they actually needed. An international policy on news and information, implemented through appropriate and effective agencies of exchange and transmission, is unlikely to be achieved if nation states are individually unclear about their media policies. Schramm's book concludes with a series of 'recommendations' to developing countries and their friends and aiders. He offers such advice as:

A developing country should examine the use it is making of the mass media in multiplying the flow of information on development ... should plan a balanced and measured growth for its mass media, with a view to relationships among the media and to those between the media and other aspects of development ... should give special attention to continuing mass media with interpersonal communication ... should provide adequate training for its information personnel ... should seek as much feedback as possible from its mass media. ...

and so on, each maxim receiving amplification at some length.[14]

This is all sound advice, but it is notable that developed countries act on hardly any of it themselves. It is a case of don't do as I do, do as I say. The media have grown up *ad hoc* in the developed countries, to serve social purposes, to make a profit, to exploit a technology. But no country is reviewing its total stock of media resources and setting that against a review of its information needs. Decisions may be made to invest in another television channel without regard to the total matrix of media available, a newspaper will be allowed to fold for reasons which have nothing to do with its social role or its journalistic adequacy.

Poor men are not overwhelmed by options. Accordingly, it is in principle easier to assess the information needs of a developing country, as prescribed by Schramm, than those of a country on the eve of the politics of choice, as envisaged in chapter 3. It is also easier to determine information needs for an autocratic regime than for a relatively open society: the people will be told what is thought necessary to sustain that regime. In the years when the Soviet Union was still a developing country, and ruled by Party dictatorship, it established a tradition of journalism about production norms and achievements, of a kind thought intolerably earnest by Western observers. A society which is both developed and comparatively free may, however, find itself with a journalism which is intolerably frivolous or in other ways quite inadequate for social progress.

Meanwhile, it looks as though in speaking rather vaguely about the role of television in making us better informed about what is going on in the world, we may overestimate it, by over-looking the extent to which television's capacity to inform us is severely affected by a lack of information available to television itself. At the domestic level, much of the information which people or politicians need is not published (or even adequately processed for more privileged consumption), and therefore not mediated by television; at the international level television is generally dependent on the same news-gathering facilities as the press, and these are biased, inadequate and in need of inter-nationally-concerted reform. Using information about politic-ally important events at home and abroad as a touchstone category to represent a larger need, the provisional answer to the question with which we started – is the information supplied by television comprehensive enough? – seems to be: lavish, but not comprehensive, seriously unbalanced in fact, because some in-formation does not flow at all, and that which does, flows most unevenly.

7 Information as Spectacle

Effects of the medium on the message

Walter Cronkite, the well-known news correspondent of CBS, spoke for many journalists, and not only in the States, when he declared to news directors at their 1970 convention at Denver:

I'm tired of sociologists, psychologists, pathologists, educators, parents, bureaucrats, politicians and other special interest groups presuming to tell us what is news or where our responsibilities are.[1]

A few months previously Reuven Frank, the president of NBC News, made an authoritative but defensively touchy speech to the Yale University Political Union, which started with these words:

Mr Agnew's Des Moines speech on 13 November 1969 has made him better known than any other Vice-President in living memory. It also has made me better known than I care to be.

Ever since 13 November we relatively anonymous men who administer broadcasting news organizations have been identified and sought out by reporters and academics. Our opinions are solicited on the acts of government, our justifications explored for things we do, and access to our files requested for content analysis.

Meanwhile, the people we employ to gather news for television spend too much of their time speaking about television news to ladies' meetings, not what they were hired for at all. ... By describing us administrators as a dark conspiracy, the Vice-President has turned us into the new glamor boys.[2]

News is not the only category of information needed by democracy, whether participatory or not. We need to consider these overlapping categories as a whole – news/current affairs/political features and documentaries/features and educational programmes providing information on a still wider range of topics ... But news and current affairs are the category on which are focused many of the issues raised by the next question: how authentically does television provide information?

The situation surrounding that question is calmer here than in the States, despite the growing mistrust by politicians of broadcasters. The public at least does not distrust them, and especially there is no parallel in Britain to the scepticism about television news felt by substantial proportions of the American population. Consequently no politician has been able to do an Agnew and acquire political visibility by articulating that mistrust. There is, indeed, no particular reason why the British people should distrust the medium as a news carrier.[3] Asking how authentically television provides information for democracy is not an inquiry into the integrity and technical expertness of media men. It is a more subtle investigation into the effects of the medium on the message, and in Britain most of the shrewdest criticisms of the medium in these terms have come not from Cronkite's bands of interfering outsiders, but in the main from active practitioners of broadcasting, with some support from media research workers. Before examining the criticisms, they must be put into perspective, since the way is prepared for the critique itself more by the achievements of television than by its failings; or rather, since the failings are now more obvious simply because of the achievements. The point was made by Reuven Frank in his Yale Speech, in terms which apply at least as fully in Britain as in the United States:

By following its own rules of craft at its own pace, television news reporting has expanded the awareness of America to the world around it immeasurably. The Hungarian rebellion and the Suez war, two concurrent events in late 1956, may have provided the first really massive example. The Vietnam war is the most obvious. In between were the opening of Africa, the independence of Algeria, the invasion of Czechoslovakia, the famine in Biafra. . . . What would these and countless other events have signified, not only to the American mind but to the American conscience, without the special ability of television to make each viewer participate in the event he sees? I refer to news subjects abroad because such domestic matters as hunger, disorder, injustice, pollution, document my argument too easily and too well.

In the States, criticism of television has begun to degenerate into political harassment. The signs are that the same damage to democracy, through governments leaning too heavily on broadcasting, could be done here; in which case those responsible for the medium could become angrily and unproductively defensive. This would be serious, for television objectively does need to improve: the remarkable medium of information which grew up within the medium of entertainment has a capacity for maturing into a superior medium of information and education, irrigating society, not merely bombarding it randomly with a prodigality of messages. There is still time constructively to consider the diagnosis of television's defects, speculate on their aetiology and conduct research, debate and experiment in reforms that will gradually lead to the achievement of this potential maturity. Nobody should glibly say 'what is news' or presume lightly to tell Walter Cronkite and his peers where their responsibility lies. What follows, in the rest of Part Two, is therefore, a tentative summary of some of the chief worries that professional broadcasters have voiced so far, in an attempt to relate them to my larger case for participatory democracy.

For too much of the time, television seems to vitiate much of its best work in informing society by its tendencies to distort and distract – distracting people from what matters with shows and distracting us by distorting what matters into a show. Television has uncritically inherited from the press the dogmas that news is what is newsworthy, that good news is no news, and that news is an end in itself. Television seems to act on the principle: if it moves, film it; if it does not move, it does not exist. It also acts on the maxim: if it is dramatic, report it; if it is not dramatic, then make it so; and if that can't be done, then it's not important anyway. Embodied in its performance is the assumption that the object of communication is impact; not, in fact, communication.

As it stands, that paragraph is as distorted and tendentious as anything that ever came off a television screen. In this chapter and the two that follow, it must be amplified so that the reality to which, unfortunately, it corresponds in varying degrees, may be determined.

The real-life show or all business is show biz

First, then, the charges that television distracts people from what matters with shows and further distracts them by turning what matters into a show, that is, distracts people with spectacle. Television's tendency to distract through spectacle is what supports the accusation that television is a narcotic diversion from the real business of living and, in particular, a diversion from wresting some control of one's destiny from the oligarchs (elected and self-appointed) who have the effective power of initiative in society. As this case was put forward at some length in chapter 4, it need not be substantially amplified here.

The case is patently overstated, but it is not patently untrue. Certainly those who work in television have no such narcotizing objective. Professionals in news and current affairs would claim that it was their job to make the public more alert, aware and vigilant, not at all to make people inert, unobservant and apathetic. Furthermore, it is a significant fact about British television that programme planners have over the years, steadily increased the amount of what, for annual report analyses, is called 'serious output' and persistently enlarged the news/current affairs section of that. Their attitude towards the audience has been at the opposite pole from that of the former *Daily Mirror* chief, Cecil King, who once uttered this notorious verdict:

It is only the people who conduct newspapers and similar organizations who have any idea quite how indifferent, quite how stupid, quite how uninterested in education of any kind the great bulk of the British public are.[4]

Yet, on the other side, a familiar insight from sociology has to be taken into account: institutional structures may produce objectively different effects from those that would ever be intended by the individuals working through those institutions. It used often to be observed that the British press was predominantly right wing, whereas British journalists were predominantly left. Some of television's greatest achievements have come about through realizing the three official objectives of British broadcasting in the same programmes – entertainment, information and education. But the purposes of information and education are often overwhelmed by the ambience of entertainment.

The ambivalence of the situation shows in many ways. Given that the bulk of the audience watches one programme after another throughout the evening, few programmes are fully appreciated – the sharp edge of the news may be blunted by the strong action drama that went before; the aesthetic richness of a play may not be appreciated by an appetite jaded by too much comedy and variety. The ambivalence appears in the *News at Ten* – this extended news programme at peak time was a daring innovation and a democratic advance, and yet the items in it are orchestrated for mood and variety like a series of revue sketches, complete with tantalizing trailers before the commercial break. It appears in the choice of music to introduce even the current affairs 'heavies'. Is it a soap opera or is it life that will follow such title music and credits? It shows in the way in which major events are handled by the medium.

Shulman (quoted in chapter 4) was worried that television was distracting the British public from its 1970 General Election. But one might have looked also at those programmes which covered the campaign itself and announced the results. This is what some of the most distinguished figures in British television news and current affairs actually did in a discussion on the coverage of the campaign arranged by the Society of Film and Television Arts.[5] The debate provided some evidence that a democratic conscience is intrinsic to professionalism in this area of broadcasting. The discussion was opened by highly experienced broadcasters and producers (Peter Morley, Alastair Burnet, Robin Day, John Grist, Jeremy Isaacs, Nigel Ryan), who were joined in the assessment by representatives of the three main parties (Geoffrey Johnson-Smith, MP, Phillip Whitehead, MP – a former producer newly elected – and Lord Byers). Several contributors to the discussion maintained that, on the whole, television had performed well on behalf of democracy during the General Election.[6]

The politicians were not all so contented. Lord Byers, for example, complained about the way television used his Press Conferences:

Here we found usually the trivial points were selected as being newsworthy. In order to keep the journalists coming every day I used to have one or two cracks, as Robin knows, to keep them interested so they would come next time. You've got to keep your customers. These were the things that got to the news....

Others were inclined to think that what at first looked like deficiencies in coverage were in fact deficiencies in the event being covered; that blame, if blame were the issue, could be attributed to politicians rather than the broadcasters. Nigel Ryan, the editor of *News at Ten* observed:

We're charged in effect with having chosen to follow the eggs rather than the issues . . . with having followed the walkabouts of the then Prime Minister rather than having covered speeches and issues, and all I want to say is this: is this really fair? . . . If the leader of a major political party decides that he will go and fight his campaign by shaking hands in the street amid a shower of praise and eggs, then that is his choice. The answer is the cameras will follow him and in my view they should follow him. All we are doing is reflecting the campaign as it is conducted by the politicians.

Perhaps television's addiction to shows forces politicians to put on an act to secure coverage? At least one producer was unconvinced by attempts to shift the blame:

I think . . . the treatment was wrong. I think Lord Byers's cracks to the press, that Powell's speeches and the chances of a punch-up, heckling and eggs thrown at Wilson, and Anthony Barber when he was trying to talk against those bells, all add up to one thing. I think we ought to be frank and remember that the entertainment factor does exist. Everyone knows . . . that journalism is not show biz or ought not to be; but television is show business, and you have to accept this; this is the sort of footage you go for.

Lord Byers clearly found it irksome to play the entertainment game, providing wisecracks as bait, having to think too much about stage management and not enough about the play:

We found the utmost difficulty in getting any coverage at all for outside speeches. We were told by camera crews, 'they'll kill it when it gets back, it's too dull, there'll be no action, you'll just get people standing around listening intelligently'. I managed to get three minutes because I was standing on a great big rubble vehicle, and that was good television, but you know it doesn't really make much sense if you have to go out and get your own eggs thrown at you.

The researches conducted over the years at Leeds University show that television significantly succeeds in informing voters during General Elections, but the misgivings voiced at the SFTA discussion need consideration.[7]

The medium's habit of diverting – and diverting *from* – is also apparent in the treatment of other major events: the results of a General Election, for example. Providing sport as an alternative to the 1970 Election was one form of distraction, perhaps, though offering a desirable freedom of choice, but what happens when the election itself is treated as a sporting event? It is one thing for Ladbroke's to run a book on an election result. It is quite another for television to present the result as though Ladbroke's understood the essence of the matter. Swingometers, computers guessing the final outcome from one result, psephologists ingeniously speculating on a future for which we have in any case only a few hours to wait, an atmosphere of carnival and gadgetry, all reduce the choice of government to the level of a game, in which the contest is more important than the contenders, the mechanics of electoral choice more important than the issues.

The very neutrality of television, in many ways a very proper safeguard, seems to make this particular distortion worse. Did Cliff Michelmore vote? Does his heart sink or is he elated as the results come through? You cannot tell. But if the umpire is *that* neutral, then the game can't be worth playing. Place your bets, ladies and gentlemen. . . .

The SFTA debate indicates that the blame lies partly with politicians who subject the medium to falsifying constraints, both through the conditions they impose on the way in which the pre-election campaign is covered and by the issue-evading way in which they often choose to conduct the campaign itself, so that when the results are announced the atmosphere of carnival and instant clairvoyance is almost unavoidable.

Some critics would lay more of the blame for turning what should be an occasion for enlightenment into an opportunity for distraction on television itself, and the way in which its styles are evolving, because the tendency for the medium to turn serious events into shows is not limited to political matters. Some of the broadcasters covering moon landings and recoveries manage to convey the somewhat immodest impression that the chief triumph is theirs, not the astronauts. These men going to the moon are, of course, brave and bright, and the programme would not be the same without them.... As Dennis Potter wrote, in some desperation: 'Even the bits of war, or the moonshots, or the hideous brutalities of starvation which we sometimes see on our screens can seem devoid of genuine meaning, true yet somehow not "true" not set in context, just stuff to feed the ever-grinding machine.'[8]

This impertinence is allied to what might be called the anteroom effect. Raymond Williams puts it thus:

Television is so good when it presents real events that it gains a power which it then abuses: nominally, to set up an anteroom, beside everything that is happening – a budget, a cup final, an election, a horse race – but actually making the anteroom the arena, the reaction the event, and the commentators the real agents.[9]

It is an insidious development, by which, as Williams observes, 'Politics and sport, in very similar ways, are processed to a desultory ritual.'

It is perfectly proper and potentially useful for television to provide interpretation of events as well as the transmission of them, and yet it is within the framework of interpretative comment that the anteroom effect often downgrades the event in comparison with those ready with their instant comments on it. As Williams wrote, in the same article:

Nobody can suppose that BBC Sport is just watching people playing games. There is the compulsive talk before and after the event; not invented by broadcasting, since supporters and fans have always done it, but in effect altered by becoming a studio ritual.

It is at this point that the similarity of the processing to which sport and politics are subjected becomes apparent. Anthony Wedgwood Benn and Raymond Williams depict the plight of the event maker. First, Wedgwood Benn:

Almost all we see of trade-union or business leaders are hurried little street interviews when they are pinned against a wall by a battery of accusing microphones.[10]

Williams:

The player is usually modest, fresh from the bath, and clearly much better at doing things than describing them. It might be the cue for some simple act of hero-worship, the persistent stance of the adolescent fan. But these interviewers, their whole stance suggests, have talked to the lot. With their authorizing microphones, they are in charge. There then begins a smooth insistence, past the compliments and the playbacks, that the player should translate his own world into theirs. The smiling pressure, often, is cruel.

Lazersfeld and Merton were among the first to sound the warning: that the act of receiving information might become a substitute for genuine democratic participation, that the necessary might come to be mistaken for the sufficient. No one can participate in democracy if he does not feel involved in its affairs. Television has remarkably enlarged awareness. Its very skill in presentation has promoted concern and the sense of involvement, has, in short, made people interested. And yet these very skills also turn reality into a spectacle, to be moved by, to applaud, to cry over, but not actually to get mixed up with. Television is providing information for surveillance and orientation, and yet the effect is alienating.

The puzzle about news

This ambivalence of television as an informing medium is implicit in the image most commonly evoked to describe it.

Television, everyone says, is a window on the world. The cliché is employed most often when describing television's capacity simultaneously to acquaint everyone everywhere with what is going on in the world (and now even in the cosmos). And clearly, without awareness of what is happening, participation is not possible.

But the trite metaphor is a give-away, as may be realized by remembering some other facts about windows. They are not only for seeing through. They sometimes distort; they can act as a burning glass, scorching what they make visible. They are barriers, keeping viewers at arms' reach, protecting the property, insulating those who watch from those who act. Windows are for fruitlessly pressing one's nose against: on the other side are goodies one can't afford, exploits to make one gasp, suffering one cannot alleviate. The image certainly summarizes the way television is used: the question is whether this is the definitive and only way in which it could be used.

There is at least a superficial sense in which television never reaches a definitive condition. That is because broadcasters do not normally rest content with any given set of styles or formats. Some of the particular examples in the previous section illustrated the transitoriness of fashions in production. Only two years after Wedgwood Benn's speech, television interviewers were already bored with trapping politicians against walls. Unfortunately, television as a medium of political information and understanding suffers from other more vitiating characteristics, which seem more abiding and could even be endemic.

One of these disabilities also afflicts the press: both media distort reality because of the nature of 'news'. There is a real puzzle here. Everyone understands about news, that is everyone knows or takes for granted, that news largely consists of a selective look at some of the more unusual or important happenings of the day. Yet everyone is misled by news into mistaking it for a portrait of reality (not that everyone is misled by all news, but that everyone accepts the distorted view which news gives of the world in some respect or other). Two examples will make the point from among scores that are possible. First, 'the generation gap'. It is natural that different generations should appraise the world through different eyes and act accordingly. The faster the world changes, the bigger the difference. To take one instance: the affluence of the late 1950s was a stunning phenomenon to those who grew up during the Depression and the war; it was an unremarkable datum line of experience for those who were born into it. Differences are also caused by gradual progress in the length and content of education. But 'the generation gap', as that vague concept is diffused by the media, usually implies that there is a general, widespread and comprehensive polarization between young and old, who view each other with suspicion and hostility. There is no research evidence to substantiate any such concept. Most young people trust their parents, model themselves on them, perpetuate their mores and attitudes – even to a fault. There are significant differences between different segments of society (from which social progress and evolution largely stem, and which are therefore worth reporting), and these have some connection with the age and experience of the protagonists, but *'the* generation gap', as commonly interpreted, is a myth, an uncritically accepted artifact of the media.

The second example – connected with the first – is on a smaller scale but perhaps more startling. In the late 1960s, the word 'student' turned pejorative. Even students could be heard discussing 'students' disparagingly, as though 'students' were by definition militant, argumentative and disruptive. *University Challenge* is one of the most consistently popular programmes on television, and yet the washed, alert, quick-witted, highly intelligent and presumably industrious young men and women who appear in it are not thought of as students, or do not modify the prevailing image of 'student'. 'Students' are only those students who have had a bad press or a 'bad screen' in the news. The vivid, highly selected fragment of reality is mistaken for the whole.

Although many press and television journalists see that there is a problem and paradox involved, they often do not believe that anything can be done about it. After all, they argue, nobody wants to be told that, say, a million passengers go in and out of the main London railway termini every day. We already know that, or can take it for granted. But if there's a strike or a fire in the signal box as a result of which trains are cancelled or delayed, that's news. No one would buy a newspaper that kept on reporting the bliss, contentment or passive indifference of the married people of Britain. But if one or two couples start expressing their feelings for each other with arsenic or hatchets, that's news.

This particular line of defence has been vigorously employed by John Whale, the former television journalist. Warding off the reproach that newsmen are over-interested in disaster and insufficiently interested in, say, what is happening in the smaller nations, Whale admits:

Journalists do have a negative approach – to take that point first. It's a favourite cigar-chewing news editor's axiom: 'Don't let's forget, we're in the bad news business.' Air crashes, stock-exchange crashes, Kremlin crashes – we love them all.

And then he parries:

It is just worth pointing out, though, that if every morning the newspapers listed every ruler who had survived the day before, every company that was still staving off bankruptcy, every air journey that had been brought to a reasonably safe landing, there'd be a certain amount of fine print. Positive thinking would set a lot of space problems.

Whale is equally unrepentant about 'that business of being bored by the doings of underdeveloped countries':

True again: you could comb European newspapers and broadcasting stations in vain for news of this year's sisal crop in Tanzania – even if the crop is an epic disaster.

Whale points out that 'there are hard practical reasons for this silence'. Some of these were mentioned above in the section on the international news flow:

Journalists need communications, in the old-fashioned sense. They need the opportunity to get into countries freely, or to have their stringers send stuff out freely. They need telephones that work, public transport systems that transport. There are not all that many African or Latin American countries where even these simple conditions are met.

Even so:

There are the commercial reasons, of course: editors have to *sell* their newspapers, and most British readers aren't interested in reading about the Tanzania sisal crop.[11]

It looks as though a position which can summon so much wit, common sense, shrewdness and indeed truth must be unassailable. But it leaves us with a puzzling consequence of an obvious premise – that since only the exceptional and the interesting are worth reporting, the world presented to us is a bizarre, violent place, and with the entry of television, there are the pictures to prove it. Sir Robert Fraser, in the speech to the Newspaper Society already quoted, was perturbed by this difficulty:

The concern of newspapers and television is with events. And events are too often troubles. It is in the nature of things. Men at work are not an event, men on strike are. The safety of life and property is not an event, theft and violent crimes are. People attending meetings of constituency parties are not events, people demonstrating in the street are. It is entirely understandable that newspapers and television turn to the troubles of society. The troubles would be less likely to be remedied, as they should be remedied, were it not so.

But I ask myself just what is the other side to this, and how we solve the problem of presenting the common agreement no less than the sectional disagreements, the normal as well as the abnormal.

In order to emphasize the social and political seriousness of this problem of intrinsic distortion, distortion as a consequence of the obvious and legitimate ends of journalism, Sir Robert concluded his speech with this quotation from the Hunt Report on Northern Ireland:

We feel bound to deplore the extent to which some press and television coverage of these events has resulted in magnifying, in the minds of readers and viewers, the actual extent of the disorders, in generalizing the impression of misconduct by the police and of bad relations between the police and public, while sometimes failing correspondingly to illustrate the calm which has prevailed in most parts of Ulster, or the degree of deliberate provocation, the danger and the strain under which the police, frequently and for long periods, tried to do their duty, as well as the fact that the great majority acted not only with courage but with restraint. Such impressions may, as in this instance, do harm to the future maintenance of law and order and the restoration of confidence up which this so largely rests. We wish to take this opportunity to correct the perspective.[12]

No doubt the suppressed and repressed violence by which life in Northern Ireland has been poisoned for hundreds of years, was more responsible for the subsequent failure to maintain law and order or to restore confidence than was television. Nevertheless, it is fair to suspect that television might have inflamed an already festering situation. And the issue raised by the Hunt report is in any case of much wider application, as the then Director-General of the ITA acknowledged in his peroration:

One should not bridle at these words nor brush them aside. They deserve to be remembered. How can we be sure, we in the newspapers and television, that we have quite succeeded in giving the balanced account, of securing the balanced picture, that self-government needs as its guide? How do we do justice to quiet virtue, to the peaceful ones?

The concept of newsworthiness which television has imbibed from the press also includes the device of dramatic over-simplification. This shows most obviously in the aggressive language of newspaper headlines, in which politicians do not criticize, they slash; people do not ask, they probe; bureaucrats do not economize, they axe. It is a world in which the only good meeting is a confrontation. Dramatization structures the news, and can sometimes do permanent damage to the information objectively available.

The fate of *In Place of Strife* was a good example. No doubt the so-called penal clauses of this Labour Government White Paper were of great importance, especially as it was published in an 'atmosphere of disenchantment with the Government which prices and incomes actions have produced'. The media, as a specialist in industrial affairs, Geoffrey Stuttard, observed, conveyed the impression that 'the White Paper, of forty pages, is a two-page leaflet, one page of which lays down compulsory strike ballots and the other, compulsory conciliation clauses, with appropriate fines for offenders'. 'What', he asks, 'happened to the other thirty-eight pages?' The public, including that section of it most directly concerned, treated the White Paper as an anti-union document, even though it was in the main an anti-employer paper, embodying proposals for many reforms advocated by trade-union leaders.[13]

For television, as distinct from newspapers, this perverse relationship between reality–events–facts–news is worsened by a specific characteristic of the medium, which is also the source of its chief strength: it deals in pictures; but not all reality is pictorial. The difficulties which this creates for newsmen in television are one of the chief themes of John Whale's discontented and much less defensive book, *The Half Shut Eye*, but all viewers are familiar with some of its effects. If the news is that there is to be an increase in postal charges, the reporter will tell us about it standing on a pavement outside a post office. It would not be much more absurd if he were to deliver the same information alongside a cardboard pillar box set up in the studio. Viewers are accustomed to the convention, and it often does no harm. But the medium is notoriously and powerfully biased towards what is visible and what moves, and this can and does lead to distortions of a more serious kind.

Much of this aspect of the critical case was summarized by Robin Day in the long, thoughtful and highly knowledgeable article in *Encounter* (significantly headed 'Troubled reflections of a TV journalist') to which I referred earlier. He wrote:

> I do not wish to exaggerate this, but the fact is that television's dependence on pictures (and the most vivid pictures) makes it not only a *powerful* means of communication, but a *crude* one which tends to strike at the emotion rather than at the intellect. For TV journalism this means a dangerous and increasing concentration on action (usually violent and bloody) rather than on thought, on happenings rather than issues, on shock rather than explanation, on personalities rather than ideas.

In consequence:

> TV can cover a riot, a war, a revolution, an assassination, more vividly than any newspaper. It also means that television tends to give much less impressive treatment of the reasons behind those events. In the case of events or issues which do not have convenient visual existence, television tends to treat them inadequately.

> This means that television is strong on visible results, weak on causes. We know from television that war means combat and casualties, but 'Television does not always take sufficient trouble to ask "who is responsible", "why is it happening", or "what is the alternative".'[14]

In chapter 4 I quoted from the late Leonard Beaton, who drew attention to the highly important matters which tend to be omitted from television news and even from current affairs programmes because the medium does not find them congenial.

Beaton was also worried by the power of television to determine the issues presented to the public:

> The most spectacular example of this was the terrible history of Biafra. Here we need not concern ourselves with the dramatic simplicity which the media brought to a situation of great complexity: it is sufficient to notice what happened to public opinion when the cameras were ordered out of the Eastern Region of Nigeria. Because the Nigerian government did not want them, the cameramen had to

go; because there was no film, the television networks dropped the subject; and because the networks dropped the subject, what had previously agonized the conscience of millions ceased to be of general concern. It is predictable that the same result would follow the expulsion of the television men from Vietnam. The long and difficult British campaign in Borneo went unknown and unreported because the government chose to run it that way.[15]

The fortuitous way in which issues of great public concern may or may not be presented to the public, or the random timing of such presentation, was considered at some length in Lord Windlesham's *Television and Political Opinion*,[15] written when he was working with Associated Rediffusion, some years before he went into politics.

Rachmanism, his chief example, became headline news in July 1963. This particular type of property racketeering (intimidating and terrorizing tenants of properties in multiple occupation, so that they would quit and enable landlords to re-let at higher rents), was not new. It had developed in overcrowded urban areas since the de-control of rents in 1957. Once it became news, however, it remained a matter of public concern, and soon after became the object of government inquiry and legislative action. But why did the abuse become news at that time in 1963? Windlesham supplies the answer:

one must doubt whether the remedial provisions of Part IV of the Housing Act 1964, would ever have been enacted, at any rate in the form they were at the time they were, without the aid of Stephen Ward, Christine Keeler and Mandy Rice-Davies.

These demi-mondaine characters (who figured at the time in the inflated scandal known as the Profumo affair) were also associated with Peter Rachman. And it was through this chance association that more serious offences against the common weal than those of a rash Minister of State were brought to light.

The selection of items for presentation in the news will depend on the criteria of newsworthiness, formulated or assumed, employed by editors, and on the sources from which potential news is derived. The criteria have to be internalized so that the constraints of a highly demanding work routine may be overcome, and research workers are just beginning to study them in use, by observing editorial meetings and through content analysis. Meanwhile, a number of descriptions of the news selection process are available from practitioners. Windlesham's book is informative. He summarizes the main sources of information inside a television current-affairs unit as 'personal observation of events and situations, stories in newspapers or periodicals, or specialist information provided on an advisory or *ad hoc* basis'. According to his first-hand experience, the process by which subjects are selected 'will depend very much on the interests and values' of those responsible for making the selection, and on what they believe to be the interests of their audience'. This judgement is affected by 'flair, news value and political fashion'. (Windlesham's list does not include 'knowledge of what actually interests viewers', though it is this essential factor that makes local newspapers the most democratic press, read by all sections of society, whatever their level of education, and which gives regional news on television an authenticity and relevance which national news often seems to lack.) Windlesham's description of what goes on round the editorial table is revealing:

In the competitive atmosphere lying behind most current affairs programmes it is crucial for a producer or a reporter anxious to get a story into a news-magazine programme, or an individual programme into the schedules, to be able to summarize his proposal concisely, even dramatically. He must make sure his colleagues recognize what he is talking about, if not instantly, at any rate within a very few minutes. While this practice has advantages in that it directs urgent attention towards the heart of a story at an early stage, the danger is that the pressure to achieve a quick sell may later be reflected in what goes on the air. Not every report prepared is actually broadcast, so that a superficial report may fall down at the final stage of selection. But by then lack of time, lack of alternatives and cost may have influenced the decision to accept reluctantly or to reject. A result of these internal pressures can be identified in those programmes which give the appearance of being little more than assemblies of five-second ideas, each likely to be interesting enough in itself, as well as being easy to present and easy to comprehend, but sometimes unsuited to being fruitfully developed after an initial statement.

Not only will a reporter, pressing for a story's inclusion, summarize and dramatize it to make sure his colleagues quickly recognize what he is talking about; when a story is presented to viewers it is subjected to similar treatment.[17] This is understandable and it is easier to be censorious about it if one has never had to select – and always select against the clock – what items of information culled from all over the world should be included in a news bulletin or current-affairs magazine. The exigencies of the process lead to what Windlesham calls the need for 'instant recognition':

Television allows little time for explanations. As soon as an item comes up on the screen a producer wants it to be recognized by the viewers at whom it is aimed. He can seldom afford a long build-up by way of explanation why something matters. Even if he has the time there is always the danger that an extended 'hooker' may turn out to be more stimulating and memorable than the central aspects of the situation on which he is attempting to concentrate interest.

Hence another limitation on television's efficiency as a means of communication in this field is that it cannot easily find the time both to present information and the additional information needed to make sense of it. It cannot, in short, adopt an educative approach, because the time and the space are limited; without such an approach, communication itself is limited. Information presented educatively is tedious; but unless information is presented educatively, it is barren.

Clearly there is a limit to the amount of news, information and background the media can carry. Are the best criteria of selection being used at present? How can concealed issues of importance come into prominence? Should the selection of news depend as much as it does on the flair and habits of copytasters? These are difficult questions, but answers must be sought so that the dramatized news which entertains the viewer may give way to the dramatic news which involves the citizen.

8 Knowledge is Power

Poverty amidst plenty:
the paradox of the ignorant citizen

Television promotes democracy by providing information about what is going on in the country and the world on a lavish scale. It generates interest and concern round those events and developments by showing reality as it is, in a way which is intrinsically impossible to radio and to print. Television fosters participatory democracy by advertising the causes and the frustrations that provoke protest, by maintaining the vigilant suspicion of those in authority which is a classic function of the Fourth Estate, and by providing pressure through magnifying popular manifestations of displeasure with authority.

But the two previous chapters have indicated ways in which television, by providing information which is distorted and distracting, fails to serve democracy. The information is inadequate for surveillance because so much of it is one-eyed. It is inadequate for orientation because so much of it persistently disorientates us. There is still justice in the inelegant verdict, that the information poured out by television narcotizes dysfunctionally, acting as surrogate for democratic involvement almost because of its very profusion, and providing an unsure grasp on reality because of its chronic eccentricity.

The reasons for these failings are enormously complex, but the explanatory clue to them is provided by looking not directly at television but past it at the audience, at the personal, social and political circumstances of viewers. (We shall see later that the clue to the improvement of television is correspondingly to be found in the relationship between the medium and viewers, in their changing social context.) At the centre of the diagnosis, is a pardaoxical figure – the well-informed–ill-informed viewer.

Even though television supplies information abundantly, and most people watch television for three or four hours a day, most of us persist in being strikingly ignorant.

There is a story in the American literature on mass communication which goes some way to accounting for this paradox. American television has a tradition, hardly in evidence here at all (with the possible exception of the party conferences), of covering political events live and whole, as we do with football matches. One of the first post-war manifestations of this tradition was the televising of the Kefauver crime hearings in 1951. Senator Kefauver was chairing an investigation into a spectacularly flagrant penetration and corruption of politics by organized crime. The hearings made such compulsive viewing that New York was literally immobilized by them. Political journalists predicted that these broadcasts would reduce electoral apathy, and educational television experts regarded them as 'a spectacular example of the power of television in informing the electorate. Millions of people were made more vividly aware of civic problems and of their responsibilities as citizens.' [1] The realism of that hopeful expectation was tested only six to nine weeks after the Kefauver hearings ended, when social psychology students from the City College of New York interviewed a sample of 260 New York citizens. It was not a wholly representative sample; on the contrary, it was 'moderately skewed toward professional and white-collar people, toward the male sex and toward the twenty-one to thirty-five-year-old age group'. In short, those interviewed were probably better educated than New Yorkers as a whole. Were they 'more vividly aware of civic problems and of their responsibilities as citizens'? The memory of the hearings had certainly survived the passing of the months; more than half this sample distinctly remembered the shock and anger they had felt at the time. This led the interviewers to find out what this sense of outrage had prompted members of the scandalized sub-sample to do. It turned out that 81 per cent of them had done nothing except talk to friends and neighbours about it, while 6 per cent had not even done that. Seven per cent wrote to their congressmen, which was indeed a political reaction, but only one had discussed the hearings with committee men of his party (probably the most appropriate reaction of those made). One respondent had prayed for the souls of the racketeers. Despite the hopes of editors and educators, 73 per cent of the sample responded to the question 'Will the hearings improve conditions?' with what the surveyors describe as 'varying amounts of scepticism'.

There was a dangerous naïveté concealed in the traditional assertion that a well-informed electorate was essential to democracy, in that the emphasis was laid unduly on the competence of the electorate and insufficiently on the accessibility, intelligibility and effectiveness of the democratic machinery. Information does not motivate people to acts of social responsibility if they do not have or do not feel that they have, an entrée to influence and power. It is fundamentally this gap, between the availability of information and the acknowledged opportunity to act on that information which is responsible both for the way in which television acts as a refracting window rather than a reflecting window on the world, and for the paradoxical ignorance of the public. Let me pursue first this question of public ignorance and then take up again later the connected phenomenon of television as a purveyor of spectacle. After the results are published, every A-level candidate can testify that information fades when there is no motive to use it. One might ask what use was the Kefauver-hearings information, directly though it bore on the lives of New Yorkers, if they were distrustful of the political system, alienated from it, unrelated to it by accessible and understandable social mechanisms?

It was not clear to the people of New York what they were supposed to do about corruption in high places except be appalled by it. Consequently, even the event itself was fading from the memory.

This lack of power, this absence of actual involvement, is the underlying political fact behind all those studies and demonstrations of popular political ignorance. It is the main reason for the daunting truth that most of us – I advisedly do not say 'most people' because I see no reason to flatter my readers or myself that we are necessarily talking about everyone else – are extraordinarily ill informed: at the level of fact, at the level of understanding the issues, and at the level of grasping the fundamental concepts that would help us to make sense of those issues. There was, for example, a famous Alan Whicker piece of vox pop on *Tonight* some years ago in which he stopped people in Hyde Park – office girls, cleaners, businessmen in striped suits, all sorts of people, any of whom could have been one of us. He asked them 'simple' questions about recent important Parliamentary business. Most of his interviewees were painfully out of their depth. The item was embarrassing because the men and women in the park were made to look foolish, and yet they were on the whole not much more ignorant than the rest of us. Other interviewers have tried the ploy since, always with the same result: by and large the public is plumb ignorant. Serious surveys and pieces of research have reached the same conclusion by sounder methods of inquiry. The American investigator Bernard Berelson, for example, makes the same point with more formality: 'Tests of information invariably show at least 20 per cent of the public totally uninformed (and usually the figure is closer to 40 per cent).'[2]

In 1954 the BBC wanted to find out how much the target audience for a television series on economics already knew. The sample consisted of professional, skilled and moderately skilled people. Eighty-three per cent knew the meaning of 'overtime', 79 per cent of 'imports', 66 per cent of 'retail prices'. Less than half knew what 'devaluation' means. Only 6 per cent could explain 'terms of trade'. All these phrases were tested in context (including 'per cent' – 53 per cent knew what that meant). People reasonably but wrongly thought that 'primary producers' are the main manufacturers, that 'commodity price' is the price of goods in general, and that 'terms of trade' is a way of talking about competition or bargaining, or about prices paid and offered. When the BBC tested knowledge of background events (sixteen questions on e.g. the wage freeze, the Korean war, the gold and dollar reserves crisis), 60 per cent were quite wrong and could give no reply on any given question. 'While the top occupational group did better on each question than did the other groups, its knowledge ... was, nevertheless, often quite poor.'[3]

In 1966, after twelve more years of television, another sample of the population was asked: 'What does the term 'inflation' mean to you?' Two-fifths of the sample could not attempt a definition, and another 16 per cent described it as something bad for the country or gave some other equally vague reply.[4]

In 1963, a sizeable minority of a British sample told Gallup Poll interviewers that Britain already belonged to the Common Market.[5]

Another American investigator, writing some years later than Berelson, provides an equally negative summary of the position: 'the vast majority of citizens hold pictures of the world that are at best sketchy, blurred and without detail or at worst so impoverished as to beggar description'.[6]

No doubt some of these investigations overestimate this impoverishment. Many people know more, understand more, than they are able to articulate at short notice in an artificial interview situation, especially one which in some unnerving way reminds them of exams. But it is too much to hope that public political ignorance is an artifact of insensitive survey techniques: some of the studies in this field have been administered with insight and the general outcome of them all is clear and unambiguous. It is also serious. Neither democratic surveillance nor personal orientation is possible if one is stumbling about in a fog.

Of course we are not ignorant in the way that a peasant, living half way up a mountain, seeing no one and not even having a transistor radio, is ignorant. What was said in chapter 1 about television the liberal educator, television the chief agent of adult education, still applies. It is perfectly possible for this to be the most aware generation, the generation with an unprecedented grasp on the complexities of political and social realities, and yet still to be inadequately informed, in relation to our needs and to the resources to hand for supplying them. The earlier claim made for television is consistent with the critical estimate of the state of public knowledge justified by objective investigations of it.

The dismal survey findings come as no surprise to élitist doubters of democracy, who have always maintained in any case, that most people are too invincibly ignorant for this fine theory to work. These aristocrats are wrong, of course. It is not that most people are too mediocre, too badly informed to justify democracy; it is that democracy is at present too mediocre, too badly structured, to motivate people towards knowledge and action.

For the same reason, it is not enough, when faced by the ill-informed public, to prescribe a supply of yet more information. Awareness of the public's lack of information and understanding has in the past sometimes led educationists or media practitioners to place enormous hopes in the powers of the media, especially if they were more deliberately applied to public education in public affairs. But it is over-optimistic to recommend that the media in general and television in particular should simply tell us more. That indeed is the spirit of the reforms often suggested by Milton Shulman (in, for example, a typical onslaught entitled 'Here is the news, but it won't take long') and proposed by Cecil King in his Royal Society of Arts lecture:

Time was when governments were concerned with such problems that had, at least directly, no bearing on the life of the ordinary man, who had no vote anyway. This has now changed, and government policy is concerned with price levels, wages and salaries, and the policy to be pursued by the vast nationalized industries. If government policy is to be more than drift, it must be explained in acceptable terms to the man and woman in the street. Hitherto politicians have supposed, quite wrongly, that when a government White Paper has been issued and a debate held, then every charwoman in the country is fully conversant with the latest development in government policy and is in agreement with it. Nothing, of course, could be farther from the truth. The general public does not read reports of parliamentary debates; does not read political speeches, and finds the television appearances of politicians unimpressive.[7]

Cecil King was undoubtedly right to complain that the state and its institutions must care more not only about the publication of information but also about its effective dissemination, but it does not follow that the media can make their best contribution simply by providing more and more information. As Jay Blumler reminds us[8] the Cincinatti campaign to make Cincinatti's citizens better informed about the United Nations Organization provided, as long ago as 1949, a classic incentive to scepticism about the effects of such a simple remedy. For six months the people of Cincinatti were deluged with information about UNO through radio programmes; films; posters; pamphlets; special PTA, church and school meetings; guest speakers; widely advertised slogans and action programme proposals. At the beginning of the campaign the percentage of the population which knew nothing about what the UN was for was 30 per cent; at the end of the campaign, the unaware section of the population was 30 per cent. 150 times a week, slogans about the UN were included in one-minute spots on radio. At the end of six months, 51 per cent of the sample said they had not heard one of them. What was he to Hecuba? Other studies do not suggest that everything would have been different had the campaign included television, but they do suggest that communication depends more on how people listen than on how loud you shout.

The clamour for more information is unrealistic because that ignores the condition and needs of the audience. In the first place, political alienation ensures that we do not know what to do with much of the information already available. Our ignorance is a function of our political insignificance. But in the second place, we are already surfeited by information. Ignorance is not solely caused by the remoteness of most men and women from the system that controls them. There are other more obvious, more everyday causes at work, and to these I must now turn.

The information overkill

We are surfeited with information, both in the information-theory sense, and in the mundane. The day starts with a mélange of news, weather forecasting, evangelism and chat from the radio. At the same time, some of us are scanning the back of the cornflake packet and skimming the daily paper, while others, listening on car radios, are exposed to road signs, traffic lights and hoardings. We 'see' hundreds of advertisements a day, in addition to unquantified worksheets, memos, recipes, knitting patterns, bills and computerized warnings from the bank and the Inland Revenue.

It seems probable that most of us are overloaded with information, supercharged with signals through all our senses, and that we are building up a neurasthenic head of pressure as a result. Tell a dog in a laboratory experiment, to do too many irreconcilable things at once, and he'll have a nervous breakdown. Most town dwellers tend to exhibit similar symptoms, some of us to a marked degree. The mental damage would be worse, and the behavioural seizure more acute, if we did not have a psychological cut-out switch, as a result of which we do not notice a great many of the impulses making for our ears and eyes. We tend only to see what we want to see; what is necessary for survival, satisfaction or self-esteem; what is essential to get on with the task in hand, watching the lathe or stopping the toddler from pitching headfirst into the paddling pool. Information is what we pay heed to; the rest is noise, and there is a great deal of it.

Despite this protective device, we are easily distracted, and when we are distracted, information fails to get through. There are many experiments which show this happening. After a lesson punctuated by loud bangs outside the classroom or the lecture hall, children and students are less able to remember what they were being told at the moments of explosion. Teachers whose jokes we remember, but not the serious points they were making, have unwittingly contributed to their own inefficiency by neglecting this phenomenon.

All this is relevant to the effectiveness of television's capacity to inform. Viewers who keep the set on more or less continuously, as many viewers do, will tend to pay less attention to the programmes than those who switch on for a particular programme and turn off when it is finished.

The power of television to inform is also severely diminished by its domestic situation. The home is an area of maximum distraction – a centre of family responsibility to be discharged, an arena in which emotional tension tends to be high, where there a many other calls on time and attention, often trivial but with the force of habit behind them. The washing up needs to be done, the baby is crying, the insurance man is at the door, the lads from across the road have dropped in for a beer. The Danes, who take television seriously as a medium for adult education, nevertheless know what they are up against. The Danish broadcasting system has made a cautionary television tape for closed circuit showing to educational broadcasters, which depicts a Danish worker, settling down to watch a programme in a series especially devised to teach shop stewards some basic economics. The telephone rings. He ignores it. It continues to ring, and he answers it because his wife is bathing the baby. He settles down again. By now his daughter has had her bath. Now she wants him to read her a story and say goodnight. ... Life is like that, and to be well informed by television requires determination in the viewer and a domestic regime which is sympathetic to such earnest, autodidactic purposes. What most of us do is to focus our attention on the undiscriminated stream of stimuli only when something special comes up – racing results, news which directly affects our lives (will there be a food shortage as a result of a dock strike, is there a traffic hold up on the A3?, the weather).

There are considerable variations between viewer and viewer which complicate the familiar picture of distraction I have sketched. Education is a factor. The more you know already, the more media you will consume to add to what you know: the better informed you are, the better the context into which to fit what will for other viewers be isolated incomprehensible scraps of information.[9, 10] It is a chronic problem for broadcasters to know what degree of previous knowledge to assume in that vast heterogeneous audience; and despite the simplicity of the language in which they are presented many current-affairs items or news reports on matters important enough to be worth paying attention to conceal their significance within some allusion to concepts which are familiar intellectual baggage for only a minority and which only a handful of specialists really understand.

Age is another factor. Show a light, the same light, to a young person and an old person, and it will appear fainter to the older person. To achieve the same response, a higher degree of arousal is needed. As we grow older, not only do they start appointing remarkably young men as policemen, but people fail to speak up and get mean with the lighting. Furthermore, the older we get, the commoner becomes the now-what-did-I-come-upstairs-for? phenomenon. Learning ability is impaired because what the psychologists call short-term memory is more easily interfered with. Go straight to bed after viewing *This Week* and you will remember what it was all about the following day; but if the next-door neighbour pops in for a chat, it might be hard to recall five minutes later. Apart from deficiencies in the medium itself, these facts of life and of psychology must also modify our confidence that because we are so addicted to watching television then we must be well informed.

We have to insulate ourselves against information because there are so many signs and signals impinging on our senses that we would blow our fuses if we paid heed to more than a fraction of them; but even when we do decide to pay attention and let some information pass through the filter, we are easily distracted, especially if we are prepossessed by worries and responsibilities, and especially if we are at home.

Partly through the prodigality of television, this excess of information presents the world to us as a passing show – our involvement is low, our incentives to master it are slight, our contextual understanding is imperfect and our ability to do anything about it is minimal.

Edit for impact

How is television to address such an audience? The millions watching the *News at Ten* or *Panorama* are, for the most part, lacking in political influence; they are enormously varied in their levels of education; they belong to diverse generations, parts of the country, subcultures. Enormous numbers of them are watching, if one may say so, 'too much', and nearly everyone is viewing in an environment which is not always conducive to attentiveness – the all-purpose sitting room.

These facts about the audience are largely responsible for the way in which television addresses that audience. They are not the whole explanation, of course. The factor of inheritance from the press, by which television reproduces the routines and news values of an older medium worked out in a different social context, has already been stressed. The circumstances in which broadcasters work is another; production takes place in a sociologically self-contained world, and is in any case so demanding and so enjoyable, that it is easy for production to become an absorbing end in itself. But the distance, anonymity and heterogeneity of the audience exercises a profound influence on programme making, so that successful broadcasting tends to be judged in terms of impact on an audience, not on communication with it. It is this, not broadcasters' perversity or vanity, which is responsible for the abuse of communication media and hence of the word 'communication' which has so angered René Cutforth. His distinguished work in radio was intensely personal and committed and this no doubt made him sensitive to the failings of television, to which he had lately turned:

It is a 'life-enhancing myth', no doubt, to believe that the sympathetic front man on your favourite programme is telling you a truth in which he is personally and vitally interested. But everybody knows it isn't so, or not very often. He's been chosen for the job because he looks and sounds like that – everybody's sincere old favourite. Somebody else had the idea; some quite different chap did the research, groaning; another man, probably, wrote it. None of it is the fruit of personal experience, and personal experience is the only thing that anybody ever has a lively desire or ability to communicate. The rest is miscellaneous information and propaganda, and totally dead. Nobody in it cares a damn except about its technical excellence. Was it successful? Did it hold the attention? Was it a good commodity? Those are now the crucial questions, and, of course, whether it hit the trend of current belief about a week ahead of its time. If so, it can be called 'controversial'.

Cutforth finds it ironical, but no accident, that

at this particular time in history ... the word 'communicate' has suddenly become loaded with sacred overtones and a mystic halo. That didn't happen until the word, and the thing itself as a commodity, had been so debased as to be almost meaningless. You don't communicate anything to anybody, or even with them, any more – you just communicate.[11]

There is a detailed account of how, in the actual production process, the effort to communicate with an audience becomes narrowed down to having an impact, in a study by Philip Elliott, the Leicester University communications researcher. The implications of this study are the more striking when it is realized that the programmes whose making he closely observed (seven half-hours in a series called *The Nature of Prejudice*) were planned as an educational series for adults. In short, a deliberate intention to enlighten the audience and challenge attitudes, with specific teaching objectives in mind, was implied. Nevertheless, the exigencies of production, the habits and routines of producers and performers, and the profound unknownness of the target audience, resulted in the content of the programmes being processed until they expressed only the unremarkable ' "conventional wisdom" current in society on this particular subject'. It also resulted in a narrowing of the production team's concern with the audience. It would not be true that the team 'paid no attention at all to their potential audience', but, says Elliott:

They did pay attention but largely in terms of *reaction*, not in terms of 'communication'. The production team's principal concern about their audience was to prevent them switching off by trying to hold their interest and attention.[12]

Instead of using television to convey substantial ideas to the audience, interest focused instead on keeping the programme moving.

The forces which encourage television broadcasters to edit for impact throughout the range of informative programming, act still more intensely than in this example in the field of news and current affairs. I said earlier that the people are largely ill-informed, despite television and the other media, because of their relative powerlessness, and that it is the audience's lack of power which conditions the way in which television addresses it in news and current-affairs programmes. In the first section of this chapter I was concerned with the effect of powerlessness on the audience's information gain. I am now dealing with the implications of that powerlessness for the way information is presented to the audience. Let me go back to that quotation from Cecil King at the RSA. It started with these words: 'Time was when governments were concerned with such problems that had, at least directly, no bearing on the life of the ordinary man, who had no vote anyway.'[13] The ordinary man read lurid broadsheets, if he read at all. The man with the vote read *The Times*. Whereas there is now a vast imbalance between the distribution of information and the distribution of power, there was once in short a rough correspondence between the two: when the readers of *The Times* were the only people with the vote and when its chief readers were also the masters of the Empire, the owners of the land, controllers of the economy, and administrators of the political and military machines designed to implement the wishes of this small minority. Now oligarchic power has been modified and restrained by the loss of imperial hegemony, by the universal franchise, by the persistent need to take account of the populace so as not to alienate it unduly, and by the development of a pluriformity of pressure groups and subcentres of power. Information is made available in vast quantities as though this shift had progressed much further, as though effective power were now spread as widely as the readership of popular newspapers and the viewership of television, which it patently is not. News, having little real function in terms of political control and economic decision making by those receiving it, has tended to become an end-in-itself and hence has turned into a consumer product. Since the political criteria for the selection of news are uncertain, they are superseded by a different concept of newsworthiness: news is fact processed into a marketable commodity. Some newspapers are almost wholly dominated by this principle. Television's task is deeply complicated by it.

This vacuum – the space that would be filled by the effective deployment and devolution of power if democracy were true to its own rhetoric – is the prime cause of television's tendency to distract from what matters with shows and of turning what matters into a show. It is wholly superficial to attribute these failings to competition between the BBC and Independent Television. That is an obvious explanation to use, but it derives in part from the stereotyped antithesis between 'public-service' broadcasting (the BBC) and 'commercial television' (ITV), and overlooks the deeper causes which influence both institutions alike.

'Commercial television' is a misleading synonym for ITV because it suggests that kind of broadcasting which exists to make a profit, in which the survival and evolution of programmes depends utterly on their ratings and their appeal to advertisers. The American model on which this stereotype is based undoubtedly diminishes the medium's creativeness. American commercial television itself had become so barren that in 1969–70 its dominance and prestige were utterly shaken by the brilliant originality of *Sesame Street*, a non-commercial educational television series designed as a form of compensatory education for children of pre-school age. Independent Television, whatever its weaknesses, and to whatever extent these weaknesses may be due to commercialism, is intended to be, and actually is, a viable alternative *public-service* broadcasting system, which happens to be financed out of advertising revenue. The Television Act 1964, lays upon the ITA the duty 'to provide a public service for disseminating information, education and entertainment . . . to ensure that the programmes broadcast . . . maintain a high general standard in all respects, and in particular in respect of their content and quality, and a proper balance and wide range in their subject matter'. In short, its responsibilities are the same as the BBC's. Consequently, ITV competes with the BBC across the board. Interestingly, during the late 1960s, the BBC's skill in light entertainment on the whole surpassed ITV's, whereas ITV was responsible for the most consistently successful news programme. *News at Ten*, which viewers liked in their millions and critics praised.

Had there been no Independent Television, the BBC would still have become less Reithian, and much more of a merchandizing organization, partly because of its growth in size as an organization, still more because of the spread of a relatively classless culture and because of the ethos of consumer capitalism with which many institutions have become imbued since the mid-1950s. These pressures (to which *The Times* and quality book publishing have also succumbed), are the source of the pervasion of television by show-business values even where these are least appropriate, and they have affected the provision of political information because of the relative powerlessness of the consumer-citizen. Programme makers would still edit for impact even if the BBC still had its monopoly. Competition only exacerbates some of the symptoms.

The need, if this merchandising form of sub-communication is to succeed at its own levels, to keep contact with this strange, comprehensive, heterogeneous audience, creates a peculiar difficulty for editors of news programmes. The technical point was well put by Reuven Frank in the same Yale speech, in a comparison between television and newspapers:

A newspaper, for example, can easily afford to print an item of conceivable interest to only a small percentage of its readers. *A television news program must be put together with the assumption that each item will be of some interest to everyone who watches.* Every time a newspaper includes a feature that will attract a specialized group, it can assume a little bit more circulation. To the degree that a television news program includes an item of this sort – like a feature on playing bridge or a column on collecting stamps – *it must assume its audience will diminish.* . . .

Perhaps it is worth looking at this way: *Print exists in space, broadcasting in time.*[14]

Under such circumstances, it is with some humility in the face of the difficulties, that one must ask: what is it reasonable to expect of television? Indeed, given the circumstances, it is remarkable that television news and current-affairs programmes are so rarely condescending to the audience, whose knowledgeability is unknown and whose ignorance is proven. How can progress be made? Clearly the cause of democracy will never be served by programmes which people switch off; equally clearly democracy is not well served by programmes whose making is dominated by an overriding determination that viewers shall stay switched on.

9 New Goals and New Values

Anything on the news?

I have said enough, probably more than enough, to show how the progress of television as an instrument of democratic advance, depends on much more than on television alone. The achievements of television are shaped and limited by the structure of the society of which it is a part, especially by the disposition of power within the society; they are also conditioned by the nature and situation of the audience.

The interdependence of these three terms – society, television, audience – does not mean however that progress in one cannot be made without some equal or parallel progress in the others. Social progress has always been and will always be uneven, partly because of the different pace at which various groups of people and institutions adapt to change, partly because all solutions create their own higher-level problems. There are changes that could be made to television without waiting for any profound transformations in society or in the public, changes moreover which would facilitate such a transformation instead of inhibiting, as at present.

Conversely, progress in one area does not automatically guarantee progress in the others. Most importantly it must be recognized that even if the most essential complex of changes were successfully accomplished, so that the balance and distribution of power within society was significantly shifted, this would not of itself ensure the straightforward clarification of television's democratic informational role, or the improvement of its performance. The explanation for this apparent puzzle lies in what was said earlier about the extent of popular participation in a participatory democracy. It is utterly illusory to imagine a hectic scene in which everyone is motivated by some comprehensive concern and busily involved in everything. Even supposing that the political structure had been reformed to make participation easier; and even granted that the educational system had quite stopped playing its traditional deflationary role as an agent of segregation, frustration and discouragement; it would still be true that people would only be able and would only wish to participate in specialized aspects of social life, from time to time or more continuously. Hence the audience's information needs, below a certain level of universality, would still be extremely diverse; this would mean that at least one of the very conditions which make that audience so difficult to address would be perpetuated.

There is a homely situation with which we are all familiar and which concretely expresses the dilemma. The point I am making now is that this dilemma might well persist into a more participatory democracy. The problem is evoked by everyday expressions, as when we ask each other: 'Is there anything in the paper?' or when with a grunt of discontent we volunteer the information: 'There's nothing in the paper today.' This strange but perfectly understood form of words has been adapted for broadcasting – 'Was there anything on the news?' The capacity of the media to inform us partly depends on their ability to interest us, which they start to do by capturing our attention with headlines which signal that here is news of importance; or of human interest, such as might arouse our sympathy or amazement at the ways of our fellow men; or which will titillate our appetites. It is an obvious feature of different newspapers that they combine these appeals in different proportions. If there is 'nothing on the news', then the broadcasters have not succeeded in using any of these stimulants to interest our attention.

There are some kinds of information and news which do not have to be useful in any direct sense. They virtually select themselves for inclusion in the media because of their universal or widespread significance. Events manifestly affecting the peace of the world, or a large part of it, fall into this category. We expect to be told and, on the whole, we are told, about such events, though we know that diplomats and businessmen arrive at decisions secretly. It is news of importance when Western Germany signs a treaty of non-aggression with the Soviet Union. All our lives are shaped by the progress of international politics and its reporting requires no further justification. News of decisions of governments about taxation or social policy are important, and its use is that it enables us to know under what conditions we are to live our lives, make personal and professional decisions which fit the situation or will contribute to changing it. Without them we cannot judge our masters, who are expected to give an account of their leadership of the nation.

Many items are attended to because they touch us directly. It is useful to know that there is a dock strike – the formation of public attitudes depends upon the provision of information about it, exporters will know when to hold back deliveries, housewives will expect shortages of tomatoes or oranges or chilled beef from the Argentine. It is useful in quite a different way to know that terrible earthquakes have destroyed large areas of Turkey and Peru. There is a humanity shared through the knowledge, and the sympathy evoked will lead to a practical response – relief teams dispatched, money collected at banks.

All this is obvious. But, for a variety of reasons, a great deal of information is useless to whole sections, sometimes large sections, of those exposed to it. Over a whole range of human activity, our involvement may differ considerably from facet to facet. This would still be true in a reformed democracy. Some items of news are likely to concern all or most viewers, but some will be of more interest to farmers than to clerks, to sports enthusiasts, animal lovers or other sub-publics. A further problem is created by the formats and frequency of the news outlets – a daily paper has to be filled every day, often with much the same proportions of domestic and foreign news. The *News at Ten* goes out every weekday at ten. Sometimes the difficulty is what to leave out; sometimes it is what to put in.

This does not mean, however, that the democratic performance, in particular the informational performance of television can never be improved. The obsession with spectacle is not incurable. Nor is it necessary to wait for the slow-insistent waves of sociological pressure to mould television into better shape for its new roles. These roles should even now be under review and public discussion. The social climate is visibly changing in which these discussions will take place. Society is already becoming disenchanted with the glittering values of the 1950s and the 1960s, and while much of the fun, gaiety and liberation of the 1960s are, one hopes, likely to persist, there are already signs that a more socially conscious epoch lies ahead. (It is a cliché to regard the United States as the prosperous society which foreshadows our own future. We should try looking at Sweden for a change.) What does such an epoch require of broadcasting?

It requires

1. A thorough public re-examination of the statutorily set goals of broadcasting.

2. A more educative approach to news and current affairs programming.

3. A changed relationship with the audience, such that the public has easier access to the medium, leading to new kinds of programme making.

Enlarge the goals of broadcasting

There has hitherto been a good deal of talk about the management of the BBC and ITV, but it should now be obvious that that is not the fundamental question. The real issue is what we, as a multi-form, pluralistic, divergent society, want to use broadcasting for. Management should be a subordinate issue to philosophy and policy.

What seems certain is that the goals set by society for broadcasting, while they have undoubtedly served well in the past, are no longer adequate. This is the real question underlying Shulman's shrill accusation of dope-peddling (which translates 'narcotizing dysfunction' into homely abuse) quoted in chapter 4.

Underlying his polemical attack on the BBC for trying to get the nation hooked on sport when it should have been turning its attention more assiduously to its electoral responsibilities, was a serious charge, which was nowhere made explicit – that the BBC was during this period perversely and irresponsibly subordinating its Charter obligations to inform and educate to its other Charter obligation to entertain. It would be difficult to sustain an accusation in these terms against either the BBC or Independent Television, but there is a prima facie case for suggesting that the injunction to 'educate, inform and entertain' is now too vague a formula to express a democratic society's expectations of its chief public communication resource. On the whole, the broadcasting organizations do well the work they have been set up to do; the question remains, is the job specification an adequate one?

The way in which these socially set goals for broadcasting have become subordinated to consumerism, as though programmes were a species of cultural consumer products to be sold and judged successful in terms of ratings (cf. sales), and as though the competing organizations making them could consequently be assessed by their share of the market, was unexpectedly illustrated by a sophisticated *ballon d'essai* flown by Brian Emmett, Head of BBC's Audience Research Department.[1] Emmett proprosed applying the operational research techniques known as 'mathematical programming' to help a broadcasting organization maximize not the audience, but 'the gratifications that viewers ... derive from the services offered'. Programmes could be rated not solely by audience size but measured in 'grats' (units of gratification). The technicalities of Emmett's paper need not concern us at all. What matters in this context is that the direction in which the discussion in Britain might profitably turn was indicated in a reply to Emmett by his opposite number in the Finnish Broadcasting Company, Dr Kaarle Nordenstreng. In effect, Emmett took for granted the British merchandising view of broadcasting with viewers left in a politically passive posture; Nordenstreng wanted to use the medium for democratic control, turning viewers into knowledgeable citizens capable of action.

At the technical level, Nordenstreng agreed that Emmett's approach represented a considerable advance on conventional audience research of the head-counting kind, but he doubted whether it was informed by an adequate concept of the aims of broadcasting. His doubts arose from Emmett's 'underlying principle' that the responsibility or aim of a broadcasting organization is 'to try to increase the satisfaction our programmes give to all kinds of people; or, to put it in more scientific terms, to maximize some function which measures the "utility" of our output to the public'.

In his reply, Nordenstreng was concerned about what is meant by 'increasing the satisfaction' and 'measuring utility':

For Emmett, the notion of satisfaction seems to imply the gratification of a number of psychological needs, and the utility of the output to the public seems to be a derivative of these gratifications. The whole model is based on how *individuals* feel about program output and the approach completely neglects any broader sociological considerations at the *macro-level* of society. Surely the aims of broadcasting and the evaluation of programme output should not be determined solely in terms of individual receivers.

Mass communication necessarily introduces social implications which cannot be tapped by simply looking at the needs of individuals – needs which to a large extent are (as Emmett also quite correctly reminds us) modified or even produced by the social network in which the individual lives. Any model which excludes sociological considerations of mass communication is seriously limited and naïve.[2]

Nordenstreng's next comment, even though a specialist observation on a British theoretical research exercise, says by implication a good deal about television's present limitations as an instrument of a democracy which will through participation work on its own transformation:

Furthermore, a model which is based on the gratifications of individuals is not value-free: inevitably it must work in favour of the social *status quo* since the needs of individuals do not develop in a vacuum but are formed within existing social structure and are not uninfluenced by the media themselves. Emmett offers one way of setting the aims of broadcasting, but ... it is by no means the only logically plausible way and not necessarily the most 'responsible' or 'democratic' way.

Since democracy will not be served by programmes which people switch off, the notion of 'gratification' remains relevant; but neither will democracy be served, and nor will the chronic political needs and dissatisfactions of the people be assuaged, by programmes which are chiefly inspired by a desire to gratify individual viewers, especially in ways meant to maximize audience size. Just as education has to work through individuals *and* meet their needs, *and* serve the proximate and long-range needs of society, so has television to accept social goals as well as aim at viewer satisfaction in Emmett's narrower psychological sense.

Emmett concedes an important point when he says:

> In order to specify the problem in such a way that a mathematical programming solution can be found, one other matter has to be considered. That is the relative importance, or weight, to be given to the gratifications of the various needs. The decision about these is not too extreme to say that they must encapsulate the philosophy or value system of the organization; in an underdeveloped country high priority might be placed on teaching, whereas in third-century Rome it would no doubt have been recreation that the Emperor decided should carry most weight. This facility may, for some, provide a welcome element of freedom in an otherwise aridly deterministic model.

Just so. And it is in this very direction that the Finns are directing their research effort. They have already concluded (perhaps going to another extreme) that 'the ultimate objective of programmes is to widen the cognitive frame of reference or world view of the audience'.

This somewhat esoteric challenge based on experience in a sympathetic social democracy helps to draw attention to the exiguousness and vagueness of the stated aims of public service broadcasting in Britain. This sketchiness is not only widely admitted: it is also thought to be a virtue. Emmett himself says of the BBC's Charter requirement to 'educate, inform and entertain' that it 'is so vague an injunction that it can be made to mean practically anything'. The Pilkington Committee considered that 'The definitions are so general as to amount to no more than broad precepts.'[3]

The Committee was content with that, registering its satisfaction in an astonishing two-sentence *non-sequitur*:

> It is no surprise that the purposes should be stated in terms so general. Opposing views were expressed to us on many particular aspects of our task; but there was unanimity on this – that no written formula for good broadcasting is possible.

Of course it is impossible to legislate for good *programmes* and all that the Report goes on to say two or three sentences later about broadcasting being 'more nearly an art than an exact science' which deals in 'tastes and values and is not precisely definable' obviously applies. But that is not to say that the *purposes* of broadcasting may not be spelled out. Since British broadcasting is already governed by three goals, broadly enough defined (or not defined at all) to encourage creative freedom to manoeuvre within them, there is no reason why the taxonomy should not be enlarged to comprise four, five or any number more objectives felt to be socially desirable.

This is a matter on which more than research is needed – it is an issue of public policy which should be publicly discussed. And the discussion should not be once and for all. No institution can now afford to ossify: all must build into their structure and procedures a capacity for adaptation. The objectives may only gradually evolve. The gloss – publicly arrived at – on how those objectives should be interpreted may need to be fairly frequently reviewed and renewed. From what has been argued so far, however, it seems necessary to prescribe for British broadcasting that, in addition to educating, informing and entertaining individuals, it should also adopt two social objectives and play its part as a chief communications resource of the society. It should (a) help the disparate segments of society to communicate with one another, and (b) foster the integrity and dynamism of democracy. Educating, informing and entertaining are not sufficient goals in a democracy. Few of the world's autocratic regimes would have a conscientious qualm about accepting them. Meanwhile, this draft proposal might be debated:

It shall be the duty of the BBC and of the ITA to provide public services of education, information and entertainment, and to contribute, through their programmes and in other ways deemed appropriate, to the extension and invigoration of the nation's democratic life, and to understanding between the different segments of society.

Even if this specific proposal finds no supporters, the fundamental issue of goals should now be placed on the agenda of statutory and unofficial forums deliberating the future of broadcasting.

Adopt a more educative approach to news and current-affairs programming

The promulgation of enlarged goals for broadcasting, though essential, would only have a gradual influence on practice. Television's democratic function could be strengthened and its informational performance improved more directly by intensifying a process which is already happening: the development of a more deliberately educative approach to news and current-affairs programming. There are two aspects of this development to be considered – negatively, the release of news broadcasting from the clutch of fallacies summed up in the slogan, 'good news is no news'; and positively, the maturing of an incipient journalism of explanation.

In chapter 7, I discussed the distortion which arises from the prevailing concepts of 'news' and 'newsworthiness'. This is a difficult problem but not the utterly intractable one it sometimes seems. One response to it is John Whale's refusal to apologize. He correctly detects a low degree of public interest in the fact that each day heads of state are not assassinated, companies do not go bankrupt and numerous aircraft flights are safely accomplished. He further perceives a considerable indifference to the fate of the sisal crop in Tanzania, even if it were an epic disaster. In Whale's view, any newspaper which went into the 'good-news business' would be a flop.

The substituting of 'only good news is news' for 'good news is no news' as an editorial policy does seem to be implied by some critics of the disaster-ridden media. Amazingly, it seems these also have been tried out in practice by a Sacramento publisher, one Bill Bailey, who is reported as having launched the first newspaper in America devoted exclusively to good news.[4] His initial issue listed only those share prices which had gone up, and its lead story reported that in 1969 in the United States 197 million people did not commit a crime, five million college students did not riot and 201 million Americans did not use illegal drugs! Whether or not Mr Bailey's venture turns out to be commercially viable, he is clearly providing a news service no less grotesque than any already available.

The traditional defence of the 'bad news is good news' doctrine is fallacious. It rests on the proposition that since viewers and readers do not wish to be told what they know already, then they are bound to be supplied with a diet of violence, disaster and the bizarre. The conclusion blatantly does not follow, but acting on it is in danger of becoming a sociologically ingrained habit with the media.

Bill Baileyism would obviously be a false philosophy for television news to adopt. There must be a place in the news for disaster, not only for the unregenerate reason that the old Adam in us takes a mischievous interest in the misfortunes of others, but also because the New Adam is humanely concerned by them – and the line is often hard to draw. Of course people do not wish to be told about aspects of life with which they are perfectly familiar, but they do wish to be told about the peaceful, constructive, non-dramatic aspects of events and issues with which they are unfamiliar.

At conferences and other events where broadcasters engage in discussion with viewers, this plea is heard more frequently. The disquiet at the back of it was expressed by the viewer who wrote to the *TV Times*:

If 20,000 hippies from all over the world had gathered for a drug and sex orgy, the TV news cameras would have been there like a shot.

Why, then, no pictures of the 20,000 Scouts at the World Jamboree in Japan – 500 of them from Britain? The vast majority of youngsters are still a credit to this country and their activities for the good of mankind should be given the publicity they deserve.

ITN replied:

There are literally hundreds of stories one could cover every day and they are featured on their merits.

In the case of the Scouts, it was in any event extremely difficult to obtain any worthwhile coverage from Japan, due to communication problems.[5]

All the difficulty lies in the interpretation of 'on their merits', of course. Awareness of changed expectations in many viewers may have affected the handling of the 1971 Pop Festival at Weeley in Essex. On the first day, the cameras were there noting an isolated outbreak of fighting between some Hells Angels and others. On subsequent days, the main burden of the reports was that the thousands of young people present had been orderly, well-behaved and accepted by the local residents.

The non-journalist's idea of what constitutes news is notoriously fallible. Secretaries of voluntary organizations, for example, frequently suffer from the delusion that utterly routine events sponsored by their members and of interest only to them, ought to be of interest to the media. But it ought not always to be necessary for active citizens, let alone the public-relations officers of public and private concerns, to contort themselves looking for some newsworthy 'angle' on some story which is already important and worthwhile in itself. Nor can professional journalists, in the debate on what news values are important in society, afford to ignore suggestions from outsiders, even though some of them will prove banal or unworkable. In a letter to *The Times* (16 April 1971), the Secretary of the Southall branch of the Draughtsmen's and Allied Technicians' Association provided an isolated but promising example of an event which was newsworthy but positive and constructive, and, consequently, largely ignored:

Sir, on 21 March, the Westland Aerospatiale Lynx Helicopter made its maiden flight from Yeovil aerodrome – Good News. However, apart from a five-second shot on a television news strip and an almost negligible report in one or two daily newspapers, the event went unrecorded. To us who worked on this machine it meant the culmination of months of hard work involving new techniques, bold thinking and a challenge to build a British winner aircraft and for us and our many colleagues who, sub-contract-wise, contributed, it was a great success story, it was Great News!

Next point, it is largely British, it could mean world-wide sales and trade, confidence and employment at home – Great News!

Next point, it was designed mainly at Hayes, Middlesex, on a very tight budget by a comparatively small design team. I think it is likely to be the last aircraft to be designed at this historic centre of aircraft design and our design team did us well – Great News!

The only bad news is how a good job, well done becomes 'no' news. The only 'good' news so it seems, is Bad News!

Yours faithfully, L. H. Beal, 53 St Marks Road, Hanwell, W7.

Westland might have got better coverage if a topless model had been on hand to congratulate the test pilot, or if the London

Rubber Company could have supplied Yeovil aerodrome with the largest condom in the world as a wind sock.

Accepting, then, that viewers do not wish to be told what they already know, does not imply the frivolous consequence that we only wish to be told about the fraught and the freakish. We need information positive and negative, about the unfamiliar world whose doings matter because they affect us. Seeking new values for news values will not be easy, but it must be attempted. It calls for a changed sensitivity in professional journalists – copy-tasters may and do change their tastes after all – many of whom resent the wastefulness of a news-gathering operation which largely exists to highlight colourful chaff; it calls for enlarged contacts between journalists and diverse centres of knowledge and power (had Shelter existed earlier for example, the exposure of Rachmanism would not have arisen so fortuitously); and it calls for a good deal less public acquiescence in a notoriously unsatisfactory situation.

Just as the standards of television advertising have led to an improvement in advertising through other media, so the relatively high standards of broadcast journalism could affect an improvement in the popular press. John Scupham, in *Broadcasting and the Community*, offers broad terms of reference for the broadcasters themselves:

Broadcasting can best serve that national need in two ways. It can, in the first place, concentrate on a few great central issues at home and abroad in all their infinitely various human manifestations – on our own economic problems, on the plight of the poor nations, and on the balance of world power – with the determination that there shall be a full and effective communication to everyone of the basic and enduring facts.

In the second place it can aim at fostering a full understanding by every citizen of those aspects of social policy which most clearly and immediately link up with his home-centred interests and affect him and his children; of education, health, housing, the care of the old, the needs of the adolescent, and the maintenance of law and justice as these come within the province of ordinary men and women. It could show that all these afford opportunities for involvement and service. On the great new housing estates, with their inward-turning family units, there is, nevertheless, an impulse towards community; in young people everywhere there is an impulse to help. If the broadcasting organizations are to play a full creative role they must face far more boldly than at present the need for exposition as well as for journalism; for the study in depth as well as the magazine item; for the series as well as the isolated programme; for continuity and repetition; and for all these at peak times and not in an obscure and inconvenient hole or corner.[6]

Scupham speaks of 'the need for exposition as well as for journalism', in itself a revealing, even an unfair, antithesis. The need is rather to step up a process which is already occurring: the development of a journalism of explanation. At present, television is stronger on events than on causes; better at description than at explanation; brilliant with the foreground detail, less cogent with the background. The plea for 'more background' infuriates some American television newsmen, but fortunately it is accepted and indeed advocated by their British counterparts. Reuven Frank (president, NBC News) for example gets really indignant that time after time groups get together to tell television how much it ought to expound on subjects that television has brought into the American home. When he made his Yale speech he was particularly incensed by the report of a committee chaired by Justice Arthur Goldberg, of which Gregory Peck was a member. Part of the panel's statement was reported in the 1 February 1970 issue of the New York *Times*. 'The panel criticized the communications media for increasing "the flow of information without providing the background within which this increased flow might be interpreted".' Frank snapped back:

Quite a change to those of us who remember back a few decades, when those concerned with foreign affairs accused American journalism of encouraging a generation of yahoos and fostering isolationism through ignorance. The cry then was: There must be more room in daily news reporting for the world around us; we must know and be ready. . . .[7]

Justice Goldberg's panel had specifically recommended: 'In-depth coverage of foreign affairs should appear on a regular basis and not have to compete with spot news.' To which Frank angrily and complacently riposted: 'We thought and continue to think it is a big deal that we present spot news from abroad so completely and so fast at so much cost and so much effort.'

Once again, the position in Britain is more reassuring. As long ago as 1962, a quite different spirit was advocated by Donald Edwards, then Editor-in-Chief of BBC News and Current Affairs, and subsequently acted on:

I believe we must do more research and more discussion in depth. We must spend less time airing opinions and more time giving explanatory facts. . . . Our duty is not merely to reflect life as it is, but also to inspire a sense of direction and purpose. . . . We want to be a vigorous creative factor in national life. We want to quicken interest and understanding of matters that affect not only us, but our children.[8]

Not all television journalists would find Edwards's sacerdotal tone sympathetic, but many of them appreciate that there ought to be a more ample provision of background information and interpretation. Without using the word 'education' they do in fact recommend a more educational approach to the provision of information, supplying a frame of reference in terms of which the eventful, topical foreground may be understood.

One way in which a journalism of explanation could be fostered would be through a more purposeful relationship between news programmes, current-affairs magazines and documentary features. At present these three fields do not phase together adequately, and all three suffer from two connected weaknesses – fortuitousness of coverage and overall lack of balance. A private, informal monitoring of *This Week*, *World in Action* and *The Frost Programme* during the autumn of 1970, for example, showed that almost 40 per cent of the output dealt with the United States (including Vietnam). The remaining programmes dealt with home affairs (including Ireland) with the exception of interviews with Kenneth Kaunda, Colonel Ojukwu, and surveys of Rhodesia and the Strategic Arms Limitation Talks in Helsinki. Domestic topics during the same period included the Labour Party Conference, problems of old age in Worthing and elsewhere, race relations in Islington, the Star and Garter Home for disabled servicemen, the casualty ward of University College Hospital, a rock musical by a Bolton secondary school, problems of the chronically disabled, price rigging by electrical contractors, the Neighbourhood Law Centre in Notting Hill Gate and a sex boutique in Birmingham. It is, on the whole, an impressive list of important subjects, and some of the programmes were very well made. Yet, on the foreign affairs side, it is difficult to avoid the conclusion that the overall current affairs output in the period under discussion was unbalanced in the choice of subject matter. It is to be expected that the USA and its current internal and external problems should form a substantial proportion of current affairs screen time, but 40 per cent seems excessive. During the period, not only did the Common Market issue lie fallow, there was nothing at all on Europe, not even on Willy Brandt and the 'Ost-Politic'. There was nothing on the role of the trades unions or of the nationalized industries in the new political context and climate being created by the Conservative Government. Some of the obvious omissions were made good on the other channel, but an analysis of its output would reveal a similar situation. The broadcasters are up against a sheer shortage of time, which limits everything they attempt, and forces difficult choices upon them in trying to meet other equally valid audience needs; but they may also be in need of a more positive philosophy of explanatory journalism.

In pleading for an educative approach, I am not suggesting that current-affairs broadcasting should abjure its familiar territory – the topical – or curb one of its main strengths – spontaneity. Nor am I recommending anything like a syllabus of subjects to ensure adequate and balanced coverage. I am, however, suggesting that specific editorial decisions to feature certain topics need to be taken within a framework of general aims and objectives, so that the output does not present a mere aggregate of interesting subjects but does provide something akin to the Finnish goal of widening 'the cognitive frame of reference or world view of the audience'. Perhaps the very concept of 'background' itself needs examination, since it conjures up a dated world in which news had to be up to the minute to catch newspaper editions, marketed with fierce competition on every street corner, when explanation was something there was never time for, and 'background' was all that could be afforded on occasion.

The old-fashioned struggle to be first with the news was won by radio, not by newspapers. Television, though capable of being 'at' the news, is also the medium which is often prepared to wait for pictures of it, and no one seems to suffer unduly from seeing film, transported by aircraft, developed and edited, of what happened as long ago as yesterday. Now that instantane-ousness is within our power, we begin to see how relatively unimportant it usually is, and this less frenetic obsession with what is happening this minute will make a journalism of ex-planation more acceptable both to journalists and to viewers.

It will also be more gradually, but perceptibly facilitated by the steady improvement in the educational level of the audience. Better education has or should have three effects: it enables more members of the audience to assimilate what television tells, to place its information in a context of understanding – a factor already discussed in chapter 8; it reduces the audience's pas-sivity in the face of television; and, thirdly, it helps the audience develop a less monopolistic dependence on television.

The spread of improved education will enable more viewers to cope with the information provided by television, the capacity for which increases according to how well stocked the mind already is with relevant frameworks, concepts and cognate information. I suggested earlier that television, whatever its own defects, would inform people better if they only watched it less. Viewers still commonly watch a very great deal. From January to July 1969, in homes which could receive both BBC and In-dependent Television, the set was switched on and being viewed by someone in the household for an average of four and a half hours a day. Nevertheless, the discrimination of audiences and their capacity to get more out of what is offered on the screen is gradually improving all the time. This is due to acclimatization as well as to education. I have already mentioned the research which Dr William Belson undertook in 1954 when only 35 per cent of the population had television (p. 73). In those days, the time taken viewing television not only had a considerable dis-placement effect on other ways of spending that time: it also had a measurable depressant effect on viewers' interests and acts of initiative. But the research showed that after about five years, these effects wore off, and television viewing was apparently assimilated into life. The novelty of television has now faded for the British public. We have also had television long enough for there to be a generational change. Viewers who have never known a world without television seem to be less obsessed and bemused by it than their elders.

Another sign of sophistication is that viewers are increasingly willing to switch channels. During the 1950s and early 1960s they tended to be uncritically loyal to one channel. Now the audience research tables show viewers shifting from channel to channel, and, gradually, showing a willingness to switch off. It is probably still only a minority of the audience that decides quite deliberately to tune to particular programmes and turn off the set when they are finished, but the majority of the audience, even if it leaves the set on, know which programmes they particularly want to see. The set is on 'so that we don't miss *Coronation Street* (or Val Doonican or Miss World or the *News at Ten*)'.

Apart from the influence of acclimatization and general improvements in education, the spread of more varied systems and technical aids to learning throughout the education service will also produce a generation familiar with the strengths and weaknesses of different media. Present generations turn to television as a chief source of information about what is going on in the world. Young people who have been through schools with a range of audio-visual and print resources, will take for granted that sometimes a need is best met by a book, sometimes by a film loop, sometimes by a stored (cassetted) television programme, sometimes by a live broadcast. The wider use of screened information, through the spread of film and film-loop projectors, overhead projectors and television itself, in schools and colleges, is likely to prepare viewers of the future to bring an *attentive* mental set to television, as appropriate. For various reasons, therefore, middle-aged viewers, with a reputation for slumping passively in front of their sets for most of the evening, are likely to be succeeded by a generation of viewers with different habits of viewing and with a wider range of mental sets – sometimes relaxed, sometimes concentrating.

Television could make its own contribution to this process of sophistication. At present the medium, operating within limited time, is subjected to the strain of unrealistic expectations, by being treated as *the* source of information, education and enlightenment. Television regularly helps specialized sections of the audience appreciate that it is only one, albeit rather splendid, instrument in a multi-media orchestra, as when educational programmes are reinforced by print, film loops, LP discs and other materials. But this significant admission, that some matters are better dealt with through other media, is not commonly made or implied in general programmes. An experiment in explicity so doing was carried out in Czechoslovakia during the 'Prague spring' when the Dubček regime was humanizing Czechoslovak communism. Television contributed to the development of Czech democracy by setting up open forums, but the television service also attempted to make clear to viewers the limitation of television as a means of disseminating ideas and information. Jiří Pelikán, the head of Czech Television who was later to amaze the world by relaying the Soviet invasion of his country as a live 'outside broadcast', explained his policy in relation to a forum series called *Public Affairs*:

In *Public Affairs* we shall confront the views of the man in the street with the standpoints of responsible authorities on issues that are universally felt at the present time, beginning with the new wages policy.

By the standards of the Novotny regime this was a daring use of broadcasting, typical of the new style of Dubček's government. But it did not blind Pelikán to the limitations of his medium. Consequently, the television series was run in collaboration with *Kulturní tvorba*, a cultural and political weekly. Pelikán:

It is seldom possible to probe all aspects of a problem during the programme. To develop discussion on the topic in print before and after the transmission is an interesting experiment.[9]

I am referring to this technically simple exercise in multimedia presentation of ideas from experts and from ordinary viewers primarily as an example of the way in which television itself can encourage viewers to be less exclusively dependent on television for their concepts and information about the world.

The larger, fundamental cause for which Pelikán and his colleagues worked so hard and, in the end, so bravely, has suffered an appalling reverse, but it remains our own cause – the harnessing of the media for the pursuit of freedom in technocracies made rigid by archaic political forms. The difference lies in the political context: working on the cause in Britain calls for imagination and adaptability, but not for heroism.*

The quality of adaptability will be most called for in the third of the three major changes that seem to be necessary. As well as expanding the goals of broadcasting, laying upon those responsible positive duties to promote understanding within a pluriform society and to stimulate the dynamic of participation in democracy; in addition to the revaluation of news values and the development of a journalism of explanation, so that information may be used more effectively not only for orientation and

* It is worth digressing in a footnote to quote from the article which supported the second programme in Pelikán's *Public Affairs* series, since its subject was 'Are we well informed?' In short, the series was relevant to one of my main themes in content as well as its method. The author, Miroslav Galuška, then a member of the Presidium of the Union of Czechoslovak journalists, made complaints which parallel the strictures voiced in British terms above. About the secretiveness of the Establishment, for example: 'No one rejects the theory that public opinion should be informed; no one attacks the principle of the freedom of the press, guaranteed by the Constitution; no one explicitly requests journalists to present the public with slanted information. In practice, however, the journalists often encounter attitudes and opinions that thwart the proper fulfilment of his responsible task. . . . Journalists find that various institutions keep information under their hats with the excuse that higher interests are involved. A little probing often reveals that these interests are not those of society. . . . Democratic control by the public is an empty phrase when problems of social importance are discussed behind the people's backs.'

Although Cold-War politics exacerbated the problem on the international plane, Schramm's analysis and other parts of the critique above, show that what Galuška regrets was not unique to Czechoslovakia: 'Information published here about the internal developments of the imperialist countries was very biased at one time. Reports dwelt on the negative aspects of capitalism: class clashes, unemployment, social injustice, industrial and financial difficultes. Little space, if any, was devoted to other aspects . . . expansion of . . . production, the introduction of new methods of management, the advance of science and technology. . . .' [10]

There is, therefore, some remarkable similarity between the fate of news adapted to the needs of communist bureaucracy and news processed for sale.

surveillance but also, as needed, for action; it is essential for the medium to create new relationships with the public. These new relationships are implied by summary demands now being heard for greater popular *access* to the medium. There are many ways in which access is being advocated, or even realized in practice. Some are more practicable than others, some express the participatory ideal more effectively and less superficially than others. Part Three is solely devoted to an examination of the alternatives.

Part Three
Programmes for Participation

10 Alternatives and Precursors

Direct access and box pop

The summary demand for access to radio and television is in keeping with the popular pressures on other established institutions described in Part One. People find it increasingly intolerable when institutions, many of them ostensibly set up for the public's benefit, seem and sometimes actually are more concerned with being able to carry on their business undisturbed by outside 'interference'. Parliament and local government, supposed to represent the people, are felt to be remote from the people; bureaucratic procedures cause all sorts of institutions to lose sight of their main purpose so that 'in hospitals patients may be woken up to be given sleeping pills, in prisons the socially inadequate are deprived of all initiative, and in schools an insistence upon obedience and punctuality may take precedence over the development of independent thought';[1] public libraries are shut at the very time when the public is free to use them; mothers of small children have to rush to catch the post-natal clinic when it is open. People are more and more impatient with institutions which function autocratically and, as a result, perversely and stupidly. Thus students want seats on the Senate, many parents want a say in the government of schools and still more want physical access to schools and their staffs. It has always been recognized that, in principle, politics is too important to be left to the politicians. The insight is being extended: education is too important to be left to educationists; housing to housing managers and committees; planning, in general, to the planners.

'Broadcasting is really too important to be left to the broadcasters.' So Anthony Wedgwood Benn, in a speech delivered in 1968, crystallized the same wood of resentment, the same sense of exclusion, in relation to radio and television. He returned to the theme in his Fabian Tract, *The New Politics*:

The public, as a whole, are denied access or representation in these new talking shops of the mass media as completely as the 94 per cent without the vote were excluded from Parliament before 1832. The real question is not whether the programmes are good, or serious, or balanced or truthful. It is whether or not they allow the people themselves to reflect, to each other, the diversity of interests, opinions, grievances, hopes and attitudes to their fellow citizens and to talk out their differences at sufficient length. . . . The press and broadcasting authorities have a responsibility for providing enough accurate information, at the time when it really matters, to allow people to acquire greater influence. The people for their part, have the right to demand a greater ease of access to the community through the mass media.[2]

At a May Day rally in 1971, Benn made a specific demand for time on television for the trade-union movement:

The time has come when the trade-union movement should demand the right to regular programmes of its own on the BBC and ITV, to allow it to speak directly to its members without having everything they say edited away by self-appointed pundits and producers.

Surely the trade-union movement, with nearly 10,000,000 members, should be entitled as an absolute minimum to, say, a quarter of an hour out of the 200 hours of BBC output each week.

Doubtless Wedgwood Benn is right when he observes (in his Fabian pamphlet): 'The democratization, and accountability of the mass media will be a major issue for the 1970s and the debates on it are now beginning.'

In his contribution to the debate. Benn has argued in favour of direct communication as distinct from mediated communication. In his May Day speech he said that if time were allowed to the trades unions on the networks that would allow them to present in depth and free from bullying interrogators, the needs and problems of those who earn their living in industry. He expanded his idea in the *Sunday Mirror*:

The trouble is that most of what we see and hear is filtered through someone who is an expert in communication – maybe a producer, or a journalist, or an editor. They feel it is their job to make their material interesting.

But making it interesting means that someone plonks himself down between us and the real situation.

You just don't hear people who are actually working in industry talking in their own language about their lives and problems.

If a shop steward in one of those car factories was given enough time to tell us, in his own words, what it was all about, or if we heard the manager talking directly about his side of the case, their words would have a special ring of truth about them.[3]

It is an attractive proposal, and the impulse behind it is similar to my own. It seems to follow from all that I have said that one of the chief aims of reform should be that viewers should have greater access to the medium, so that it is much less a one-way medium through which a select band of communicators may address everyone else, and much more a medium through which the heterogeneous sections of a society in process of confusing transformation may effectively communicate with each other. But is Benn's proposal the best way either to democratize television or to use television in the service of a participatory democracy (two separate questions, frequently confused)? The Dutch are attempting something of the kind through the Nederlands Oucroep Stichting, which allows interest groups to create broadcasting societies with direct access for presenting their views in proportion to their membership. It will be important to observe the successes and failures of the Dutch scheme and it would probably be worthwhile to conduct similar experiments in Britain.

Wedgwood Benn's idea has encountered considerable scepticism, but this could be a short-term effect of its novelty. Some critics doubt whether trade unionists are articulate enough to pull it off ('most trade unionists are at a considerable disadvantage compared with people who have always regarded words as their natural means of communication').[4] This is not a serious objection. It is basically a snobbish objection. The spoken word is in fact a tool of trade to every shop steward and trade-union negotiator, and in any case people with a capacity for expressing themselves can learn to adapt to the exigencies of an unfamiliar medium. More telling perhaps, is the fear that trade unionists are articulate enough, but boring:

Has Mr Benn ever watched the TUC at their annual conference when trade unionist after trade unionist gets up and has his five-minute say?

Anyone watching three days of *that* would conclude that the less trade unionists exposed themselves unfiltered and unedited the better. The fact is that most trade unionists, as do most politicians, churchmen and businessmen, talk more conventional, cliché-ridden nonsense about themselves than not.[5]

British experience of direct access has not been reassuring – outside broadcasts from party political conferences, the party political broadcasts themselves, for example, do not do much, if anything, to irrigate the arid channels of democratic communication.

Wedgwood Benn himself anticipated one of the difficulties. If the trade unions had the right of access, presumably management would want it too:

If that meant giving the same time to the Confederation of British Industry as well, at least we should be hearing from managers who are also experiencing complex problems of human relations in industry.

One of Mr Benn's supporters was the secretary of an ex-serviceman's organization, who wrote to *The Times* envisaging a place for his society in such a scheme. Somehow it would be necessary to ration scarce time on a handful of channels not only between the TUC and the CBI, but on behalf of the British Legion, the Boys Brigade, Toc H and the Townswomen's Guilds, Rotary and Round Table, ACE and CASE, Shelter and Snap, the British Humanist Association and the Salvation Army, Release and the Adult School Union, rank upon rank of interest societies, voluntary bodies and pressure groups. Not impossible in practice, but daunting.

More importantly, would it be worth the effort, even if (as some see reason to doubt) the resulting programmes were viewable, interesting, peopled by passionate enthusiasts with a reality to communicate and 'with a ring of truth about them'? I fear it would not. Benn was demanding a quarter of an hour a week in which to present 'in depth' the needs and problems of the industrial workers. Fifteen minutes: and it could not be more, with that press of industrialists, ex-servicemen and vegetarians all queuing up for their share of time. But how could any of them present themselves *in depth* under these circumstances? Who would view? How effective would they be in communicating or in promoting dialogue and social change? Experience of such a scheme might prove otherwise, but on the face of it those who demand access to the networks are on a false trail. No doubt many of the resulting programmes would have a valuable authenticity and freshness, but to claim parity of opportunity with professional broadcasting is to want an equal right with the broadcasters to a medium of staggering inefficiency and ineffectiveness, as analysed in Part Two. Advocates of 'direct access' are recommending the wrong message for the wrong medium. They are really hankering for a multi-channel situation, for cable television, for the wired city. What they propose would be socially desirable and feasible in practice if the technology were right, and it is in that direction that the argument based on their premises should run.

It is largely in order to promote such direct access that the extension of cable television is being seriously considered in Canada and the United States. 'The wired city' is an extension again of CATV in conjunction with other electronic devices. Wilbur Schramm is one of many authorities who regard such a project as realizable before the end of the century:

The wired city ... means essentially that most homes, schools, industries and businesses will be served by coaxial cables with a capacity of twenty to forty television channels each, and a far greater number of voice channels. These will enable business and industry to do much of their work, and operate many of their automated factories at a distance. Much marketing will be done on these new channels, and many meetings will be held on them. The wired city will connect our homes with storekeepers, lawyers, doctors, libraries and an adult education centre for life-long study and retraining. It will provide us photo-telephones, and let us choose from much more news and entertainment than we can now receive.[6]

The demand for direct access is in tune with the temperament of the time, but the demand is vitiated by the technology of the time. Its impracticability does not show the demand to be unreasonable – it exposes the contemporary technology of open circuit network television as for some purposes old fashioned.

There is not much point in attempting to broaden the range of voices with the right to suffer from the same communications blocks which make television, and much of the professionalism associated with it, ineffective and spurious.

Another attempt to use television for democratic participation, employing quite a different communications model, nearer in concept to the wired city, has been attempted in West Germany. The system (called ORAKEL) combined televised documentary and discussion with the techniques of phone-in and electronic opinion poll. Three programmes were transmitted on consecutive evenings in the summer of 1971, the first starting at 9.30 p.m. and going on until 1.30 in the morning. It started with a cartoon criticizing the gap between government and people on the pollution question, and went on with documentary film to remind viewers of the kind of problems created by pollution. There the resemblance to a conventional programme ended. The rest of the time consisted of 'organized conflicts' on television, phoned-in questions from viewers, and viewers' answers to poll-type questions processed by computer. The 'organized conflicts' were aggressive exchanges of opinion between representatives of industry, government, doctors, consumers and other interests. These exchanges were influenced by two panels, one consisting of thirty representatives of the general public who could join in the discussion at any time on open telephone lines; the other a group of experts in the studio whose task was solely to supply factual information, interrupting participants when necessary if they made factually false statements or unjustified generalizations. After each bout of conflict, viewers phoned in answers to questions – 3000 were able to do so, using thirty available lines. At the end of each line a student recorded the viewer's answer (rated on a five-point agree–disagree scale), and noted the demographic characteristics of respondents. No names were taken. The resulting data were punched directly on to cards and analysed by the computer. The answers were then considered in the next round of organized conflict.

It is reported that the Federal Government was suspicious of this experiment but that viewers were enthusiastic. Clearly the technique could be abused, and fears were expressed that this could lead to a reversion to manipulative government by plebiscite, using the most up-to-date techniques. The organizers, a group of scientists from the Heidelberg Study Group for Systems Research (largely financed by the Federal Ministry of Education and Science) were encouraged by the success of the experiment, methodologically and politically. The programmes went out on the third (educational) channel, and therefore the poll results (based on an unrepresentative sample suffering acutely from what social scientists call 'volunteer bias') were not at all a scientific measure of public opinion; nevertheless the force of the arguments deployed and the reaction of 3000 viewers to them did persuade the Government to give more funds and support to pollution control. As an effective expression of public opinion, the Heidelberg experiment was at least as proper, democratically speaking, as the exercise of influence by pressure groups or the changing of a political climate through the correspondence columns of *The Times*.

The Heidelberg team proposed repeating the experiment later in 1971 and the BBC attempted something similar but technically much less ambitious on BBC-2. On 1 October 1971, the BBC staged a three-hour debate on the Common Market. One thousand viewers (selected as representative by Gallup Poll) had been asked to vote on the Market issue a fortnight previously; they were then assembled in six studios and asked to vote again in the light of the Great Debate, as the programme was called. However, the computer went wrong and Robin Day, the chairman, had inelegantly to confess that 'After the great debate, now follows the great cock-up.'

The ORAKEL model is more promising, under present technical conditions, than Wedgwood Benn's plea for direct access. But it is still not the only possible one. Mounting it calls for a suspension of normal broadcasting procedures and the creation of *ad hoc* machinery. These are not arguments against it, but they are factors indicating that though change could come along this route, or something like it, it would come slowly, especially in Britain, where we are not given to the enthusiasm for gadgetry which is implied by ORAKEL.[7] It would be more fruitful to look for models which extend present practices and which would grow more securely because they derive more organically from already accumulated experience.

I am not making the cynical recommendation: if you want to achieve something new in Britain, disguise it to look like tradition. I am saying that to make progress it is worth looking at the resources, experience and traditions that we already have and then pressing for their adaptation so as to achieve something new. There is to hand the inheritance that is wanted as a foundation, but it needs looking at from in front, with the eyes of the future, instead of from behind.

Three approaches

It appears that the slogan, 'Broadcasting is too important to be left to the broadcasters' is too vague to be much of a guide to action. Even demands for 'access', for enabling people to talk to each other through the media, conceal a good deal of confusion. The weakness of Benn's analogy of Parliament with the media is that the various Reform Bills which gradually democratized Parliament obviously did not enable fifty million people to sit in the House. The discussion so far about democratizing broadcasting has tended to confuse two distinct issues – (a) how broadcasting is governed, and (b) how broadcasting is used. I am primarily concerned with the latter, while recognizing that the two are connected.

At the level of use, three different lines of reform may be distinguished, all of which could be based on existing experience. The first is Benn's more precise advocacy of air time for trades unions and other interests, which I have already discussed. This is the mode of which we have least experience, and that not altogether encouraging. It would be an attempt to democratize use by making the broadcasting organizations act as publishers, relinquishing all or some editorial command to outsiders but providing technical support for them, creating more programmes on the analogy of party political broadcasts.

Some of the most creative workers in television have demonstrated a second approach with a potential for reformist growth: they pay socially sensitive attention to the formats and contents of their programmes, producing for empathy instead of for impact. As specific a production matter as set design, for example, may contribute to the sense of remoteness, of show biz out-thereness and artificiality which can work so much against real audience involvement that the impact achieved is democratically counter-productive. The tendency for television to turn what matters not only into a show, but into a 'mere' show, is often due to such design decisions. When a chairman, for instance, sits on a rostrum, elevated and removed from those he is 'confronting', who sit behind elegant panels, or on strange fantasy furniture, it may make for a clean, visually 'interesting' set. But it is also likely to make for a visually inappropriate set, dominating the proceedings instead of serving them; turning the medium into an end in itself; emphasizing studio contrivance and presentation at the expense of what has to be presented; oppressing and moulding those who take part. This kind of subordination of communication to style emasculates even experts and professionals: how should laymen survive it? Why should it persist at all, this obtrusive legacy from the Ziegfeld Follies?

It is important that there are a number of producers who are aware of the ideological aspect of production style. Sometimes they make mistakes by going to the other extreme. John King, for example, the bold BBC producer responsible for a series of programmes with the significant title *Free for All*, deliberately eschewed over-production and went instead for an undisciplined, unstructured form of presentation in a raw studio, packing it with, say, a crowd of students (or of students' critics) and virtually letting them sort themselves out. Doreen Stephens attempted something similar when she was at London Weekend, with a series of programmes called *Roundhouse*. They tried to recreate in the Roundhouse the vigour, spontaneity and raucousness of Hyde Park's Speakers' Corner. These experiments turned out to be unworkable, confused rather than free, raucousness getting the better of spontaneity, but they were a healthy reaction against 'over-produced' programmes which cause format overkill. More such daring explorations are needed. When successful they create a more democratic tone for the output, which too often distances itself from the public and reduces that public's real psychological involvement through an authoritarian professionalism.

Some producers also attempt to use the medium in a more democratic way by having non-professionals taking part in the programmes. In principle, there is nothing new or intrinsically democratic about such participation. For years ordinary members of the public have been variously encouraged either to make contemptible idiots of themselves, or, more humanely, to show off their skills for the entertainment of others in talent contests (such as *Opportunity Knocks*), and party games (*Take Your Pick, Double Your Money, The Golden Shot* and others whose enormous popularity make their own comment on the power of the get-rich-quick fantasy in an alienated age).

It is much more innovatory, however, when producers apply this approach in other kinds of programme. John King has tried to make programmes quite literally in the spirit of Wedgwood Benn's plea that 'the people' be allowed 'to reflect, to each other, the diversity of interests, opinions, grievances, hopes and attitudes to their fellow citizens and to talk out their differences at sufficient length'. He has summed up this philosophy in the maxim 'People *are* television' and he has been quoted as saying:

The medium is shackled by pre-set ideas of what is good, bad, or even possible, basing the measurements on what has gone before. I believe we must open it up to the audience.[8]

Early in 1971 King invited people 'virtually to walk in off the street and take over a television studio' in Bristol. The result was an interesting shambles. It was an attempt to make television as free as an Arts Lab or like a meeting of the London Film Makers' Cooperative, and it failed. This is not to say that nothing of the kind could ever succeed. At their best, even the much more deliberately produced David Frost programmes began to show that it was possible for television to stimulate real discussion, involving, thought-stirring discussion, between experts and ordinary members of the public, as distinct from over-dramatized argument which often has about as much cognitive value as all-in wrestling. It may be that King's drastically radical interpretation of 'direct access' would work on CATV or on local radio, even though it may fail on network television. Like the broader case for 'direct access' itself, this may be another instance of the wrong message in pursuit of the wrong medium, a good intention at odds with the available technology and the existing institutional structure.

There is, however, a third approach to programming which would release television's power on behalf of participatory democracy. This approach would satisfy the impulse behind the approaches already considered (television as a form of publishing; and participation programmes), it would overcome some of the difficulties they seem to entail, and it would occasionally even require the kind of programmes they envisage, but as part of a larger and more articulated process. In so doing it would begin to help television establish new relationships with the audience, thereby enabling the medium to cure itself of some of the weaknesses discussed in Part Two. I shall call this third approach Participatory Programming.

Participatory programming is a democratically responsive social process, in which television programmes are a component in a multi-media mix, or in a multi-agency complex acting in consort to achieve social, community or political change and development. This approach, which will be concretely described in the chapters that follow, would not only enable us – broadcasters and public together – to make television more than a *mirror* (which symbolizes its quietist effect), and much more than a *window on the world* (which symbolizes the screen as alienating barrier). It would also do more than enlarge its representativeness as a *forum*, which is what 'direct access' implies. It would give television another capacity altogether, turning it into a *chief instrument in an orchestra* of means of communication organically integrated with society, so that we may use it as a power tool for shaping our destinies instead of being wagged by them.

There are two essential preliminaries to a description of what would be involved in participatory programming: first, the 'neutrality' question needs to be faced; and secondly, existing precursors to participatory programming should be identified, both because they make the exposition more intelligible and because their very existence shows what is proposed to be feasible. The 'neutrality' issue is unavoidable because this approach to the use of television is without doubt interventionist. To misquote the most famous expression of Marx's impatience with academic philosophy (in the eleventh of the *Theses on Feuerbach*): 'The broadcasters have only *interpreted* the world, in various ways; the point, however, is to change it.'

To those who fear that broadcasters already editorialize too much, such an interventionist policy may sound dangerous, implying an abandonment of the editorial neutrality enjoined on the broadcasters through the BBC Charter and the Television Act. Although some working in the medium may chafe at the constraints imposed by the need to be impartial, most would probably insist that while giving information about the world and endeavouring to interpret that information in various ways was a chief part of the job our society gives to television, changing the world is emphatically not. In short, this could seem like a recipe more likely to find sympathy with totalitarian governments or with the new crop of democratic regimes suffering from a bout of neo-Bonapartism.

In fact, as will appear, television may be both interventionist and neutral: indeed, its neutrality is essential if its interventions are to succeed. But it is wise to recognize that the neutrality of broadcasting does not always work in democracy's favour. Broadcasting has to be impartial on controversial matters; controversial matters are usually important; yet such issues are often handled in a way that induces boredom, and boredom is not the frame of mind in which a democratic public should approach areas of significant disagreement. To take a typical example: an ambitious programme with the altogether laudable aim of rendering intelligible the Conservative Government's Industrial Relations Bill concluded with a debate. It was predictably chaired by Robert McKenzie; it was inevitable that Vic Feather would appear, and that made it equally unavoidable that he would be balanced by Campbell Adamson, along with two other similar–dissimilar pairs. The unintended disservice to democracy was effectively diagnosed by the critic Philip Purser:

You can almost hear the yawn that convulses the nation whenever the kindly but immovable face of Mr Feather fills the screen. Does anyone cry, 'Goody, it's Campbell Adamson again'?

Purser was not being flippant:

In this instance the presence of the big guns was justified. . . . But their presence has been devalued by too many occasions when some routine piece of industrial news has been expressed in terms of a collision between these two men, or their predecessors, as if they were hereditary champions of worker and boss. Since both of them occupy positions which are by definition fixed, there is never any real swirl of ideas. It's equally the fault of television for reaching for them so often, and their fault for accepting.[9]

There are many occasions when producers decide on a less conventional interpretation of an issue and engage less predictable, more provocative, spokesmen or scriptwriters to display it. This approach frequently precipitates protests from weighty interests such as the motor industry, the film business, the medical and teaching professions, who resent it the moment a producer shows a sign of having a view of his own which is perhaps less flattering to the interest depicted than the one it maintains of itself. Programmes which dare to such candour sometimes properly, sometimes less responsibly, have helped to nourish a campaign to make television more accountable (in itself a desirable end), which sometimes masks an altogether undesirable pressure to make television more conformist and less of a Fourth Estate.

It is harmful to note only those occasions when producers seems to be insufficiently democratic by being unaccountable, without also noting those probably more frequent occasions when they are insufficiently democratic because they are too conventional, making programmes that damage debates which are supposed to lead to surer understanding. The trouble goes deeper than the stereotyped casting of top spokesmen of established opposing interests. Spokesmen are spokesmen; they would not be doing their job if they really talked together: they are condemned to thwacking each other with verbal bladders. Furthermore, broadcasting tends only to be neutral within a subtly shifting area of mainstream disagreement. It is rarely neutral when the dispute is between a representative of some strand of the conventional wisdom and someone outside the respectable or fashionable consensus of the day, who could be a dangerous bigot but could equally well be Moses or Jesus. If broadcasting is to serve an increasingly pluralistic democracy, then it has to be more rigorously neutral than at present and not treat certain groups which exist within British society as though they were interlopers from alien cultures, to be ignored or guyed. The polarization of American society shows only too luridly the perils of playing a consensus game, trimming now to liberalism, now to the silent majority, while always overlooking the fundamental ideological stresses until they erupt on campus and in ghetto.

So, television must be neutral if it is to be a trusted vehicle shared by all the Alternative Societies within society, all the Counter-Cultures within the culture. But it also has to be interventionist. It can be both, and the dissolution of the apparent paradox – a more active, interventionist role for television as a chief instrument of a participatory democracy – will readily occur to anyone familiar with the theory and practice of community development. Community development workers accomplish change by enabling the people among whom they move to clarify their own objectives, improve their own relationships, overcome for themselves the obstacles in their way. The community worker is not primarily a leader, inspiring people with his goals; he is primarily a catalyst, helping them to diagnose, clarify and implement their own. His neutrality is consequently an essential asset, not an embarrassment. For the same reason, television's neutrality and objectivity is one of the chief advantages it already possesses which will enable it to be the effective carrier of other people's voices, not its own.

The neutrality of community workers is not absolute. They are not equally impartial towards democrats and anti-democrats, for example. They cannot be because the *raison d'être* of their work is democratic; but they will normally be objective in their dealings with different sub-cultures, attitudes and policies within the frameworks of values actually subsisting in a society.[10]

The policy I shall propose, for new kinds of programme and new sets of relationships with society and the audience, does not therefore presuppose any fundamental departure from accepted practice on this particular point of principle. Broadcasters will need to extend the range of their professional ethic, and apply it more fastidiously, not abandon it.

British precursors

Since the purpose of participatory programming is to precipitate creative social change, there is a good deal more to it than the programmes themselves. Nevertheless, television programmes are still at the heart of the process, and they need to grow out of experience already acquired of programmes which are interventionist in intent or effect, and of programmes supported by materials in other media and actively responded to by people working in non-broadcasting institutions and agencies.

There are at least five classes of programmes which could be regarded as useful precursors, since they have a potential for provoking participation, sometimes in a quite rudimentary form but sometimes achieving more significance and effectiveness. These are:

1. Programmes which strengthen the participatory moments in the processes of representative democracy.

2. Programmes which crystallize or intensify a public mood that creates an ambience for participatory activity.

3. Ombudsman-type programmes.

4. Programmes which provide a channel through which social change may be promoted.

5. Programmes which, by changing the way members of particular professions act on society, may begin to change society.

1. The most important programmes that strengthen the participatory moments in the processes of representative democracy are by definition those which inform viewers about the parties and policies competing for their votes at a general election. Despite the healthy self-criticism expressed in the SFTA discussion (see above pp. 109–11), there is ample evidence from the research of Trenaman, Blumler, McQuail and others that television's influence at such times can be substantial.[11] This particular case illustrates a more general point. When there is something that people are expected to do, and can do, because the social mechanism for action is at hand (i.e. in this case, voting), and when the issues touch people in their daily lives, then the information pouring off the screen becomes, for a few weeks, unusually useful; consequently, it is attended to; consequently it sticks, and viewers become measurably better informed, more receptive, more thoughtful. For most people most of the time however it is not clear what if anything can be done with the information received, so it is badly assimilated, if at all.

2. The key example here is of historical significance, though 'transmissions' is a more appropriate term than programmes. By televising the Soviet invasion of their country, Czech television enabled a great deal of the world to monitor the operation; more importantly, it involved and strengthened the Czech people throughout the inevitably changing forms of their struggle to preserve their new socialist democracy so that, in defeat, they were better able to maintain the spirit of it. Without television in those key days in August 1968, run by men and women of courage and resourcefulness, the Czechs might quickly have become confused; many could have succumbed to the Soviet newsreel interpretation of those crucial events.

The most notorious domestic example of this category in recent years was the documentary drama *Cathy Come Home*, which vividly depicted the persistence of poverty in a prosperous society, the continued crisis in housing, and the associated harassment of vulnerable citizens. By capturing the imagination of viewers, and provoking the indignation and comment of these in authority, both the conscientious and the complacent, this play provided an emotional climate humid enough to promote the growth of Shelter's fund-raising and political agitation.

3. Ombudsman-type programmes have been produced in a number of different forms in recent years. They all push television well beyond its mere window or mirror functions, because they all make the medium interfere with ongoing social processes. *Cause for Concern* (BBC), for example, set out to investigate prima facie cases of injustice and sometimes succeeded in righting past wrongs.

By using an outside broadcasting unit linked with a studio in Manchester, *On Site* (Granada), confronted representatives of authority with people with a grievance against that authority. The conflict would sometimes be between parties between whom communication had broken down. By arranging for them to meet without meeting, *On Site* avoided the embarrassment of pre-transmission sociability and enabled viewers to see the aggrieved party in their own setting. The choice of Ray Gosling as Granada's man on location was a wise piece of casting – in terms of his credibility in the role on television and in terms

of his own active social conscience. (He used to follow up particular issues after the programme was over)[12]. The first series
of *On Site* ran for forty-one weeks and was up to that time (May
1969) Granada's most popular local programme. No cautious
planner in broadcasting need fear that the new mission for the
medium being proposed in this book is a prescription for plum-
meting ratings. *On Site* was so successful that Granada converted it into a network programme. It suffered. In order to make
it appeal nationally, Granada dropped Gosling, probably a mistake, and heightened the dramatic aspect of the format. Instead
of being a catalytic link in a chain of real social conflict, the
programme exploited real conflicts as an end in themselves, in
short turned them into a 'show'. Dramatic overstatement went
too far, even for its own good, when some unemployed men
from Netherton were taken to a gale-swept, frost-bitten piece
of waste ground on Merseyside, there to discourse with their
bosses, cosily relaxing in the warmth of Granada's studio. There
have been other such ombudsman programmes on both channels.

4. Programmes in this category are either meant to get things
put right, or to get new things tried. *Campaign* (another of
Granada's local programmes) combined both. The last programme in the 1970 series looked back over the progress
achieved. It claimed that because of *Campaign*, a farmer's simple
gadget for testing cattle for brucellosis would soon be commercially available; a temporary day nursery had been set up in
Rochdale while a new one was being built; clubs and organizations were being formed all over the Manchester area to help
epileptics; and Lancashire's coastal towns had become aware of
their pollution problems.

The National Suggestions Centre (now the National Innovations Register) which aims 'to provide a platform for ideas and
to stimulate action: to encourage innovation and experiment'
(both technical and social), collaborated with Thames Television
to provide the *What? Spot*, every Monday night on Eamonn
Andrews's local magazine programme, *Today*, in the first quarter of 1970. In three months, viewers sent in 1000 suggestions,
the best of which were featured in the programme, the 'inventor'

discussing his suggestion with critical experts. The Post Office Corporation and the Housewives Trust agreed, as a result, to discuss the practicability of a dial-the-price telephone service (up-to-date information about the retail prices of perishable goods); London Transport took seriously the notion that buses on tourist routes could provide taped information (paid for by those mentioned) – 'Stop here for Swan & Edgar's, Lillywhite's and Simpson's ... *Woodstock* is showing at the Empire, Leicester Square....'[13]

Richard Luce, director of the National Suggestions Centre, was understandably impressed by the more ambitious Norwegian programme *Bank of Ideas*. In two years, this programme, with more resources than Thames's modest but effective *What? Spot*, achieved many social reforms and practical innovations, especially benefiting the remote areas of the country which are easily forgotten. Those responsible for *Bank of Ideas* are proud of it, but they have nevertheless stopped making it. The more seriously such a programme is taken, the more it becomes a social service fronted by a television feature. To sustain *Bank of Ideas* required a larger administrative apparatus than the Norwegian Broadcasting Corporation (NRK) could manage within the resources available to it as a *broadcasting* organization. This is an organizational point of some significance, for which a properly articulated policy of programmes for participation will have to provide.

5. The series mentioned so far are precursors of fully fledged programmes for participation chiefly because of their subject matter. *What? Spot* and *Bank of Ideas* also begin to indicate some of the problems of methodology and administration to be faced if television is to be fully harnessed for a more active democratic life. Experience in the solution of these problems is now being acquired by many broadcasting organizations throughout the world. Educational broadcasters are already working out ways of combining television with other media, to strengthen the messages of each, and also with ways of connecting multimedia *teaching* materials with an appropriate face-to-face organization on the ground, to make comprehensive *learning* systems, without which the media acting on their own can ac-

complish little. There is some irony in the realization that educational television, which tends to be regarded by many mainstream broadcasters as an aberrant form, is actually at work on techniques and approaches which will enable current affairs broadcasting as a whole to find a major new role within a new kind of democracy.

Since I shall have to look abroad for examples of programmes which clearly exemplify the part that television could be playing in the development of democracy, it is encouraging that the illustrations in this last category of precursors are all British. This is not to strike a banal chauvinistic note: it is to make again the important point that practical experience relevant to participatory programming is already being built up in this country and that this is happening within the present constitutional framework of British broadcasting. Although the future route I am outlining may seem in some respects unfamiliar, at least we set out from a base in the present. No utopian wholly-new-start will be necessary.

My three examples are, then, all from educational television; but they all highlight matters of importance to the practice of participatory programming. They are *Living and Growing*, a sex-education series for primary-school children, made by Grampian Television; *Heading for Change*, a series on the application of management techniques to secondary-school administration (Harlech Television); and *Representing the Union*, a BBC series on productivity bargaining for shop stewards.

When a producer wants to make a feature programme, documentary or item in a current-affairs magazine, he decides what it will be about and then usually picks a good many brains before he goes into production. He will retain an expert in some capacity, as presenter, writer, researcher or consultant. The object is to make the best possible programme on the subject with the widest possible appeal. When the producer of an educational series (educational programmes, as distinct from educative ones, are in series by definition) makes his programmes, then from the start he has a different relationship with his advisers. Some of them (in the Schools Broadcasting Council, or the ITA's Schools Committee, for example) may have suggested the subject for the series in the first place. Others will suggest ways in which matter and manner should be tailored to fit the needs of teachers working with children of a given age range. The advice is not meant to help produce good television, attractive to the largest possible audience and a threat to the ratings for the other channel; it is meant to produce good television relevant to the specific educational needs of a highly age-specific segment of the audience, viewing in groups under the guidance of teachers. The relationship producer–adviser–audience is a much tighter one because the audience must be able to *use* the programme as well as enjoy it.

When Grampian Television decided (as a result of advice from educationists) to make a series of sex-education programmes for children on the edge of puberty, the company found itself obliged (as did the BBC some two years later) to create an even more elaborate net of pre-production relationships. In addition to the normal processes of consultation associated with schools television, the aura of taboo affecting the subject made Grampian adopt a procedure like that used in community-development work. An extended series of meetings was held throughout the region not only with educational administrators and teachers, but also with clergymen and above all parents. Should the programmes be made at all? For what age group? Dealing with what particular topics? Pilot programmes were shown and evaluated at a second round of consultations with parents and teachers. By the time these programmes finally went on the air, Grampian knew precisely what was wanted, knew what problems to deal with, what type of expert presenter to engage, using what varieties of vocabulary, with what sorts of visual illustration. As a result, the programmes themselves quickly broke down embarrassment, unleashed talk of a kind never possible before between the curious, nervous, eager children and their shy, inhibited, ill-equipped parents and teachers. The procedure was like that of community development; but the objective was educational (though with consequences for home–school relations and for personal relationships between the generations going far beyond that specific goal). What is wanted now are experiments using similar community-development approaches for programmes with community-development objectives.

Whereas conventional broadcasters customarily unloose their arrows with optimistic prodigality, hoping they will land somewhere and not get caught up in the trees, the enormous success of *Living and Growing* portends a much less speculative, wasteful situation for the broadcaster making programmes for participation. His audience will help him select arrows of the right calibre, advise him on the most effective trajectories and then busy themselves actually putting the butts into position. Effectiveness of communication instead of hit-and-miss, responsiveness on reception instead of indifference to 'chewing gum for the eyes' – these are the rewards for the participatory broadcaster prepared to undertake an unwonted amount of consultation and, as will appear, as yet rather unfamiliar collaboration with other agencies and media.

Grampian's programmes were made for schoolchildren. To enable teachers to make best use of them, the company also published a booklet summarizing each programme, with advice about the place of the series in the curriculum, and suggestions for following up the programmes in discussion projects. This combination – programmes plus teachers' notes, occasionally plus wallcharts or workbooks for pupils – is the standard kit for any school programme whether on Independent Television or BBC. Although embracing several media it would be an affectation to say that this combination embodied a multi-media approach. It is not, however, pretentious to describe Harlech's *Heading for Change* as a modest multi-media system. The *preparations* for *Living and Growing* provided an elementary model (in a cognate field) of how to set up a participatory programme. The *components* in *Heading for Change* are similar in principle to those needed in successful participatory programming. In two other respects, this project was useful as a model from which to learn: it was prepared for adults who could as easily opt out as volunteer to take part; although it constituted an episode of in-service training for the teachers who viewed, since its subject matter was management, the programmes (or rather the multi-media system of which they were a part) led to changes in the way that some schools in Wales and the West of England were run. Changing institutions through changing the professionals who work in them clearly points to the next step;

changing society through changing the people who live in it. There is no reason why it should be surprising to employ television for the critical reform of society, since it is already engaged in *recyclage* (as the French neatly call professional updating), one of the by-products of which may often be to change the texture of society as well.

The *Heading for Change* programmes were also transmitted, simply as programmes, in the Midlands, where they apparently had some effect. But the full system (used in Wales and part of the West Country) consisted of eight television programmes which went out at 4.25 p.m., the end of the school day, between April–June 1969; 250 viewing groups meeting in secondary schools, teachers' centres, institutes and colleges of education, with a total membership of 3000 viewers; a workbook consisting of white pages (notes on the subject matter of each programme) alternating with blue pages (simulated 'in-tray' materials evoking the range of challenges faced by the management of any modern secondary school). The success of this simple multi-media system depended on the creation of a partnership between HTV and the educational world in its region. The company started with an advantage in that its education officer had a reputation in his own right in the region. He and his small staff established a sound working relationship with the Director of the University of Bristol School of Education, Professor William Taylor, who wrote the workbook, scripted and presented the programmes and briefed the leaders of viewing groups. Because the need for such a course had been accurately diagnosed, local education authorities readily used their own machinery to set up the viewing groups. Significantly, it was not necessary for HTV to employ extra staff to create the face-to-face component in the system. Enthusiastic partners in the field did it for them. There is much to learn from this experiment.

The lesson to be drawn is not, in this context, the pedagogic effectiveness of multi-media teaching systems which are based on television or include television in a media mix. If that were the point, the Open University in Britain, the NHK Correspondence School in Japan or the Telekolleg in Bavaria would provide more sophisticated illustrations. The Grampian Television and HTV projects are important because they begin to demonstrate the potential for social change through audience participation in this approach. It is no coincidence that they were originated by two of the smaller companies in the mosaic that makes up Independent Television, working at their local regional level. It is easier for such a company to be in relatively close touch with its audience, and much easier for its personnel to get to know those with responsible positions in other agencies. (Some years earlier in 1964–5, Westward Television, another small company, proved this by anticipating the HTV project using a less elaborate system. Westward collaborated with the Department of Education at Exeter University on the production of in-service training programmes for teachers called *Teachers' Workshop*. On that occasion, grants from the Department of Education and the Gulbenkian Foundation gave the programmes an extra life at home and abroad by paying for their transfer to film.[14])

Since it was also a success, my third example proves, however, that it is possible to mount a project of this kind on a national scale; to the key features present in the two local projects, this new dimension was added. The system on this occasion embodied these main characteristics: (a) collaboration between a broadcasting organization and major organizations outside broadcasting; (b) television as part of a multi-media teaching system; (c) strengthening viewers' capacity for participation as a consequence of education (an instance of what the French, in another felicitous phrase, call *Télépromotion*). The BBC's chief collaborator in *Representing the Union* was the TUC. Even working together (which at national level they usually do not) the agencies of trade union education (the TUC itself, the Workers' Educational Association and university departments of extra-mural studies) could have only reached shop stewards by the score or the hundred. By working with television it was possible to reach thousands – in principle to reach all 160,000 of them. But if the BBC had decided unilaterally to educate shop stewards, its target audience would have been missing. As many trade unionists still suspect that the BBC is the voice of the Establishment, they would expect trade union education from that source to be managerial brainwashing; but it follows, from the processes of news selection already discussed –

the conscientious distortion built into the very concept of news
– that shop stewards have a public reputation as the irritants of
industry, rather than its lubricants (the distinction in fact made
by the producer of the series). They know that television, Establishment or not, is largely to blame for this image. So, in order
to do effective work – not only trustworthy but trusted – a
collaboration between the BBC and the TUC was essential.
The TUC was able to advise the BBC on content and relevance, was in a position to stimulate the formation of viewing
groups, was able to give its approval and the benefit of its joint
auspices to the programmes and other components in the system.
The BBC, through its field liaison officers, also had to consult
management representatives whose blessing for group viewing
in works time was sought. Just as many union leaders looked
for the management fist concealed in the BBC's velvet glove,
so many managements feared a touch of subversion, a school
for militancy. And it was not possible to please everyone.
Modern managers accept the necessity for example of showing
union representatives the firm's books; more traditional managers shudder at the sacrilege committed by such disclosure. For
broadcasters to win and deserve the confidence of those with
whom such difficulties have to be resolved, without contracting
anaemia in the process, it is essential for them to interpret their
neutrality in a vigorous and positive manner, reinforced in such
a case by academic integrity towards the subject matter of the
programmes. Unless they respect the body of knowledge identified by responsible experts as the core of, say, productivity bargaining, they cannot hope to gain the respect and cooperation
of the audience or of other outsiders on whom they may depend. Such problems are soluble, and in this instance, they were
solved; as I write, the BBC has decided to run the project for
a second year, encouraged by the enthusiasm among shop
stewards for the series, as discovered by research carried out by
the Commission on Industrial Relations.

Apart from the ten half-hour programmes on different aspects
of productivity bargaining, the system comprised a BBC special
programme publication (also called *Representing the Union*) with
notes and background information (26,000 copies were sold),
plus a set of TUC booklets (*Work Study and Payment by Re-*

sults, Job Evaluation and Merit Rating, Productivity Bargaining and *Costs and Profits*), all these to be used by individual viewers but chiefly by the leaders and members of viewing groups, following and discussing the programmes in their factories and workshops. (11,000 of these packages for groups were sold.)

Dr Fred Bayliss, formerly Senior Economic Adviser at the National Board of Prices and Incomes, has estimated that the successful operation of a national prices and incomes policy depends crucially, on half a million key people – on the management side as well as the union – understanding the issues. I have already noted the widespread ignorance of economics which exists; Bayliss finds it also at this very level where it matters most. Words he used in 1967 have since proved abundantly true:

Unless there is an understanding of what some current issues of economic policy involve, these policies simply cannot be mounted. The main one . . . is the prices and incomes policy. The links between incomes, prices and productivity are extremely complicated. They are not self evident. And only when there is an understanding of the relation between these main economic factors is there going to be a serious possibility of an incomes policy working in this country. If there is to be a coordinated, concerted attempt by government and by trade unions and employers to regulate the movement of incomes and of prices and productivity in the interests of a faster rate of economic growth, then an educational policy has to be built into it.[15]

No educational policy was built into it. The outcome is painfully familiar to everyone who is daily amazed or distressed at how quickly wages and salaries lose their value. Although a small effort when measured against the need, the BBC–TUC project is the most ambitious attempt yet to do something effective (not only good teaching, but good teaching on the right scale) about one specialized, but complex aspect of economic policy. In that it helps shop stewards to represent their members more ably in productivity bargaining, it also strengthens their power to take part in the running of modern industry. In this sense, these educational programmes are already indirectly a species of programmes for participation.

Participatory programmes in the full sense, however, are those which address viewers not merely as workers or professionals with an influential purchase on society at large, nor merely as citizens; but as citizens expected and expecting to act, to create an active society by showing that action is possible and that it works. For examples of such programmes it is necessary to look abroad.

11 Foreign Experience

Informing their discretion

The most substantial body of foreign experience to illustrate the character of participatory programming is to be found in the United States. America is notoriously the country in which most of the profligate excesses of traditional capitalism have been committed. It is also American capitalism which has most blatantly exploited new technologies, with little attention to the social consequences, so that the aggregation of policies which in themselves may be rational or plausible results in an irrational society. On the other hand, the same energy and prodigality have also inspired in the States a proliferation of reforming experiments in democratic social engineering, and some of the most acute social criticism, both having application in other technocratic countries. The American treatment of television exemplifies this same duality. No nation has abused the medium more or used it more vigorously in the pursuit of their own corruption. Yet no country has more experience of socially organic broadcasting, of using broadcasting as a means of creating an active society, than America.

One trouble with foreign experience, is that it is *foreign* experience. We can learn from it, but not transplant it; be inspired by it, but not replicate it. Programming for participation in the States derives its rationale from the Jeffersonian heritage, a democratic dream which must become real today if the tenuous hold of democracy is not to give way. Jefferson, author of the Declaration of Independence and Third President of the Union, wrote, for his times and ours:

I know of no safe depository of the ultimate powers of society but the people themselves; and if we think them not enlightened enough to exercise their control with a wholesome direction, the remedy is not to take it from them, but to inform their discretion through education.

Participatory programming in the States is also inspired by folk memories of an ancient institution, to which reference is constantly made in promotional and interpretative material and in the very titles of programmes themselves – the town meeting. When New England was still a Puritan colony, a 'town' was any settlement large enough to feed and provide for itself, but small enough for all the inhabitants to congregate in one place of worship or to protect their lives and cattle against an Indian attack within one stockade. The system of land tenure – common land plus equal plots – prevented extremes of wealth. Out of this closeness and rough equality developed the habit of assembling together to decide how their own local government should be run.

This 'town meeting' is a kind of nostalgic Athenian component in the American dream. It features prominently in American writing and rhetoric about the history of adult education, but at least one authority, in trying to correct a bias in this mythology has drawn attention to a duality of purpose which applies also to participatory programming. In his scholarly study, *The Adult Education Movement in the United States,* Malcolm Knowles writes:

The New England town meeting is frequently characterized as an important adult educational instrument, and perhaps it was, to the extent that it served as a training ground in the art of self-government for the colonists. Possibly it also provides a general formula on which later adult educational programmes were based, such as public forums. But the town meeting was essentially a *problem-solving, decision-making instrument, not an educational institution.*[1]

The phrase in my italics is, as I have suggested, a clue to a fruitful ambiguity, which is also to be found in the concept and practice of participatory broadcasting. Looked at from one point of view, it is a species of adult-education broadcasting, first cousin to the avowedly educational series using mult-media approaches as mentioned in the previous chapter. Looked at from another point of view, it is a species of news, informational, current-affairs broadcasting, first cousin to programmes that are meant to inform citizens for their democratic role, often similar in appearance (but not in consequences) to programmes such as Granada's *On Site*. The 'town meeting' was essentially a decision-making instrument which educated those who used it; the town meeting of the air is essentially an educational instrument designed to improve the decision-making process by strengthening the capacity of ordinary people to take part in it. In Jeffersonian terms it is an instrument for informing the discretion of the sole reliable depository of power. Whatever nuances of interpretation may surround the American town meeting as a seventeenth-century institution, the fact is that we now, descendants of the Puritan colonists in both countries, are in need of every 'training ground in the art of *self* government', which is also a 'problem-solving, decision-making instrument', that we may lay hands on. Their titles cannot have the same emotional impregnation for us as some of them have for Americans, and we cannot directly imitate them, but inspiration for and an understanding of participatory programmes is to be found for us in such projects as *The Whole Town's Talking*, *Town Meeting, Inc* and *Metroplex Assembly*.

The Whole Town's Talking was an early experiment in community-based television by Iowa State College, Ames, Iowa, an enterprising state-supported land-grant college, and the first institution of higher education to be licensed by the Federal Communications Commission (1950). The object of the series was to bring together each week representatives of some particular Iowa community to discuss a serious local problem which would interest people in other parts of the state because they shared it. The representatives were encouraged to consider alternatives, weigh costs and arrive at a decision on a course of action which they recommended to their community. The very first broadcast in the series came from Cambridge, Iowa, a small 'town' of 600 inhabitants with a serious school problem and (according to the College report) a reputation in the state for 'the worst type of community apathy'. At first Cambridge citizens resented and resisted the intrusion of television, but whether or not they should participate in the programme became itself an issue for democratic decision in a town's meeting, and ultimately twelve people (selected because they were articulate and because they represented the actual range of opinion in the town) appeared in the programme. An introductory film sequence showed them at their daily work so that viewers could see them as particular individuals with their own problems arising from the schools crisis, not simply as mouth-pieces for different viewpoints. Then the cameras recorded their discussion: television acted as a catalyst by enabling factions which would have nothing to do with each other to talk together, by encouraging in them the self-confidence to press for reforms on teachers and administrators, and by giving them more than a mere role-playing experience of arriving at a decision by majority vote. They and their fellow citizens moved from apathy and stalemate to agreement and action.

Producers' experience and viewers' reactions led to gradual changes in the format for the series which resulted in an innovation which seemed startingly novel when it was used years later in the BBC satire show *That Was The Week That Was* – the cameras were visible. As the College report says:

Our cameras, our equipment, our technical crew, are shown freely. ... There are two advantages in the procedure. ...

1. The number and variety of camera angles is greatly increased. The set can now be shown from all four sides, and this gives the opportunity for discussion 'in the round' instead of the limited picture of flat classroom rows. ...

2. The open acknowledgement of the camera allows us to create the impression that news is taking place, that history is being recorded, that the viewer is truly 'on the spot'.

The effects of this experimental project were not researched, but observers related how it stirred people up throughout the state. The producers were understandably excited by its effects:

When we entered Cambridge we found an apathetic, dispirited community, afraid to discuss its problems. In the past few weeks we have watched a ferment growing in this town. We have watched people as they began to talk about their problems in the open – for the first time. This talk need not, must not, end with the television programme.

Discussion groups ('town talk' groups) were set up even in several communities which were not featured in the series. Training sessions for discussion leaders were organized by the

College. Printed outlines were prepared for pre-programme distribution. Those associated with the project concluded:

1. The people themselves – not experts, but the people themselves, talking, thinking, coming to personal decisions on the problems of their community – are the material for an exciting and entertaining television programme.

2. This programme offers a new and effective way to get expert knowledge to the people who are in most need of that knowledge.

3. By using such a programme as a springboard to organized community activity, television can be made to serve – in a totally unique fashion – the fundamental processes of democracy.[2]

The Whole Town's Talking, for all its originality as a television programme, was an application of a well established broadcasting tradition in North America. It represented the conversion into television of experience acquired in radio by Iowa State College itself, by the Canadian National Farm Radio Forum, and others – the use of broadcasting to foster the long-standing twin objectives of agricultural extension work, i.e. the economic and cultural viability of the countryside during an epoch of rapid urbanization. The validity of this kind of educational activity in rural areas continues to be tested in India and many other developing countries, but also in France and Eire.

In France, the chief project, known as TPR, started in 1966 and has continued since. The essence of TPR – *Télé Promotion Rurale* – is to use television (for exposition and for debates by *téléparticipants* typical of the target audience), film, printed materials and discussion groups as a means of stimulating social change as well as agricultural efficiency in Western France. It is a collaboration between French television (ORTF); teachers and research workers of the *Centre d'Economie et de Sociologie Rurales* of Rennes and of the *Institut National de Promotion Agricole de Rennes*; agricultural associations; and the farmers themselves, many of whom appear in the programmes, and some of whom have been trained as *animateurs* (discussion group leaders).[3]

Something similar, though more ephemeral in organization and impact, was an enterprise called *Telefis Feirme* (Television

Farm), in which Radio Telefis Eireann cooperated with the Irish Department of Agriculture. The messages of forty-eight television programmes, transmitted in prime time, were reinforced by printed backup material in mass circulation newspapers (since the target audience had no tradition of buying books), in the RTE programme journal and the weekly *Irish Farmers' Journal*. Viewing groups were set up in association with farmers' organizations, young farmers' clubs, the Cooperative Movement and a Christian vocational body whose name in Irish means literally 'people of the countryside'. There were crash courses and a special guidance booklet for discussion leaders. Since agriculture is the dominant industry in Eire, affecting farmers has some influence on society as a whole, and involving farmers in a process of what the French call *promotion sociale* is itself a step towards social participation. Furthermore, if a series of programmes, with mainly vocational aims, is to relate realistically to people's lives and to help them get the better of their circumstances, then it will begin to penetrate beyond techniques into more controversial areas. The author of *Telefis Feirme* (an academic authority on veterinary science, himself a farmer, but then also working for RTE and later a Member of Parliament in the Dail), expresses the dilemma forthrightly:

Serious programmes arriving at social amelioration must try honestly to pick out the real sources of difficulty, which in the case of small-scale agriculture are not technical but socio-economic. There is a continuous choice: purvey pap and nobody will take you seriously, or tell the truth and offend the political powers-that-be.[4]

Justin Keating alerts us to an undoubted hazard of participatory programming.

While participatory programmes, often with a social-educational emphasis rather than a directly political one, continue to be made in different countries as a contemporary extension of traditional services of rural animation, American media activists in association with enterprising adult educationists, social scientists and others are experimenting in new directions. They are testing the proposition that techniques of community development using the media long recognized as relevant in the backward countryside or in developing countries may also provide a solution to some of the most profound ills afflicting the metro-politan heartlands of post-industrial civilization.

Metroplex assembly and other town meetings

Of all the projects designed to meet conditions of contemporary crisis, those which are of most interest to us in Britain are the 'Metroplex Assembly' and its successor 'Town Meeting'. I shall also make some reference to the radio-based San Bernardino Valley Project, from which 'Metroplex Assembly evolved, and to *Cancion de la Raza*. These four projects together provide certain guiding principles for participatory programming, and a number of practical techniques which could be adapted to suit British conditions.[5]

1. *The San Bernardino Valley Project* was the first of the four. It started in 1952 with a grant from the Fund for Adult Education (itself an offshoot of the Ford Foundation) as part of the FAE's Test Cities Project. It was centred on San Bernardino Valley College in Southern California and had as its chief objective the involvement of 'greater numbers of people in the study and im-provement of the communities in the Valley College District'.[5] The College expected also to learn from it 'how to make such a program of community development an experience in liberal adult education for those who participated' (once again, the same combination of aims which was less consciously present in the seventeenth-century town meeting). The chief media and agency components in the project were radio shows and Metroplex forums, newspaper articles, discussion groups in listeners' homes, residential conferences and workshops. The entire enter-prise was under the overall leadership of a prominent adult edu-cationist, Eugene Johnson, later Executive Director of the Adult Education Association of the USA.

2. The term 'Metroplex Assembly' was in fact coined during the fourth year of the San Bernardino Valley Project, but it was ap-plied to this second experiment (also under Eugene Johnson's leadership, and also supported by a grant from the Fund for Adult Education) from the very beginning. The foundation money was made over to the mass media arm of the Civic Educa-tion Center of Washington University in St Louis. The elements

in the system were similar to those used in California except that this time television took the place of radio. The project was launched in 1958 (after a successful pilot project partly financed by Sears-Roebuck) and lasted nine years.[6]

3. The two projects directed by Eugene Johnson were highly imaginative exercises in adult education, enabling people to understand and to master their environment. 'Town Meeting' emphasizes the political, rather than the educational, aspect of the seventeenth-century conception on which it is based. Town Meeting Inc. is primarily interested in communication, literally in the fostering of contact, argument and dialogue between people who need to act together but are increasingly separated by social, ethnic or generational barriers. Its literature expresses the more desperate tone of the late 1960s, whereas Eugene Johnson's reports have the confidence of possible progress that was a more understandable mood in the America of the 1950s. According to Osgood Magnuson (President, Town Meeting, Inc. and an associate professor at the University of Minnesota), 'Town Meeting utilizes public television and the viewing citizen to present points of view' in a process designed to 'maximize the pooling and sharing of ideas'. Town Meeting uses a saturation technique which associates the media with 'dissertations, discussions, dialogues and deliberations' in many different forms.[7]

4. *Cancion de la Raza* (Song of the People) belongs here even though it was in fact a soap opera, a sixty-five instalment *novella* tailor-made for the Spanish-speaking Mexican–American population in Los Angeles (produced and transmitted by KCET in the fall and winter of 1968–9). It is significant partly because of its format, but mainly because it involved KCET's production team in collaboration with the social research staff at the University of Denver's Communication Arts Center. As Denver's Professor of mass communications has claimed, 'the series ... represents a major attempt to wed the usual mass communications creative processes with social science knowledge'.[8] The results of this collaboration (and some of the problems it creates) have a more general significance for the planning and production of participatory programmes.

The rationale of Metroplex Assembly and Town Meeting provides a bridge between the two theoretical concerns of this book (the progress of democracy and the evolution of television) and a detailed description of the projects themselves. In earlier chapters I contrasted the lavishness of the information available to viewer citizens with the fact that most of us are ill informed or, even if well informed, remarkably inactive. The social outlets for action or decision making or decision influencing are for the most part not available or not felt to be available. Hence the rise of protest and demonstration as ways of signalling political dissatisfaction or at least as ways of giving vent to political frustration or seeking a release from the pressures of social subservience. There are three interconnected failures underlying this situation: (a) a style of communication through television which actually frustrates communication; (b) a lack of organic relationship between television and the channels for social action; and (c) a hardening of the constitutional arteries of democracy so that people are or at least feel themselves to be powerless, however well informed they may be by television.

Participatory programming is an attempt to make a direct attack on the first failure, for which the traditions and habits of broadcasting are themselves largely responsible; it is also an attempt to experiment with reforms that might begin to cure the second failure. The third failure is a profound affliction of society as a whole and it would be unreasonable to expect it to be ameliorated in any major degree by changes in the uses of television (indeed it would be alarmingly dangerous were there to be such a direct relationship between the conduct of the medium and the political health of the society). But nevertheless, changes in the structure of communications could have far reaching effects on other aspects of the matrix.

I also suggested earlier that remedying the first two failures could require much more explicitly worked-out goals for broadcasting. The present aims – to educate, inform and entertain – are so vague as to be as consistent with a policy of escapism or of authoritarianism as with the regeneration of democracy. As guides to how broadcasting should be used in the restless decades leading up to the twenty-first century they are useless.

The policy statements of Metroplex and Town Meeting are

relevant not only to understanding what was attempted and achieved in practice in the States: they also illustrate the kind of argumentation that must fill out the trilogy of objectives set before broadcasting in Britain.

The Metroplex Assembly was based on broadly the same analysis of what is needed to improve the communication process as my own:

Communication does not take place simply because radio and television programs are broadcast and newspapers printed. The reception of the material offered needs to be organized and its study encouraged. Given the diversity of the material offered to people and the need to overcome the built-in screening mechanism that blocks perception of important news, we need to turn as much time and effort to the task of organizing the reception of mass-media offerings as we do to their preparation or broadcast.[9]

This conviction was partly based on practical experience in the San Bernardino Valley Project, during which it appeared quite clearly that 'There is a vast difference between putting *out* information and putting it *in* – into the hearts and heads of the people.'[10] Set down like that, the point is obvious, but it does not come naturally to broadcasters to pay much heed to the reception end of the communication process, still less to think of getting organizationally involved at that end. Audiences are typically so vast, so remote, so heterogeneous; making programmes is in itself so absorbing and enjoyable that production can easily be treated virtually as an end in itself. This is not to suggest that broadcasters are self-indulgent: they often pride themselves on their communication skills, and such skills are mainly other-regarding, not self-regarding. Broadcasting organizations recognize the importance of finding out the size of the audience and of discovering whether audiences like or dislike what is offered to them. But it is extremely rare for audience research to investigate whether viewers have understood a programme or whether the information it contained was useful to them. 'Broadcasting' suggests the scattering of seeds on a vast scale, adopting the recklessness and generosity of nature itself to ensure that some propagation and reproduction takes place somewhere. Now it will be more necessary for broadcasters to show an active interest in what happens to those seeds, to justify their dispersal by knowing more about the soil on which they will settle, even by helping to prepare that soil.

Town Meeting expresses this view with greater urgency even than Metroplex Assembly because of the extent to which the American polis has disintegrated in the last decade or so. A statement prepared for a conference in Minneapolis by Town Meeting Inc. and the American Institute of Planners describes the polarization of attitudes in the States, and the historical setting in which this polarization is taking place. The setting applies equally to Britain, since it affects the species as a whole. The terms of the polarization naturally vary between countries according to their political traditions and social structure.[11] First, the human context:

We ... know that man is achieving the power to alter fundamentally the physical environment in which he lives. It is also clear that he does not yet know how to control this power nor how to calculate the consequences of the actions he decides to take. In the past man has concentrated on gaining the power to do anything he wished: now he must decide what he wishes to do out of the enormous range of options open to him.

Today's institutional structures were not designed for facilitating choice; rather, they were designed to increase man's domination over the physical environment. Therefore, if man is to survive we must work together to create new methods and institutions to decide on our goals.

Next, the communication crisis in the States, which is not precisely paralleled in Britain, but which is confusedly developing here in terms of political conflict, revived class struggle, and to some extent (significant albeit persistently exaggerated in the mass media) of antipathy between the different generations:

We are confused about our aims and goals because we still do not really understand the new world into which we are moving. We do know that changing conditions have already been responsible for the collapse of the dominant liberal consensus that first began to develop in the 1930s. This consensus saw its full development in the 1940s and 1950s: there came to be rather general agreement ... that it was necessary for the federal government to intervene in the economy and society to prevent economic recessions and to remedy social problems.

This consensus was so complete at the beginning of the 1960s that it led to massive legislation. The consequent planning and policy developments have, however, proved highly unsatisfactory to many groups in the society, partly because the developments did in fact favor some groups against others and also because there was no sense of involvement in the process of decision making. . . .

If the American society is not to be split beyond repair we must develop a new basic understanding of . . . the two profound dynamics that are now emerging. . . . There are those who feel that America would continue to develop satisfactorily if only its inherited traditions were restored: and there are those who believe that profound, rapid change is required to move us into the future.

Creative dialogue is possible only if there is relevance within each point of view. Each of these attitudes does, in fact, have valid aspects; but they can only be perceived if viewed from the perspective of a larger whole. It is true that a complete overturn of all present structures would destroy America. It is true that the widespread ignoring of the fundamental values inherited from our past is deeply dangerous. It is true that man cannot ignore the nature of the new realities if he is to survive.

When one contemplates the dead students on university campuses in the United States, and the response to their death expressed by Timothy Leary's maxim 'to kill a policeman is a sacred act', then it becomes desperately important to endorse and act on the moderate propositions with which this joint statement continues:

We must get beyond the view that the two dynamic approaches in the United States today are contradictory: we must come to see them as different ways of looking at the issue, 'How can mankind participate in creating the future?' In today's situation we must, in particular, examine how man can benefit from the environmental and technological change that he himself has started. We must, therefore, find ways to enable communication among all active groups to ensure that the insights of each group are widely understood and the inadequacies of each stance challenged.

The statement is concerned not to succumb to a stereotyped diagnosis of the social location of the conflicting attitudes that need to be subsumed within a larger synthesis, however necessary:

There has been, and indeed still is, a rather general belief that all those in the 'disinherited' groups – minorities, the poor, the young – see the need for fundamental change and that those presently in 'power structures' all want to retain the present. Those who believe in the potential of communications usually argue that there are change-agents in all classes and areas of society who can be brought to recognize each other through open dialogue and then be able to act more effectively together.

In this situation, the mass media of communication need to be used literally to foster communication, instead of which they have either provided blocks to such communication or, in T. S. Eliot's phrase, distracted us from distraction with distraction. I attempted a partial analysis of television's part in this failure in Part Two. The Town Meeting statement summarizes the change in these words:

The mass media have largely failed to tackle the difficult problems involved in moving information about the controversial issues of the day: even their best efforts have been flawed by failure to provide opportunity for feedback. This is largely because they have perceived reality in terms of objective 'facts' and 'trends' and have not developed techniques to deal with subjective controversy about goals nor about the ways of creating new potentials for the future. In addition, their structure as profit-making businesses and vehicles for merchandising goods has limited their potential as change-agents.

The authors go on:

Nevertheless, there is a need for massive movement of valid but controversial ideas: we must find ways to overcome the present extremely efficient barriers. New methods must be devised to encourage the movement of the concepts essential for responsible decision making in the era we are entering.

The programmes and their social nexus

It is time to describe Metroplex Assembly and Town Meeting concretely as 'new methods ... to encourage the movement of concepts essential for responsible decision making'. Since Britain is itself in the throes of reorganizing local government, it would be pertinent to start with a particular series of Metroplex Assembly programmes – 'The Metropolitan District Plan' – to illustrate the method employed.

The Metropolitan District Plan

In the autumn of 1959, the citizens of St Louis had to vote on a plan to take certain public services – transportation, police, fire and others – out of small-community control and to put them under a newly created metropolitan district. Metroplex transmitted four programmes over KETC, channel 9, to help viewer voters make up their minds. In itself, there is nothing remarkable about that. Almost any broadcasting organization with a public service commitment would have done the same. The significance of these programmes lies in how they were created, how they were responded to and the effect they had.

Normally a producer making such programmes would study the proposals, so as to provide viewers with a synopsis of their most salient and/or newsworthy features. Against a lightly researched or profoundly investigated background, according to the professionalism, time and budget available, reporters would interview those responsible for the plan and leaders of lobbies or pressure groups with principles or vested interests threatened by it, partly to ensure 'due impartiality' in presenting the issues, perhaps to dramatize the attendant controversies through studio confrontations of the chief protagonists. Abstract questions about such services as fire protection, police protection and sewage disposal would be concretely illustrated by specially-shot or library film of some suitably vivid conflagration, police car chase or effluence gushing from a conduit into a foaming river.

The production team would naturally be interested in attracting as large an audience as possible, but the size of that audience would depend on factors such as the skill of their publicity colleagues, on whether the programmes would inherit part of the audience from a previous top-rating show or gain from viewers switching on the programme to follow, and on what was on the other channels. If well-made, the programmes could hold that audience and provoke five sentences of critical praise in the papers next day. If, as in this case, viewers knew they had a chance to vote on the questions raised, then probably some members of the keen minority that actually votes in local government elections would have their understanding of the issues improved. But on the whole, most viewers would probably choose another channel, or, if they tuned to these programmes, they would treat them as an end in themselves, just part of the evening's viewing, perhaps good for a touch of light conversation the following morning.

The Metroplex Assembly approach is fundamentally different. In the first place, the themes for the programmes have to be developed, as Johnson and his colleagues put it, 'from the inside out'. This means that instead of the programmes being based on how the issues look to a producer and his research team, or to the leaders of the different political parties or interests concerned, or even to academic experts on the subject, 'a living, vital problem ought first to be stated by the people who have the problem and are most deeply involved in it'. After that, it is possible for academic experts and others to know what insights, what aspects of knowledge, it is necessary to bring to bear on the problem and the public's understanding of it.

The Assembly's approach stems from its general philosophy of social change:

Social change will be accomplished with less disturbance and with maximum understanding and acceptance if widespread citizen participation is encouraged in studying the circumstances of change and formulating policies to guide it.

Assembly series are, therefore, not plotted out, packaged and sold. They are built 'slowly out of material the community itself provides'. Since there was to be a referendum on it, the Metropolitan Plan practically selected itself as a theme. But how was it to be handled? The staff held a series of public meetings to discover what people were saying and thinking about the Plan and to identify the main issues round which public opinion would probably shape. These meetings showed that there was quite a lot of public interest in the Plan, but very little knowledge of its specifics. At this stage the staff thought the programmes would probably have to be about the services themselves.

The next step was to organize Neighbourhood Forums all over

the affected area; to familiarize more people with the Plan's general outlines; and to discover 'television talent', people who were articulate, unofficial proponents of attitudes beginning to circulate in the community and who might later take part in the programmes. Each forum meeting took the form of a debate between representatives of two well-organized community groups which were in vigorous opposition to each other over the District Plan, followed by general questions and discussion.

These forums led the Assembly staff to realize that to relate to the interests of viewers, the programmes would not after all be about specific services: they would have to deal with three main questions: would the Plan work, i.e. would a metropolitan district perform better than a variety of municipalities plus a county? How much would it cost and how would costs be shared? Would the Plan result in the absorption of small communities either by the city of St Louis or of both by some new entity? Not only did the forums suggest the themes for the programmes and sharpen their focus on a complex of issues: they also had news value in themselves. Publicity arising from them helped alert the community to the fact that the broadcasts were coming up. When the forums were over, individuals who had been identified as able spokesmen, regardless of their point of view, were invited to take part in a special meeting in the studios of KETC, which was taped. The meeting opened with a résumé of the forums by the Assembly moderator, followed by statements by representatives of each of the opposing factions. Then others in the studio audience asked questions and made comments. Portions of this tape were included in the three main programmes on the Plan, and the whole tape transmitted later as a programme in its own right.

Metroplex Assembly programmes were transmitted twice a year, each spring and autumn. The way in which the series theme was chosen varied from series to series, always using appropriate processes of community consultation and discussion. But after a pilot project in 1957 (*Operation Greater St Louis*) there was a consistent method of presenting the programmes, once the theme had been decided and the programmes made. A Metroplex Assembly in operation on any one evening followed this standard routine:

1. Documentary programme on television – thirty minutes.

2. (i) Discussion of programme in viewing posts, one hour.
   (ii) Viewing posts telephone in questions arising from discussion to television station, one hour.

3. Half-hour discussion of viewing-post questions by experts, produced as an extension of discussion, not as a mere answering of questions.

There were hundreds of viewing posts all over the transmission area. They were in effect discussion groups led by specially selected, trained and briefed group leaders. These groups were formed and their leaders recruited to achieve the widest possible variety of people who would be most closely involved in an issue. A 'segment' strategy was used to make this practicable within a limited budget. The St Louis area had a population of more than two million. Only a fraction of that population could participate fully in an Assembly. It was essential to interest and involve people who were representative. The Assembly staff included Civic Education Representatives (always known as CERs) whose job was to set up viewing posts in all relevant segments, using a wide variety of promotional techniques. 'Segment' was variously defined, according to the nature of a project theme. It might stand for working women, Catholic men, the Railroad Brotherhoods, amateur music groups, block unit officers, Mexican-Americans, and so on. Members were not necessarily members of organizations, although organizations were naturally used as a means of contact. Many viewing posts, including many of the best, consisted of informal groups of friends and neighbours.

Most projects were supported by supplementary printed materials for viewing-post members, for post leaders, and, through large metropolitan newspapers which were pleased to cooperate because of the newsworthiness of the entire enterprise, for the public at large. (*The St Louis Post Dispatch*, for example, reprinted on its editorial page a document intended for viewing posts watching a series called *The New Immigrants*.) These newspapers, along with local radio and television stations, would also report the results of opinion ballots which were conducted through viewing posts as a way of sharpening discussion to a point of individual decision and as a way of stimulating a wider diffusion of the debate.

This battery of devices was used in connection with The Metropolitan District Plan. The vote was heavy, or much heavier than usual for such referenda. The plan was thrown out. Some proponents of the Plan complained that had Metroplex Assembly not stirred up such a lot of interest in the subject, the vote would have been lighter and, by and large, only those who were knowledgeable about and favourable to the Plan would have bothered to vote; but official spokesmen from all sides felt CEC had done a useful public service, and done it impartially.

Eugene Johnson modestly denies that Metroplex was as influential as its critics claimed on this occasion, but it seems clear that this Assembly enterprise was politically effective: it helped more people to talk, think, decide and act. Metroplex Assembly was also educationally effective, especially in that aspect which most troubles the conscience of those professionally involved in the education of adults: the marked tendency for opportunities to be disproportionately taken up by those who are already well educated; 60 per cent of the participants for one Metroplex series had never engaged in any such activity before; and 40 per cent of those involved in another series had had only the statutory minimum of formal schooling. So Metroplex tends to reach those sections of society most resistant to social action in general and educational activity in particular.

This unusual concentration on the reception, assimilation and use of information does not imply a neglect of production values. Preparing programmes which people are more than usually motivated to view is no excuse for treating them to poorly produced programmes. Johnson warns:

Possibly the push of effective community organization can carry an activity such as Metroplex through an occasional poor television performance, but viewer interest will fall and participation suffer if the television production is consistently poor or mediocre. The quality of the television product is crucial.[12]

The warning is especially relevant in the United States, whence came the cartoon showing one television producer putting down another by saying 'Educational TV? Isn't that for people who are not strong enough for real TV?' In his survey *Television Teaching Today*, Henry Cassirer noted the tradition in America for educational producers and directors to efface themselves and to adopt an austere approach to production, partly in reaction to commercial entertainment television, which overstresses production values and underestimates content. *Sesame Street*, the pre-school series which turned out to be the best programme of any kind on American television in 1970, has one hopes, finally killed the old antithesis between good television and sound education. Some years before, and on a smaller budget, Johnson and his colleagues insisted on programmes being well produced. British broadcasters, who may have seen some American and some French participatory programmes, should be reassured: I am not advocating a genre which will turn television into a mere telephone with pictures, or convert producers into long-range vision mixers controlled by unimaginative academics or devout but dull social workers.

'Client participation' in deciding the themes for participatory programmes is a chief characteristic in their preparation. Metroplex experience shows that producers who consult only experts will be misled. The collaboration between broadcasters and social scientists in setting up *Cancion de la Raza* also provided a telling demonstration of this paradox. Experts and selected community leaders were asked to advise on what the projected programmes, aimed at Mexican–Americans, should be about. The result was that the producers were told that Mexican–Americans were still resorting to *curanderos* or folk-healers, instead of to qualified physicians, and that this was partly due to their dissatisfaction with the orthodox medical facilities available in the Los Angeles area. The experts urged producers to find ways of dissuading Mexican–American viewers from dealing with *curanderos* and to push for better medical provision.

A social survey of the target audience showed this advice to be quite unsound (assuming that the survey itself was valid, of course). Fully 78 per cent of a representative sample said that they, or someone in their immediate family, had been to a doctor in the twelve months before the interview. No more than 1 per cent of the sample had consulted a *curandero* during the same period. As Mendelsohn puts it, 'a heavy focus in *Cancion de la*

Raza upon the necessity for avoiding *curanderos* would have appeared ludicrous to its viewers'.[14] On the other hand, the targeting survey showed that more than four people in ten from this ethnic group believed that in the face of social adversity they could either do nothing at all about it, or, at best, gripe to friends and relatives. A third of the targeting sample was expressly dissatisfied with the political processes through which they were governed; another third, though eligible to vote, had not registered to vote. These findings provided more important themes for the resulting soap opera than the avoidance of an allegedly dubious species of fringe medicine. The people interviewed were found to be profoundly anomic; their sickness was social, and it was this with which the programmes would have to deal.

The research provided guide lines for the scriptwriters of a kind which would never have emerged from consultations with experts or specialist advisers. They were encouraged to work out scenarios which implied that Mexican–Americans should be proud of their own unique heritage, that they were entitled to use public services without embarrassment along with all other Americans, that they should stand up for their rights, that they should train for steady work, get more value from their religion than just praying about their problems, that not all 'Anglos' are prejudiced against Mexican–Americans, and so on.

Eugene Johnson explains the paradox: experts falsify on account of their very expertise.[14] This became most apparent in preparing programmes for the Metroplex series *The New Immigrants*. The staff consulted the leaders of the relevant community action agencies – school administrators, police, city officials, directors of welfare organizations. In itself this was a sensible move. Such people confront the realities of a problem area and are in this sense the best sources of information about it. In this situation – as in similar situations in Britain – they were acutely aware of the financial burden on central-city police, health, welfare, recreational and educational services; the visible deterioration of many neighbourhoods; delinquency among immigrants. The staff concluded from these discussions:

The community's attitude can be summed up in one short phrase: 'It's a hopeless mess.' Each year, the community spend more and more on education, welfare services, law enforcement, hospitals and health. Yet, each year, more poor whites and Negroes flood in, services are strained still further and the in-migrant ghettoes expand.

The problem seems to defy solution ... at least, the standard solutions of exposure to education, law enforcement, welfare services and the assumed American urge to better oneself. The newcomers are not assimilating; if they are Negroes, they may still be newcomers, culturally, after two generations in the city.

This finding was also in line with the general rhetoric of community discussion in St Louis at the time:

'The problem' was the problems newcomers were giving police, schools, city administrators, welfare agencies. 'The question' was 'how can we cope with these people?' 'how can we make them conform to our requirements?' or, even more simply, 'how can we shut off the flow?'

On this basis, the staff provisionally concluded that the series would have to be about the formidable problems created for St Louis by the large numbers of newcomers displaced from the rural south by the mechanization of agriculture. Afterwards it became obvious to them that they narrowly missed addressing themselves to the wrong question. Improved understanding came about not, as in *Cancion*, through research, but through the use of the sensitivity skills of the expert community worker, the ability to listen to what was not being said as well as to what was. The staff began to see that it was natural for an agency administrator to define a community problem in terms of the work or even trouble it gives his agency, 'not only because that is how he first perceives it himself but also *because that is how he is asked about it*; by his board, by his superiors, by news media'.

There are discipline problems in the schools: Why? There is a growing welfare caseload: Why? The crime rate keeps going up: Why? Slums keep spreading: Why? The answer, time after time (and sometimes with questionable fairness) was 'in-migrants' and in this manner a metropolitan area grew aware of a 'problem'.

Furthermore, when CEC staff asked these administrators 'what is the problem?' they had replied as though they had heard a different question – 'Why is *your* agency falling down on the job?' The staff gradually broke down this defensiveness by persisting with their discussions in smaller, informally convened, groups. As a result, a fundamental change occurred in the way the problem was perceived, both by staff and by expert consultants. The final staff report describes this transformation:

St Louis is exceedingly well aware of the problem the newcomers present to *it*. But how many people seriously consider that the community may present rather formidable problems to the newcomers: particularly to those newcomers who would like to conform to urban standards, who have a desire to better their skills, who would respond to opportunity and incentives?

The difference in approach is important. To define the 'in-migrant problem' only in terms of the problems individual poor whites and Negroes from the rural South present to police, to social agencies, to schools and welfare agencies is to rivet our attention only on the trouble makers among the newcomers. . . . We are aware of the aberrants among them, we conclude they are all like this, and we define the process of human change as the unpleasant business of forcing 'our' standards on 'them' . . . the mass of invincibly backward white trash and colored.

Given this definition of the group, it *is* a nasty business. So we have not done it. Charity for those 'who don't know any better' (and never will) has intervened time after time to weaken the enforcement of laws in in-migrant ghettoes and to lower achievement standards in slum schools.

But how do the in-migrants who are *not* like the stereotype feel about this? They have seldom been asked; by and large, the community is not aware they exist . . . it is necessary to confront community leaders and residents with the kinds of in-migrants they have not yet met; first, the poor whites and Negroes who do aspire to improve their living standards, who want education, who would like to acquire higher skills, and second, those who would strive for any or all of these *if offered any incentive to do so*.

This new perception informed the six programmes which subsequently went out. Each week Phase 1 presented a documentary on one of the major problems faced by the new immigrants in the metropolitan area – finding a job, getting somewhere to live, fixing their children up with adequate schooling. Immigrants and agency officials were then interviewed in relation to *that* set of problems, and consequently viewing posts sent in such question as 'Why don't the States from which the in-migrants come provide help – education for example – ... before they migrate?' 'Is this a national responsibility calling for a national policy or the responsibility of individual cities who feel the heavy impact of in-migration?' 'What can the different agencies ... do to focus their different services on helping the new immigrants?' 'Why doesn't ... St Louis provide a "reception centre" in which these newcomers could get an adequate introduction to the nature and opportunities of city living?'

Apart from involving ordinary viewers all over the city in these discussions, this Metroplex series prompted the staff of different institutions actually to come together for six seminars in order to exchange ideas and achieve a more comprehensive view of what they should be doing, separately and together. They all became aware that the in-migrant problem was not just the problem as it affected them. These seminars were attended by representatives from the Health and Welfare Council, the public schools, the police department, the Mayor's Council on Human Relations, the Department of Public Welfare, the Department of Public Safety, the Urban League, the YMCA and YWCA, the Citizens' Council on Housing and Community Planning, the Missouri Commission on Human Rights, the Inter-Association of Neighbourhood organizations and others.

Metroplex Assembly used television on current affairs in educational ways, supported by other media and agencies, instead of in the traditional way – a running commentary on events beyond the viewer's influence. It prompted not resignation and passivity, but social and individual change, caused by active engagement between viewers and the political texture of their environment. Several agencies and organizations wishing to take constructive social action found it politically more feasible to do so in the climate of informed questioning promoted by Metroplex series. For example, *The New Immigrants* and other programmes made it easier for the Mayor's Council on Human Relations to secure the passage of a 'public accommodations law' ending discrimination based on race, religion or national origin, in all establishments serving the public. The Metropolitan Church Federation in St Louis, which had talked for ages about setting up a department of research and planning, swiftly did so during the creative turbulence stirred up by Metroplex. Many new neighbourhood associations were formed in the city as a result of Metroplex' stimulus.

Metroplex provided much more than stimulus, of course. A good deal of orthodox television does that. Metroplex, because of its multimedia, pluriform approach, turned the stimulus into an educational experience which began to transform people's minds, and which, by providing them with outlets for socially based talk and action, actually developed in them the confidence and the citizenship skills needed to be active participants in an active society engaged in realizing its own best values. In helping individuals to argue and discuss and then to act together, Metroplex obviously helped to change individuals as well as St Louis. A St Louis housewife and mother of two, with no connection of any kind with any neighbourhood organization, took part in the first CEC leadership conference in 1957. She then organized a viewing post and stayed a keen Metroplex Assembly supporter, growing in awareness and self-confidence, until in 1962, she ran for office in the local elections. A suburban family, impressed by what they had seen on Metroplex about the possibilities opened up by active neighbourhood associations in certain areas of St Louis, decided to move there. A Washington University faculty member bought a house in St Louis and found himself lobbied into inheriting a viewing post which had met there under the previous owner. A young architect, appalled by the difficulties faced by professionally trained Negroes trying to find work, of which he had been unaware before Metroplex, personally saw a young Negro through college and then employed him in his own firm.

The experience of growing, in personal and social competence, as a result of a television-based programme is rare as yet because real communication through television is so unusual. Many producers of participatory programmes consider some audience feedback device essential as part of a complete communication pattern. Metroplex Assembly had its follow-up programme based immediately on the discussions and phoned in questions of the viewing posts. Town Meeting Inc. has experimented with direct telephone access to programmes by individual viewers, a process which, Osgood Magnuson says, not surprisingly, 'contains some hazards'. In Minneapolis, Town Meeting used television and radio in combination. A pre-recorded television programme examining three attitudes to anti-ballistic missile systems (pro, con and moderate) on channel 2, KTCA, was followed by a radio programme on WLOL, in which three participants in the television programme argued about the ABM system with viewers who phoned in. The Northwestern Bell Telephone Company ran a busy signal count on the radio station for two hours following the telecast and recorded 1413 busy signals. Town Meeting, anticipating ORAKEL, has also developed a punch-card system which provokes viewers into responding on issues and makes it possible to analyse and publicize their responses. In Ireland, RTE adopted a less instantaneous approach to feedback. This is how Justin Keating describes their method and the way it had to be modified:

During the second year, we obtained for a period an extra ten minutes. Instead of lengthening the basic programme we tried to develop a feedback mechanism from the groups called *You Tell Us*. It had been the habit of those responsible for making the programmes, all through the series, to watch the actual transmission with a viewing group somewhere in the country. Generally we did *not* participate in the discussion, but just watched and listened to reactions. Usually we just dropped in, unannounced. During the *You Tell Us* phase, we tried to bring chosen people from the viewing group into the studio to discuss (and often adversely criticize) the previous week's programme. This failed because we could not find enough people who could handle the situation naturally and normally. So we chose groups at random and notified them (three or four at a time) that we wanted a lengthy written comment on the programme for transmission a week later. We showed a slide of the place, and of the group if we had it, and discussed their response. This worked well, serving as a revision and unifying 300 scattered groups, through the sense that they were all, in different corners of the country, sitting down to do the same thing at the same time.[15]

ORTF has used similar techniques as part of *Télépromotion rurale*. The Metroplex Assembly experience with such forms of feedback was quite unambiguous however, and relates to what was emphasized earlier about production quality:

While the second television broadcast on the same evening may be designed as 'feedback' for the viewing posts, it also has to qualify as a good television program in its own right. Viewing posts will not watch the program simply because it provides feedback. The questions asked and the discussion of them must be focused, interesting and meaningful, if the interest of the participants is to be sustained.[16]

While it was in operation in St Louis, Metroplex Assembly ran series on, among many others, the improvement of neighbourhood organization (*Operation Greater St Louis*); the meaning and relationship of five different arts – music, painting, drama, motion pictures, television and architecture – to city living (*The Humane City*); The Metropolitan District Plan (already described); and *The New Immigrants* (mentioned above). Any of these themes might have been featured in the normal output of orthodox public service television. The mode of operation ensured, however, a highly active response from a nucleus of the target audience; a high degree of attentiveness and reaction; and a heightened awareness of issues among a much wider public, making possible effective interaction between that public and the environment. Participatory programmes give the words 'public-service broadcasting' an altogether new depth of meaning.

Swedish case study

The Metroplex model, the most sophisticated of these examples, could be adapted to British conditions, but it would be unnecessarily limiting to think that participatory programming has to follow Metroplex, well devised though that was. An example from Sweden takes quite a different, less tightly structured form.

In a speech made in 1969, when he was the Minister responsible for the environment, Lord Kennett conceded that Sweden has:

gone furthest along the road towards treating the control of environmental pollution as a separate new social objective, cutting across old divisions of labour, and needing a single coherent machine for its achievement.[17]

Sweden established this 'coherent machine' (coordinated by a powerful National Conservancy Board) in 1967, three years before European Conservation Year. In doing so, the Swedish government was responding to the combined pressure of expert scientific and popular opinion. Why was Swedish opinion so enlightened – at least as enlightened then as it has since become in some other countries as a result of ECY – and so politically effective? A full answer would have to take account of the traditions established in Scandinavia to base political change on widespread public debate. For the moment it is sufficient to notice the role of participatory programming in the transformation of Swedish attitudes.

In the mid-1950s scientists in Sweden as elsewhere, became increasingly worried by the deterioration of the lakes, by the acidity of the rain, and other indices of environmental pollution. Then the pheasants started dying in large numbers. The cause was isolated: mercury in seed dressing. This and similar episodes began to arouse public anxiety. In 1962 Sweden's chief newspaper *Dagens Nyheter* invited leading scientists to write a series of articles on environmental pollution. The series was so successful that more popular newspapers imitated it. Journalists were horrified by what they discovered. Public pressure led to the establishment of a Royal Commission on Natural Resources in 1964. Three years later in 1967, Dr Hans Palmstierna, then a university research scientist, published a best-selling polemical book accusing the authorities of negligence and passivity. In November of the same year, the Royal Commission submitted its report, arriving at similar conclusions to Dr Palmstierna. Thus the familiar power of a journalistic campaign to initiate social and political change was demonstrated. The problem, in democratic societies, is to ensure that such an initiative does not peter out; that it leads to appropriate and effective political action, and to the changes of attitudes among the population at large without which reforms in law and machinery may be neutralized.

However, at this point, Hans Palmstierna and a team of colleagues persuaded the Swedish Cooperative Insurance Society (Folksam) to provide 500,000 kronor (about £40,000) for a campaign of information and education (the grant was later in-increased to 1½m kronor when the campaign began to make a significant impact).

The sequence of events may be schematized in this way:

1. Public sensitized to problems of conservation by press and television features.

2. Establishment of National Conservancy Board.

3. Adult education agencies enable members of public to study problems facing Board in depth.

4. Adult education agencies train corps of keenest students to take social action to maintain political pressure in this area.

5. Resulting social action becomes in turn attractive to press and television.

6. Momentum sustained by programmes which extend the debate.

Such a scheme is no doubt facilitated by the small size of Sweden's population, and by the informal interlocking of key organizations which is a feature of Swedish political life (in this case the Social Democratic Party, Folksam and the Swedish Workers' Educational Association). Instead of such links, something more formal would probably be needed in Britain.

In reality the sequence of events was less tidy and more spontaneous than I have suggested above. It was nevertheless a more deliberate and planned sequence than would occur in Britain. Dr Palmstierna and his colleagues prepared a short course for use in study circles and classes organized by the ABF (the WEA in Sweden), adult schools and other agencies. They prepared a booklet and made films. During 1968–9 they reached between 150,000–250,000 people who attended at least two meetings on the subject. Of these, 10,000 attended at least half the meetings in a ten-week course, and out of these 1000 volunteered to turn themselves into a popular pressure group. They were described in a brief report in *The Times* (22 September 1969) as 'vigilantes', making themselves responsible for alerting their communities to threats from pollutants.

These vigilantes have acted as 'problem shooters' in their localities. They have deliberately looked for problems, used the information made available in the course to suggest possible solutions, and pestered town councillors and industrial managements. The principal instrument used in this phase of the campaign was a public tribunal, organized by the ABF and other organizations, usually in this form: representatives of the vigilantes would put their charges against the authorities or local industry at a public meeting, with the support of a scientist or other expert (sometimes Palmstierna himself). These charges would be discussed or rebutted by representatives of the authorities and industry facing the protesters at the other end of the platform. By October 1969 there had been about thirty big hearings attended by at least 500 people and about 250 smaller ones. The halls were often crowded to overflowing: the meetings were well covered by radio and television, which reinforced their effect and diffused their basic message still further.

Apart from news and features programmes focusing on pollution and campaigning against it, the National Swedish broadcasting corporation (Sveriges Radio) has kept the debate going and extended its terms of reference. Before European Conservation Year Sveriges Radio engaged Dr Palmstierna to make a series of programmes for schools, using television and radio in a co-ordinated scheme. The series opened with a brilliant exposé of the pollution problem, using a vivid montage of visuals and an uncompromising commentary to disturb the audience. But because television is better at showing how things are than at explaining in any detail how they came to be so, this first programme, an impressive documentary in its own right, was followed by three radio programmes dealing in turn with the pollution of water, air and soil. To show concretely how pollution is caused by the political and economic decisions of responsible leaders and acquiescent publics, the next programme was a television portrait of environmental damage in Gothenburg. It was packed with sufficient information, forcefully presented, to cause considerable offence in Gothenburg itself. Programme 6 (radio) and the final programme 7 (on television) concentrated on possible solutions, on what was being or could be done to reverse the dereliction of the environment. There were also two regional school-radio programmes in each of the SR regions to give regional and local aspects of problems dealt with in the project. A work book for pupils and a guide for teachers were published to support the programmes.

The schools series, remade to take account of actual progress in Swedish attitudes and action, was repeated in 1970, and towards the end of 1970 Sveriges Radio returned to the subject again by presenting a series of documentary adult education programmes. They had to recognize that, after a year of ECY propaganda, it was important not to bore the audience. They achieved this in three ways – in general by making the programmes to a high production standard and presenting them with conviction at a peak time (9.30 p.m., with a morning repeat three days later); by engaging one of Sweden's most popular comedians, Carl-Gustaf Lindstedt, who gives a subtle, comic performance as the environmental fall guy; and by taking the issues in new directions, for example, by exposing the long-term genetic and other hazards of a diet polluted by nitrate, mercury, DDT, phosphorous pesticides and other similar achievements of modern food technology or consequences of our being at the apex of numerous nutrition chains.

There was one further ingredient in this series that should be noted: the contribution of the Fools Group Theatre, since this illustrates the courage with which the Swedes mobilize a variety of communications resources to stimulate awareness, commitment, consensus and action on a theme which the debate within the nation has identified as important. There are several experimental theatre groups, usually performing in factories and public halls, hardly ever in theatres as such, using drama either as an overt form of agitprop or implicitly to provoke thought about moral and political issues. These groups are almost all politically well to the Left of the Swedish Establishment, and yet many of them are subsidized out of public funds. They visit schools, where many teachers – not all by any means – find their very partisanship an educational asset. Swedish radio – TV has on a number of occasions employed the Pocket Theatre, one of the best known groups, to produce special plays which dramatize the issues to be explored in a more orthodox didactic way in schools programmes on, say, the geography and economics of developing countries. In this and other ways, the work of these theatres is *extended* by television, not merely featured on it, still less taken up and emasculated by it as a gimmicky radical eccentricity. (It is sad and ironical to note that it was just such a British theatre group which refused to allow Stuart Hood to make a programme about them: their distrust of television as a medium which would distort them was too great.) On this occasion, the Fools Group Theatre was asked to make a play as the first programme in the 1970 environment series; they produced a sharp-edged pantomime about a mother in a supermarket unable to find anything but poisoned food on which to feed her baby.

It seems that the mood of the Swedish public has not only changed, but that the change is consolidating – not just because of television – but because of a dynamic congruence *and* tension between leadership, critical media coverage and social action promoted through agencies of adult education (special trade-union meetings, travelling exhibitions provided by museums as a form of education in the remoter areas of the country, and other activities as well as the ABF meetings already mentioned). Many Swedes are less tolerant of the destruction of amenity even though the development of industry or the maintenance of full employment may in the short run seem to require it. They are beginning to recognize that, in a phrase of Palmstierna's, 'waste is just resources in the wrong place', and that, if waste can no longer be regarded as a terminal condition, ways have to be found of incorporating it into productive cycles. Industry and the public are acknowledging that these procedures raise costs at the same time as they increase social benefits.

European Conservation Year seems to have sensitized opinion in Britain too. It was made the occasion for numerous projects in schools and elsewhere. The contrast with Sweden must not be overdrawn. But the information-education-action processes lacked the coordination achieved, apparently so informally, in Sweden. Consequently, although exposure to the issues has been considerable, this exposure will not of itself lead to continuing commitment, understanding, sacrifice of short-term self-interest, and positive action of the kind which the ecological crisis demands. The scepticism one inevitably feels about the British conversion to conservation was expressed in one of the reviews praising a programme in the BBC's 'Horizon' series. The programme was aptly titled *Due to Lack of Interest Tomorrow has been Cancelled*. The *Observer*'s critic, Mary Holland, had her doubts:

about the tricksy title, but I think it was justified if it persuaded people to give a try to yet another programme about the environment. Last year's fashionable cause is this year's big yawn. Pollution is one of those subjects like the Common Market, the Economy, Vietnam of which most viewers have just had too much.

(which again raised the paradox of the information glut). After admiring the programme's 'grim and vivid' cautionary tale of the making of the American Dust Bowl and its contemporary equivalents (the crops which no longer grow in California because the air is so laden with motor fumes, healthy trees being kept healthy by being wrapped in polythene), Miss Holland concludes:

What good will it do, what difference will it make? Very little, I suppose. But if the job of the media is to educate, to raise awareness, to make sure that we no longer, like the Dust-Bowl farmers, have the excuse of ignorance, then 'Horizon' is doing part of the job for all of us.[18]

Educational broadcasters from other European countries with a less favourable political climate have asked Keity Klynne, the producer of the Swedish environment adult-education series, to say what good she expected *her* programmes to do – full as they were of alarming information of trends apparently beyond the influence of ordinary viewers. She was able to reply categorically that such programmes have already proved their capacity to mobilize discussion about the public support for the initiatives of scientists and other experts exercising their social responsibilities. The Swedes have begun to do what the British scientists quote earlier say that we must do – involve citizens far more in scientific policy making, and improve both education and communication procedures to make that possible. It is time for us to move on from the phase of pious hopes and make sure that television does actually educate and prompt participation; that means a good deal more than diminishing ignorance and raising awareness.

12 Mobilizing British Resources
for Democracy

The strengths of participatory programming

These foreign examples were modest but effective demonstrations of a new use for television. Revitalizing democracy, making it easier for more people, including those most unfamiliar with power, to take part in the business of democracy, is more important than democratizing television. But participatory programming shows that when it is purposefully used on this work of democratic invigoration, television itself becomes more democratic.

People from all strata and milieux sometimes find themselves involved in the selection of themes for programmes, that is they have access to the medium by influencing its programme planning; sometimes, once the theme has been chosen, they are in a position to affect the contents of the programmes and the way they are treated. The definition of issues, the delineation of the actual areas of controversy, the selection of protagonists become much less top-down and authoritarian than in conventional broadcasting.

In television as we know it, everything is left to producers whose antennae are attuned to the consensus as currently defined by the Establishment and influential élites. In participatory programming the people also have access by influencing programme research and by providing a community stimulus for editorial response, counterbalancing the normal pressures of oligarchy. And sometimes, when the theme and treatment demand it, representatives of the people have access by taking part in the programmes.

In participatory programming broadcasting professionals do not dominate the proceedings, as in conventional programme making, but they do not abdicate either, as they are apparently expected to by some radical advocates of an alternative television. In participatory programming, current-affairs topics are the basis of socially relevant adult education through television, helping people to decide for themselves what policy they wish to adopt or action they wish to take. Having helped the people move themselves, television can then report the news generated by the resulting social change. And throughout the process it can do this because of its trusted neutrality, or, as in the Swedish case study, because of its trusted objectivity (Swedish SR was hardly neutral as between polluters and anti-polluters, but it was not propagandist either – its social concern expressed itself through confronting the Swedish people with the stunning results of disinterested academic research).

Participatory programming enables people to clarify their ideas and wishes, and then to channel their responses in a socially or politically effective manner. Thus the information provided by television becomes worth having, assimilating, evaluating, accepting or rejecting, because it is information which can be used. There are visible outlets for social action to hand, an integral part of the social machinery into which television itself is fitted.

These tentative experiences of integrating television with other media, media with other social agencies and institutions, experts with laymen, information with education, education with debate and dialogue, talk with action, show how the problem about television itself should be redefined. We should not be dealing in isolation with the question: how can broadcasting be made more accountable? or how can the people have access to television? The issue that calls for discussion and experiment, research and development is this: how can the media resources of society be brought into relation with channels of social decision and action so that the people are involved in an increasingly participatory democracy?

The future of television is central to the main issue, but it is not in itself that issue. By focusing too exclusively on the politics of broadcasting, we are in some danger of missing the fundamental matter; the future of democratic politics itself and the role of broadcasting, as the key figure in a family of media, in that future.

Review of British resources – television

Participatory programming is, then, a process in which the media are used chiefly as a stimulus to participatory democracy but also in part as themselves a forum or outlet for participation. Television must (at least at first) occupy a central place in attempts to use the media for these ends because of its popularity and its reach.

As I remarked at the very outset, television still predominates in what social scientists now call the 'time budget' of leisure – watching it consumes more time for more people than any other activity apart from work or sleep; and no other spare-time activity begins to rival it. No one knows for how long this sociological phenomenon will persist, but it is now two decades old and it continues to be a central fact about social life in Britain today. Furthermore, as we have seen, television is now for most people the chief source of information about what is going on in Britain and the world. This is a much more recent phenomenon and it is too soon to assess its stability. For the time being, however, it is another social fact of major significance, which gives to television a strategic and tactical importance in any process designed to improve communication and action within a would-be participatory democracy.

Television is popular, not only in the sense that the great majority of the population use it and devote most of their spare time to it, but also in its related sense that they like it and trust it. Despite a growing volume of public criticism of broadcasting, the confidence in it of most members of the public is undimmed. The sheer size of the audience which exhibits this trust was made possible by the attitude of successive British governments towards the provision of broadcasting. Until the advent of local radio, Britain has always maintained a strictly egalitarian policy, in that a listener or viewer living in a rich city would receive no more and no less broadcasting than a crofter in the Orkneys. Capital investment decisions and engineering choices have always had to be made on the basis that any signals have to be provided equally in all parts of the kingdom. Everyone paid the same licence fee; everyone had as many channels and programmes to choose from. The creation of Independent Television has made no difference to this principle, and engineers regard it as a cardinal duty to find ways of sending signals over or round obtuse mountains, however few people there might be living in the valleys on the other side. This egalitarianism is in marked contrast to the traditional policy of the United States, which has adopted a market approach – different places have as much broadcasting as advertisement revenue can sustain.

The result of official policy and engineering pertinacity is that the country is almost totally penetrated by television, a fact of considerable political significance, whichever political way you look at it. It could continue to be significant as Britain moves away from oligarchic democracy to participatory democracy. At certain levels of action, political effectiveness depends on this reach and penetration. Community action on a small scale can lead to the erection of a bus shelter, even to the provision of a bus service, but community action cannot be restricted to such parochial endeavours. To achieve results on a regional level, as through Metroplex, or on a national level, as in the concerted Swedish assault on pollution, the use of television is essential.

We could make a start now, on participatory programming spearheaded by television, without changing fundamentally the constitution, organizational or managerial structure of the broadcasting organizations. I have argued already that an explicit reference to democratic goals should be included in the legislated responsibilities of broadcasters, to strengthen the development of policy and clarification of planning, but a revision of the terms of reference (which would condition many other kinds of programme) is not a prerequisite for action in this particular direction. There may be good reasons for advocating, as many do, reforms in the administration, and it is possible that organizations which are themselves hierarchic may turn out to be insufficiently sympathetic to participatory programming as a socially desirable objective. On the other hand, even syndicalists are not always as sensitive to the democratic responsibilities which an institution has to those outside and whom it is meant to serve, as they are to the internal democracy of the way the enterprise is run.

Such a role for television would, however, require some strengthening of the external relations of broadcasting, though not at all along unprecedented lines. The relevance of the adult and further education output of the BBC and ITV to the needs of its target audiences already depends in large measure on consultative machinery. Educational programmes (including those for schools) are always planned in the light of advice from the educational world. This is channelled through to the broadcasters not only by a series of advisory committees, of a kind which do not (as yet) exist in any other programme area (except religion), but also by small teams of specially trained field-liaison staff, capable of listening to what educationists want, of interpreting their wishes to production personnel, and, in turn, of interpreting the broadcasters back to the world of education. This system is especially well developed in the BBC, and the success of *Representing the Union* was largely due to it. Participatory programming would be encouraged by an extension – in their numbers, skills and terms of reference – of these specialized liaison workers.

It might be objected that education is itself a specialized sector of social life, whose institutions and leaders are readily identified and located. It is one thing to liaise with them over the levels and subjects of series tailor-made for educational use; it would be quite another to negotiate with the whole population over the infinite range of political, social and cultural issues which, with participatory potential, might be treated in documentary, current affairs and news programmes intended for mass consumption. This valid contrast is easily overstated, however. Although education, as a system, is readily isolated for contact, the possible subject matter for educational programmes is also as infinite as life itself. This has not made impossible the pragmatic application of criteria of priority. Furthermore, nobody would or could advocate a wholesale conversion of large segments of the output to the participatory mode. It is inevitable that such programmes should constitute only a modest proportion of serious output, especially while they are being tried and tested; but even later, when broadcasters have more experience of them, they would still only take up a fairly restricted amount of air time, concentrating inevitably on a few projects of cardinal social value (but establishing thereby a new mode of relationship with the audience which would begin to leaven the tone and approach in the more conventional forms of programme, and to influence the criteria by which their success with audiences would be judged – 'understanding' and 'usefulness' finding their place alongside 'impact' and 'appreciation').

It is important that the participatory sector of the output should be enlightened by the work of community liaison staff who would not have to shoulder the entire Metroplex-like burden themselves. They are necessary because consulting the audience, and moving among the population segments that make it up, are as important as – indeed cannot be separated from – efficiently addressing that audience. In participatory programming, as much professional attention needs to be devoted to reception and use as to production and transmission.

Although some enlargement of field forces would be necessary, participatory programming would not call for any increase in production resources: they only need to be partly re-routed in this new direction. That could call for certain inter-departmental adjustments within broadcasting, notably closer collaboration between features, education, news and current affairs (so that, for example, some documentaries would become part of a thought-out system of stimulus – educational input – coverage of social effects). It would also call for the familiarization of production personnel with the new social values.

Furthermore, the broadcasting networks do not transmit networked programmes all the time. All Independent Television companies are committed by their contracts with the ITA to provide programmes of many kinds (features, news, regional magazines) solely for their own regions (and never intended for networking), so that some participatory programmes could count against their 'local origination' obligations. The BBC still produces some television output exclusively for regional use. These existing categories of provision could readily be adapted for contributions to Anglicized Metroplex Assemblies.

Also, both broadcasting bodies are already devoting considerable air time to educational series for adults. Education is one of the two areas, religion being the other, in which the BBC and ITV regularly plan together instead of competing. Participatory programming, in at least some of its phases and in one of its major dimensions, is, as I have suggested, a species of educational television. Accordingly, it is not fanciful to envisage a project in which, for example, an ITV company contributed regional programmes dealing with its *content*, while the BBC (which has a well-established 'community' strand in its further-education output) could make a complementary series (for wider transmission) on the *methodology* of this and similar projects (e.g. how to conduct a community self-study, or how to create and sustain a pressure group).

Review of resources – local radio

Participatory programming is good for society, for audiences and for television itself, because through its methods it disavows the preposterous presupposition of present practice – that television is or can be an all-purpose medium dominating the other media in a competition for audience loyalty. Britain is becoming increasingly rich in communications resources, but haphazardly, and they are in no clear relationship with each other. We need to experiment with different ways of associating them. Potentially the most important collaborator with television in the participatory programme process is local radio.

National radio still has an important part to play in the creation of an educated public, for the moment overshadowed by the supremacy of television as as information medium. Its limitation – that it can only describe events which television can actually show – is obvious; its strength – that oral exposition can be more explanatory, subtle, complex and comprehensive than a sequence of pictures with or without commentary – is too often overlooked. Moreover, audiences do not at present have the habit of using television and radio in conjunction, deliberately turning to programmes such as *Analysis* or *From our Own Correspondent* to make better sense of items of which the colourful iceberg tip has been glimpsed on television. Nor, apart from modest attempts at collaboration in the curricular educational field, do the controllers of the BBC do much to encourage such a habit. The alternative media are just there, alongside each other, the one upstaging the other, their complementariness unexplored. Participatory programming would provide opportunities for joint-media production by broadcasters, and joint use by the public.

In developing strategies for participatory programmes local radio seems likely to have a strong place. It is difficult to treat people as people through network broadcasting: reduce the scale to a locality, even to a region, an area in which the broadcaster will meet his listeners in the street, send his children to the same schools, be as well known to the Rotary Club and the Trades Council as an editor of a local paper, and broadcasters find themselves more easily adopting a tone which would be too real, too human for the show business audience grabbing ethos of the networks.

The authority which local radio may acquire, young though it still is, and restricted as yet to VHF, was shown in the summer of 1971 by a documentary programme on BBC Radio Merseyside. It dealt with aspects of life in the terraces of Toxteth in Liverpool 8, with its black population, its cosmopolitan character and high crime rate. The programme criticized the local police for harassment and brutality and it opened with a statement by a Liverpool City Councillor who said:

I have seen people soon after these allegations of harassment or brutality. As a medical practitioner, I have occasionally been called on to examine people, and I have certainly formed the opinion in some cases that brutal behaviour – unnecessary brutal behaviour – has in fact occurred. I am further strengthened in this belief because on one or two occasions – and I don't want to exaggerate this – I have had an opportunity of talking informally with members of the Force. From these conversations, and from having heard a little from the other side, and putting two and two together, I have no doubt at all that in some cases it certainly adds up to four and adds up to an unnecessary display of violence.

The programme quoted from a statement made to its makers by a Liverpool policeman, and then commented:

As a serving constable, this is a clear breach of police discipline, and it is a measure of the concern that some police officers feel that they should risk their careers in this way. It could also be taken as an indictment of existing procedures within the organization of the police force. The officer said that in certain police stations, particularly in the city centre, brutality and drug-planting and the harassing of minority groups take place regularly. On one occasion, the officer witnessed a police sergeant attack a teenage youth who had reported to the station while on parole. The sergeant poured insults on the youth, picked him up by the coat lapels and banged his head against the wall several times, before throwing him into a chair. The youth was then dragged out to a police jeep and driven away. After hearing the word 'agriculture' used on a number of occasions by plain-clothes police on duty in Liverpool 8, the officer asked what it meant. The reply was: 'Planting – but you can leave that to us.'[1]

The programme was scrupulous, recognizing that the police have a difficult task in the city, but it was a bold piece of investigatory journalism. The Chief Constable of Liverpool undertook to investigate its allegations.

This authoritativeness is important, especially in the early days when listeners will judge local radio by expectations derived from network radio. But it is essential for local radio to acquire new styles and a new manner if it is to be an apt instrument for participatory programming. Fairly soon after its formation, Marghanita Laski experienced this change of tone. She wrote perceptively of getting 'over the shock and into the feel of local radio':

The shock is at entering a dimension radically different from that of national broadcasting. It is like knowing your place on a map of five miles to the inch, then moving to one of five inches to the mile. People are on a new scale. Radio London's 'experts', for instance, are the parish priest, the small shopkeeper, the local pensions officer, the borough councillor. You have to get used to less competent speakers, but speakers who know, from the ground up, what they're talking about. The most potent effect seems to be an entirely different quality of discussion programme.[2]

She cites a discussion, typical of the regular slot in which it appeared, about the demolitions and rebuildings in Christchurch Street, Chelsea, which were debated by the Chairman of the Chelsea Society, the leader of the residents' association, the vice-chairman of the borough's planning committee and others who 'all knew the place on the ground':

The principles involved – the value of mixed-class housing, the laws on demolitions and local-council grants, the significance of preservation as against conservation orders – emerged because each had had to find out, for his protection, his passion or his job, how far these were relevant and could work for him. It was only on hearing this that one realized how much, and necessarily, nationally broadcast discussions start from or must quickly pass to the abstract, invoking the particular only illustratively; and we have tended to accept, no matter how ill founded, discussion based on largest-scale principles as the norm.

Her verdict on this programme, which certainly did not achieve its success just because it was local (which could have meant poorly produced parish pumpery), but because the producer had already learned how to address his physically close audience with a new kind of seriousness which often eludes producers of national programmes:

This debate about a Chelsea street, which perhaps a quarter of the listeners would know at least roughly, lasted only half an hour but seemed spacious and elbow-roomed, and left us with applicable knowledge of concretely-founded principles.

Marghanita Laski's summing-up is pertinent:

For high-grade entertainment and for intensity it's necessary to turn to national programmes, but for enrichment of ordinary living at most ordinary levels, I suspect that, at least potentially, local stations may have it over national ones.

This combination of broadcasting's traditional authoritativeness with localness of tone and allusion has enabled local radio to go beyond investigatory journalism, often allowing a wide range of representative members of the public to take part. Radio Merseyside has already contributed to a project which was a Metropolex in miniature, with local radio as the spearhead medium.

There is a great stirring of community feeling and action in Liverpool. Much of the best community-development work and adult education in Britain is to be found there, inspiring self-confidence and political participation among people who face daunting social conditions. Community councils are being formed and hitherto gravely disadvantaged people are succeeding in talking, on something more like equal terms, with 'the Corpy', as everyone calls the City Corporation. The EPA (Educational

Priority Area) Project director, Eric Midwinter, can provide abundant evidence for the claim to 'have nailed conclusively the myth of apathy and lack of concern among lower-working-class parents'.[3]

In this physically depressed but spiritually reviving atmosphere, Radio Merseyside and the Workers' Educational Association mounted their mini-Metroplex. At the kernel of it were six fifteen-minute discussion programmes – pointed up with relevant popular songs and dramatized inserts – called *Living Today*, dealing with the family, the neighbourhood, the church, the school, the local authority and the government. They were well enough made to interest anyone on Merseyside, but they concentrated on the problems social change was creating for men and women living in the EPA. House to house canvassing in the EPA led to the formation of a dozen listening groups, meeting in houses, community centres and pubs, led by 'resilient' (i.e. not stuffily academic) *animateurs* recruited by Mr Tom Lovett, the WEA's so-called 'unattached' worker who also wrote the scripts.

The group discussions were successful. Bob Jones, the producer, said: 'When you see forty men and women talking about common problems in the Seven Stars pub off Scotland Road you feel that education can be brought back to the people.' These were emphatically not the kind of men and women normally recruited for more formal courses and classes run by university extramural departments, the WEA or even by what used to be called 'night schools' and 'evening institutes'. One group, for example, consisted entirely of young housewives. All except one left school at fifteen and did unskilled factory work before marriage; they all had two or three children; most of them lived in houses under compulsory purchase orders – two bedrooms, no bathrooms, outside lavatories – owned by often unscrupulous landlords who saw no point in doing repairs, however urgent. Several of their husbands became unemployed during the 'term'.

These women were eager but unused to handling ideas, like most of the other participants. Yet the discussion groups produced practical suggestions and important questions to or criticisms of authority on such a scale that Radio Merseyside remade the series, including this time representatives of the groups face to face with councillors and local government officials to talk with them. The housewives felt that discussions like theirs should be tape-recorded for use in secondary schools – with the aim of disabusing girls in particular of their sentimentalized picture of marriage and parenthood; they wanted schools and church buildings used more as community meeting places; they urged schools to be more open and responsive to parents instead of referring to them only when there was trouble; they recommended that the Corpy should have an efficient, adequately staffed centre for complaints and information. Given the network of functional relationships between voluntary and statutory agencies in Liverpool, the advocacy of such suggestions stood a good chance of success, reinforced by the continuing dialogue between the people and authority taking public and audible form through Radio Merseyside.

I have described this venture in some detail because of its effectiveness and more general validity. The scale was small, the resources were exiguous, but the method is capable of imitation and development, especially in harness with regional television, and especially when the issues, locally defined, affect people everywhere.

Review of resources – other media and agencies

The popularity and penetration of television, its status and resources, mark it out as the chief component in participatory programming aimed at major social or political effect. The localness of local radio makes that medium the most appropriate for local situations or for the local treatment of national questions. But it is now apparent that this philosophy of communications use may be applied to any media resources, the media chosen and the mixture of media involved depending on the nature of the issues and the geography and demography of the participating population. Apart from broadcasting, the most neglected resource is CCTV (closed-circuit television) and mobile VTR (video-tape recording).

All forms of broadcasting share one democratic virtue of considerable significance: they are public media whose signals are available to anyone with the right receivers. They reach into every home, not merely into those of the influential, the leaders or those on a subscription list. This virtue is denied, by definition, to closed-circuit television. Those running closed-circuit systems would have to recruit audiences specially if they were to play a part in a participatory process, and members of the public would have to be keenly motivated to gain access to such systems or their offerings. Nevertheless, the community has already invested many millions in the installation of the CCTV plant operated by four local education authorities (Glasgow, London, Plymouth and Hull), by most universities, many colleges of education and further education, and even by several enterprising schools. These systems could be used to transmit specially prepared materials for particularly dedicated sections of a community, looking at a theme intensely within a smaller geographical area, or from the point of view of people with special responsibilities for leadership, or whatever. This could sometimes be a planned follow-up to broadcast programmes, sometimes the initiating component. Discussion could be fostered at a level midway between the relatively impersonal level of broadcasting and the intimate level of face-to-face groups. But as yet, except for student magazines at Leeds, Sussex and other universities, these facilities are used only for academic, curricular purposes.

The democratic possibilities of CCTV were hinted at some years ago – many years ahead of time in that these CCTV systems did not then exist, when the now defunct Television Viewers' Council sponsored an experiment using *ad hoc* equipment at Loughton Hall, the base of Debden Community Association. Using improvised gear, a community was able to talk to itself in a way never possible before.[4]

The community use of CCTV for democratic participation may gain impetus from the as yet tentative experiments being undertaken by such groups as TVX (an Arts Lab spin-off, associated with a former film editor, Gordon Woodside, and the same imaginative Underground 'entrepreneur', John Hopkins, who helped initiate *IT* and the Pink Floyd) and members of the staff at Goldsmith's College, London. VTR already has a wide range of applications – in industrial training (salesmen can see their own negotiating demeanour as it really is); in many forms of sports coaching (golfers and athletes are learning to improve their individual performance; rugby players to gain insight into the group dynamics of the scrum, the line-out and rucking in the loose, by seeing themselves on tape); in police work (Lancashire police with a VTR can courteously convince errant motorists by playing back a tape of their road behaviour); in schools (one Nottingham head is reported pleased by the power of VTR to persuade long-haired pupils to get their hair cut; others are making serious educational use of it) and in colleges of education (student teachers can see themselves as others see them). The technique could be applied to community self-study projects – an appalling environment to which inhabitants have become inured confronts them and others with its horror on VTR – and to the necessary business of fostering communication between people and bureaucrats; why should an elderly unlettered council tenant have to cope with forms and telephones when a community service VTR could easily provide a document on tape showing that she does have rats in her basement? Why should a housing association not present its case for a zebra crossing across a dangerous road by presenting a tape on which the hazards are visible instead of a written report that has to prove the authenticity of its arguments? These are the first thoughts on early experiments, but they are clearly acorns with a future.[5]

Metroplex experience in the United States has already shown the useful part that local newspapers can play in participatory programming, by providing news coverage, by acting as a recruiting agent for viewing posts and discussion groups, by reproducing the texts of significant documents in the case. Works magazines, professional journals, parish magazines and other forms of print could all be involved, according to the theme of the project and the population segments taking part. New reproduction techniques make it easy for people to produce attractively designed newspapers of their own. In the Vauxhall area of Liverpool a newspaper provides information about, e.g. pre-school playgroups and holidays for old people, and acts as a sounding board for community feeling on local issues. The paper is produced by a part-time community worker with the voluntary help of twenty local people. It is financially viable with a sale of 3000 copies.

In Stavely, a small town in Derbyshire, a band of volunteers from all parts of the community produce an occasional newspaper which sells 3000 copies. Its originator envisaged that:

our newspaper could be *prospective*, describing and influencing matters as yet unsettled, not *retrospective*, describing events already past. It would not use information as entertainment (like most newspapers). We might assert the individual's right to control anything that affects him/her. The thing would have to take root among local people, become *their* paper.

It apparently did so.

Ad hoc publications could also be prepared for use in any Metroplex-like operation. The BBC and ITV customarily produce pamphlets, wallcharts, tape-slide presentations, film-loops, discs and other devices as supports to educational series, any of which could be made available as part of the data input for a participatory project.

Data has not only to be fed into this system. It also has to be gathered for diffusion (which suggests a new mode of extension work for universities, libraries and other centres of knowledge), and critically assimilated by its recipients (involving informal and traditional agencies of adult education). The recipients have to be recruited (via the gamut of voluntary associations and also through schools and other institutions with means of evoking the interest of the many people who do not join organizations), and provided with channels of participatory action (statutory channels, relevant pressure groups, *ad hoc* instruments for articulating need).

It remains to be seen whether cable television will in due course become available for this and other communications purposes in Britain. It is as yet a remote prospect here, but not in Canada, the most 'cabled' nation, per capita, in the world. In 1971 over four million Canadians watched cable TV, and their numbers were growing at the rate of 25 per cent a year. *Challenge for Change*, published by the National Film Board of Canada, has supplied practical advice to interests and groups wishing to make programmes and to promote feedback to them, and illustrates the programme possibilities by such examples as:

a documentary on the unemployed *made by* the unemployed; live city-council meetings, with home audiences phoning in questions ... before or after the meeting; what the militant poor mean by welfare rights; ... regular accountability sessions with federal and provincial MPs; ... a picture of the local Indian reserve, made by the Indians themselves; a lively Ukrainian feast-day celebration; a rap session with young long-hairs in a drop-in center, and a discussion with a church youth group, followed by an exchange of ideas between the two sets of young people. (Add a couple of parents!)[6]

Cable TV would help complete the mesh of communications needed. Meanwhile, it would pay us to experiment with different permutations of the various media that we do have, starting with combinations which demonstrate convincingly one of the main strengths of participatory programming; by using different media, national and local, in a multi-media system, the advantages of each are combined, so that large-scale issues may be brilliantly presented, and their repercussions in different localities considered in depth by people with the authority of their place in the place, which may be quite unlike the authority of experienced performers.

There is no reason why experimentation, based on the experience derived from the British precursors described in chapter 10 and on the foreign projects reviewed in the previous chapter, should not begin in this country, using available institutions acting in accordance with their own limits, and broadly within existing budgets, but acting, deliberately, together.

It should be entirely feasible, for example, to mount something like a Metroplex Assembly in one of the regions served by an Independent Television company. The media and agency components in such a project would, by definition, depend upon the ultimately selected themes, and determining these would, again by definition, not depend solely on the broadcasters (or any other collaborating agencies). The population has to be and can be involved in the pre-production planning stage. One can envisage many topics keenly exercising the inhabitants of a particular region, but (remembering the policy of the prototype *The Whole Town's Talking*) not them alone – the siting of an airport; the conflicting and even irreconcilable pressures on land and water in, say, the Lake District or the New Forest; the ambivalent effects of motorways; cultural deprivation of the countryside; conurban planning, and many others not necessarily taken from one aspect of political life as these examples are.

Participatory programming increasingly feasible

To say that participatory programming is feasible is not to pretend that it would be easy. The broadcasting organizations in Britain have sometimes found it difficult to collaborate with other media and agencies, using different logistical styles, attitudes, and so on. The relevant American experience shows in particular that it is often peculiarly difficult to weld production personnel and research workers (survey research or production-reconnaisance research are often valuable ingredients in such enterprises). But nevertheless British experience in educational broadcasting, the experience of RTE in mounting *Telifis Feirme* and ORTF's close association with Rénnes, show that the mode is possible. It now needs trying out on a broader political–social–cultural plane.

There are reasons to expect, however, that certain changes are taking place, some short range, others longer term, that will make participatory programming increasingly manageable and demanded. These are

1. Changes in the relationship between broadcasting and other institutions at national level, being brought about for strictly educational reasons but relevant in their consequences.

2. Changes in the rationale and remit of field agencies of adult education, which is that part of the educational system potentially closest to the democratic process, and changes in the organization of the social services.

3. Most long term, but fundamentally most significant, changes in the expectations and capacity of the public.

The kind of programming I am advocating does not even exist at present, but it is important to see it is not only in tune with the fundamental political dynamic discussed in Part One, but also that it will become more feasible, not less, because of other developments in the environment of broadcasting.

1. The broadcasting authorities are expected, as I write, to have seats on the governing body of the new national organization for educational technology, destined to be the successor to the National Council of Educational Technology (NCET). This apparently dry piece of constitutional information could turn out to be relevant. The new organization will, among other functions, provide a more satisfactory framework for collaboration between the different providers of educational software and between them and the users of the software, at all levels of the educational system, and in industry and the Armed Forces. When NCET was set up, its terms of reference emphatically made it clear that it would not intrude upon the autonomy of the broadcasters. The broadcasters now accept that the new body does not need to be more sensitive about the broadcasters' sovereignty than about that of the many other institutions with which it will deal. Furthermore, the broadcasters recognize that collaboration is right and inevitable in this field. It is an important shift of emphasis, and likely to go further, especially as the partnership with the Open University becomes second nature, and especially as the new centralizing and coordinating body should display more interest in adult education as a sector of provision in its own right. And it is precisely through adult education that the boundary between education as such on the one hand, and social work, community development and politics on the other becomes so blurred. NCET will foster the habit of systematic association between autonomous agencies, and one result of that could be increasing confidence among several of the potential parties to participatory programming.

2. The field of adult education is itself changing in ways that would make the field component in participatory programming more sophisticated and able to provide an adequate infrastructure for the media effort. Whereas in the United States, adult education has had such a community orientation that 'community development' and 'adult education' often seemed to be coterminous, the British tradition has hitherto been individualistic, and this despite the social conscience of the WEA and the declared aims of the National Federation of Community Associations. Community associations certainly played a develop-

mental role before and shortly after the war in helping to humanize new housing estates, but their energies have tended in the last twenty years towards providing sociable activities in community centres. This is often a long distance from promoting social change through the encouragement of grass roots democratic activity. The community claim of the WEA is stronger because the Association has always shown an active interest in the politics of education (at all levels, not just adult education) and because its ideology relates the pursuit of education to active citizenship. There is a big difference, however, between addressing education to individuals in the hope and expectation that they would become better trade-union officials, city councillors and citizens, and addressing education to groups of people or to strategic segments of the population in order to mobilize their energies for informed, self-determined social change. Now however the word 'community' is on everyone's lips in the adult education world, and many agencies are beginning to think about how they may service the needs of the community, whereas once they were introvertedly obsessed with the problems of recruiting people to their routine programmes of courses and classes. In addition to this general change of emphasis, some agencies are deliberately exploring adult education as a resource for social change – not as a device for solving problems, but as an instrument to help people analyse problems and devise their own solutions to them with more confidence. This is happening notably in the Liverpool Educational Priority Area, as we saw, but the outward-looking techniques and approaches being tried there are in principle appropriate to any environment, not simply to one officially classified as deprived and disadvantaged. This change of climate in adult education means that when the broadcasting organizations attempt to work with the heterogeneous mass of different agencies which that sector comprises, they will meet with much more understanding of what they are talking about than they would have done less than five years ago.

Furthermore, the exploitation of media stimulus at the receiving end, permitting better consideration of issues and information among the public to fructify in action, will be facilitated by the growing coherence of social organization at the regional and local level. The reform of the social services is the most obvious change in this direction especially as it will bring the provision of education, welfare, cultural and recreational amenity closer together. It is also to be expected that educational bodies will increasingly see the importance of peripatetic personnel whose job is to put those with control over educational resources into contact with those whose needs or interests are amenable to service by education. At present the WEA has one experimental 'unattached' tutor, and only a few local authorities employ roving development officers, but it will become obvious that the new community ambitions of adult education cannot be achieved by a handful of organizers, many of them part-time, and all of them prepossessed with, at best, running centres, or at worst, administering programmes of classes. As a result, in the wake of the Russell Committee (the Committee of Inquiry set up by the Secretary of State for Education to report on this field), there should be an enlargement of the liaison field force necessary to relate broadcasting with other agencies. The burden will not rest unilaterally on the limited numbers of field staff employed by the broadcasting bodies. Approaches for collaboration may stem from a variety of sources.

These changes, in the national organization of educational technology, in the coherence of local government, and in the orientation of adult education towards participation and conscious community growth, will also predispose important agencies to look to broadcasting for new forms of cooperation and support. Physicists use the concept of critical mass to indicate the minimum quantitative levels that must be achieved before any qualitative change in an object or process occurs. For adult education to make any socially significant mark in any specific direction, it needs to mobilize enough people in particular situations for their influence to be felt on the political or cultural fabric. To achieve critical mass in areas of informed, participatory social change, it is necessary to employ mass media. The field agencies will increasingly recognize this. Consequently, any one of the interested parties could take the initiative in setting up a Metroplex partnership of media and agencies.

3. Far more significant in the longer run will be the increasing numbers of people in the population who are better educated;

who actually enjoyed and were not humiliated by their experience of school, so that they do not regard education as a kind of aversion therapy; and who are more and more sophisticated about the media themselves. As well as benefiting quite disproportionately from the petty perks of our privilege-ridden society, the better educated will also continue to press for the humanizing of it. And more and more of them will have attended that growing number of universities, colleges of education and colleges of further education which use closed-circuit television as a teaching resource. A growing number of these establishments are allowing students to produce television equivalents to student newspapers and magazines. This is even beginning in schools. Anyone who has seen primary-school children (like those at Oxhey Wood Primary School near Watford) or secondary-school children (like those at the Community College in Ilfracombe) making programmes – learning about cameras and microphones, designing graphics, manipulating video-tape recorders and simple telecine systems, will become aware that pioneers in the educational system are beginning to produce a generation for whom television (not just watching it, but making it as well) has become healthily demythologized. A capacity to communicate on and through the box will not be limited to a handful of performing talents.

At the same time as society becomes increasingly participatory, there will be a new population of younger people capable of making the maximum use of the media, both the centralized ones and the local, more spontaneous media mentioned in the preceding review of resources. This use will comprise both participatory programming and participation in programmes, in increasingly sophisticated forms.

Meanwhile, and in the short term, the transition has to be made from conventional television to the new use for television explored in this book. In ordinary television, programmes are an end in themselves, or they vaguely serve a vague objective: the diffusion of awareness in the population of what is going on among them and beyond their boundaries, a population which often could not care less. In participatory television, as I have tried to show, programmes are addressed to people more or less already made aware of what information, concepts and ideas about alternatives they need; able to deepen their knowledge through access to complementary information in other media with other strengths; able to develop their sensitivity to other viewpoints and their grasp on their own value systems through face-to-face discussion and dialogue; able to articulate their wishes and press their views through social machinery with some purchase on the levers of power.

Participatory programmes are intended to promote social participation. That is their chief objective and *raison d'être*. They work by addressing people in terms which they understand, on issues which they really care about and which they have in some way shared in selecting. The programmes are supported by specially contrived arrangements at the reception end for ensuring that a representative core of the audience may assimilate and evaluate the information received; and they are related in some way to political and social instruments through which citizen viewers may press the conclusions at which they have arrived.

By taking part in participatory programming, television simultaneously advances democracy and promotes its own development: it advances democracy by acting as a communications resource for public dialogue, and by providing a stimulus for social action; it promotes its own development by learning how to convert itself, at least in one of its modalities, from a medium of multiple diffusion which haphazardly succeeds in communicating, into a means of communication to which recipients of its messages actively attend, to which they respond and through which they may reply.

The question facing television is: will it continue to alienate us from the world and from the possibility of effective action, by transforming an environment we are powerless to affect either into an object out there about which we are continuously but patchily informed, or into a spectacle to divert, titillate and uselessly appal us? Or will it help us create a society in which effective action is possible?

It is not an anaemic, theoretical question. In advanced industrial nations the best endeavours of responsible men are leading to irresponsible societies; the rationality of the parts adds up to a dangerously irrational whole; the air is full of messages but there is little communication. In the confusion, there are ugly portents – wild behaviour by disaffected individuals and groups matched by disciplinarian governments.

Representative democracy could be wrecked in the near future (here and abroad) by a dangerous conflict between populist anarchy and oligarchic reaction. The second half of the 1960s rumbled with the premonitory tremors of this incipient struggle. Democracy must become more democratic if it is not to succumb to chaos, or to tyranny, or, as already seems possible in the United States, to a sordid mixture of the two. The issue is as urgent as any our society faces. Television can work for dialogue and against disintegration; for freedom and against a technological barbarism, not just by reporting the events to passive people, but by collaborating with an active people in making the news, the continuing story of the remaking of democracy.

Notes

Chapter 1

1. Independent Television Authority, *Annual Report and Accounts 1970–71*, HMSO, 1971.

2. See, for example, H. Himmelweit *et al.*, *Television and the Child*, Nuffield Foundation and OUP, 1958.

3. National Viewers and Listeners Association, *Report on the Schools Broadcasting Monitoring Project covering Programmes dealing with Ethical, Social and Personal Topics*, 1971.

4. Peter Black, 'Bad news', *Listener*, 18 April 1968, p. 153.

5. Milton Shulman, *Evening Standard*, 14 July 1971.

6. Sir Robert Fraser, 'Independent television: the first fifteen years' (speech at Goldsmiths' Hall, 24 September 1970), ITA Notes no. 21.

7. Milton Shulman, *Evening Standard*, 24 July 1969.

8. D. McQuail in J. Tunstall (ed.), *Media Sociology*, Constable, 1970.

9. L. Anderson in T. Maschler (ed.), *Declaration*, MacGibbon & Kee, 1957.

Chapter 2

1. E. M. Forster, *Howards End*, Penguin, 1941, p. 74.

2. G. Radice in B. Lapping and G. Radice (eds.), *More Power to the People*, Longman, 1968.

3. G. Radice, op. cit.

4. H. Thomas (ed.), *The Establishment*, Anthony Blond, 1959.

5. J. Osborne, *Look Back in Anger*, Faber, 1957, p. 20.

6. J. Osborne, in T. Maschler (ed.) *Declaration*, MacGibbon & Kee, 1957, p. 67.

7. A. Jay, *Listener*, 29 July 1971.

8. T. Maschler (ed.), *Declaration*, MacGibbon & Kee, 1957, p. 7.

9. J. Osborne, op. cit., pp. 84–5.

10. R. Williams, *The Long Revolution*, Chatto & Windus, 1961; Penguin, 1965, p. 319.

11. D. Ogilvy, *Confessions of an Advertising Man*, Longman, 1963.

12. G. Allport, 'The psychology of participation' reprinted in D. F. Sullivan (ed.), *Readings in Group Work*, Association Press, 1952.

13. C. Wright Mills, *The Sociological Imagination*, Oxford University Press, 1959; Penguin, 1970, p. 9.

14. G. Radice, op. cit.

Chapter 3

1. R. Williams, *The Long Revolution*, Chatto & Windus, 1961; Penguin, 1965, p. 112.

2. H. Kahn, *The Times*, 9 October 1969.

3. D. Marquand, 'Questions of value', *New Society*, 16 October 1969.

4. Ministry of Housing and Local Government, *People and Planning*, Report of the Committee on Public Participation in Planning, HMSO, 1969.

5. Department of Education and Science, *Youth and Community Work in the 1970s*, HMSO, 1969.

6. E. P. Thompson (ed.), *Warwick University Ltd*, Penguin, 1970.

7. D. Marquand, op. cit.

8. S. Lal and D. Dickson, 'Science and social crisis', *New Scientist*, 28 May 1970.

9. B. Dixon, 'Science and the silent citizen', *New Scientist*, 27 August 1970.

10. S. Lal and D. Dickson, op. cit.

Chapter 4

1. M. McLuhan, *Listener*, 11 June 1969.

2. W. K. R. Richmond, *The Education Industry*, Methuen, 1969.

3. M. McLuhan, *Understanding Media: The Extensions of Man*, Routledge & Kegan Paul, 1964, 358, 344.

4. A. Cockburn and R. Blackburn (eds.), *Student Power*, Penguin, 1969.

5. C. Booker, *The Neophiliacs*, Collins, 1969.

6. G. and D. Cohn-Bendit, *Obsolete Communism: The Left-Wing Alternative*, Deutsch, 1968; Penguin, 1969.

7. A. Cockburn and R. Blackburn, op. cit., pp. 9–10.

8. G. and D. Cohn-Bendit, op. cit., pp. 105.

9. P. F. Lazarsfeld and R. K. Merton, 'Communication, taste and social action', in L. Byron (ed.), *The Communication of Ideas*, Cooper Square, New York, 1948.

10. The research was conducted in 1954–5 and is summarized in W. Belson, *The Impact of Television*, Crosby Lockwood, 1967, pp. 258–94.

11. L. Beaton, *Listener*, 27 August 1970.

12. Milton Shulman, 'The big fix', *Evening Standard*, 8 July 1970.

Chapter 5

1. G. Radice in B. Lapping and G. Radice (eds.), *More Power to the People*, Longman, 1968.

2. A. Etzioni, *The Active Society*, Free Press, 1968.

Chapter 6

1. Independent Television Authority, *Annual Report 1969–70*, HMSO, 1970.

2. British Broadcasting Corporation, *Annual Report and Accounts of the BBC, 1968–9*, HMSO, 1969.

3. Opinion Research Centre, *Sunday Times*, 10 May 1970.

4. Independent Television Authority, *Attitudes to Television*, Opinion Research Centre for ITA, 1970.

5. Sir Robert Fraser, 'The troubles of democracy', ITA Notes no. 16, January 1970.

6. A. Barker and M. Rush, *The Member of Parliament and his Information*, Allen & Unwin, 1970, p. 8. The authors summarized their main findings in *The Times*, 6 July 1970.

7. J. G. Blumler, *Does Mass Political Ignorance Matter?* Editions de l'Institut de Sociologie, Université Libre de Bruxelles, 1971.

8. The Open Group, Social Reform in the Centrifugal Society, *New Society* pamphlet, 1969.

9. C. King, 'The press and television today and tomorrow', *Journal of the Royal Society of Arts*, June 1969, pp. 496–501.

10. W. Schramm, *Mass Media and National Development*, Stanford University Press, 1964, pp. 58–69.

11. R. Day, 'Troubled reflections of a TV journalist', *Encounter*, May 1970.

12. Sir Robert Fraser, op. cit.

13. R. Day, op. cit.

14. W. Schramm, op. cit., pp. 253–71.

Chapter 7

1. W. Cronkite, *Television Quarterly*.

2. R. Frank, 'An anatomy of television news', *Television Quarterly*, USA, winter 1970.

3. Since writing that sentence, the controversy over reporting events in Northern Ireland developed. Even though opinions differed over the reliability of broadcast news on those events, nearly everyone recognized the uniqueness of the problem they created for the media. The main point still stands.

4. C. King, quoted in B. Groombridge, 'Popular culture and personal responsibility: a study on time', National Union of Teachers, 1961.

5. 'Television and the 1970 election', *Journal of the Society of Film and Television Arts*, no. 40, summer 1970.

6. Robin Day, for example, despite the misgivings of his *Encounter* article, thought 'this country can be pretty proud of

the way television covered this election'. He itemized several respects in which he considered that there was 'better and freer coverage' on this occasion than on the other three general elections handled by television. Sir Geoffrey Cox, Chairman of ITN, was also impressed by television's advances. Many contributors felt that the Representation of the People Act and the strict way in which it was interpreted was a more important cause of inadequacy than television itself.

7. J. Trenaman and D. McQuail, *Television and the Political Image*, Methuen, 1961; J. G. Blumler and D. McQuail, *Television in Politics: Its Uses and Influence*, Faber, 1968; J. G. Blumler, 'The political effects of television', in J. D. Halloran (ed.), *The Effects of Television*, Panther, 1970.

8. D. Potter, *The Times*, 5 July 1969.

9. R. Williams, 'There's always the sport', *Listener*, 16 April 1970.

10. A. Wedgwood Benn, speech in Bristol, 18 October 1968.

11. J. Whale, *Listener*, 15 October 1970.

12. Sir Robert Fraser, 'The troubles of democracy', ITA Notes no. 16, January 1970.

13. G. Stuttard, 'In Place of Strife', *Adult Education*, vol. 42, no. 1, May 1969, pp. 66–7.

14. R. Day, 'Troubled reflections of a TV journalist', *Encounter*, May 1970.

15. L. Beaton, *Listener*, 27 August 1970.

16. Lord Windlesham, *Television and Public Opinion*, Cape, 1966.

17. See the important case study of this process, J. D. Halloran, *et al.*, *Demonstrations and Communications*, Penguin, 1970.

Chapter 8

1. *Public Opinion Quarterly*, 1952.

2. B. Berelson, 'Democratic theory and public opinion' *Public Opinion Quarterly*, vol, 16, no. 3.

3. W. Belson, *The Impact of Television*, Crosby Lockwood, 1967.

4. H. Behrend, H. Lynch and J. Davies, 'A national survey of attitudes to inflation and incomes policy', Occasional Papers in

Social and Economic Administration, no. 7, Edutext Publications, 1966.

5. D. Butler and D. Stokes, *Political Change in Britain*, Macmillan, 1969.

6. J. P. Robinson, *Public Information about World Affairs*, University of Michigan, 1967.

7. C. King, 'The press and television today and tomorrow', *Journal of the Royal Society of Arts*, June 1969.

8. J. G. Blumler, *Does Mass Political Ignorance Matter?* Editions de l'Institut de Sociologie, Université Libre de Bruxelles, 1971.

9. J. G. Blumler in J. D. Halloran (ed.), *The Effects of Television*, Panther, 1970;

10. J. Trenaman, *Communication and Comprehension*, Longman, 1967.

11. R. Cutforth, *Listener*, 4 March 1971.

12. P. Elliott in J. Tunstall (ed.), *Media Sociology*, Constable, 1970.

13. C. King, op. cit.

14. R. Frank, 'An anatomy of television news', *Television Quarterly*, USA, winter 1970.

Chapter 9

1. B. Emmett, 'Gratifications research in broadcasting', *Public Opinion Quarterly*, winter 1968–9.

2. K. Nordenstreng, 'Comments on gratifications research in broadcasting', *Public Opinion Quarterly*, spring 1970.

3. Committee on Broadcasting, *1960 Report*, HMSO, 1960, p. 12.

4. *Guardian*, November 1970.

5. *TV Times*, 3 September 1971.

6. J. Scupham, *Broadcasting and the Community*, Watts, 1962.

7. R. Frank, 'An anatomy of television news', *Television Quarterly*, USA, winter 1970.

8. Quoted in J. Scupham, op. cit.

9. R. Kavanova, 'Mass media man', *Czechoslovak Life*, February 1967.

10. M. Gaļuska, 'Are we well informed?', *Czechoslovak Life*, February 1967.

Chapter 10

1. C. Hannam, P. Smyth and N. Stephenson, *Young Teachers and Reluctant Learners*, Penguin, 1971.

2. A. Wedgwood Benn, *The New Politics: A Socialist Reconnaisance*, Fabian Tract 402, 1970.

3. A. Wedgwood Benn, *Sunday Mirror*, 2 May 1971.

4. Mary Holland, *Observer*, 9 May 1971.

5. Milton Shulman, *Evening Standard*, 6 May 1971.

6. W. Schramm, 'The future of educational radio and television', Japan Prize Lecture, NHK, Tokyo, 1970.

7. On 2 December 1971 several papers reported that a similar scheme, initiated by Peter Fairley, science editor of ITN, was being prepared when the 1970 General Election intervened. It is characteristic of the British scene that the project has been called 'Friday night is voting night' and that the *Guardian* called it 'a political version of Hughie Green's *Opportunity Knocks*'.

8. J. King, *Daily Sketch*, 17 March 1971.

9. P. Purser, *Sunday Telegraph*, 14 March 1971.

10. See, for example, Calouste Gulbenkian Foundation, *Community Work and Social Change: A Report on Training*, Longman, 1968: T. R. Batten, *Communities and their Development*, Oxford University Press, 1957.

11. See references for chapter 7, note 7.

12. T. Gould, Profile: Ray Gosling, *Listener*, 17 July 1969.

13. R. Luce, 'Switching on ideas', *What?*, vol. 2, no. 2, 1970, p. 30.

14. B. Groombridge 'Adult education: the formative phase', in G. Moir (ed.), *Teaching and Television*, Pergamon, 1967, p. 89

15. F. Bayliss, Address to the Annual Conference of the National Institute of Adult Education, *Adult Education*, vol. 40, no. 4, 1967, p. 212.

Chapter 11

1. M. Knowles, *The Adult Education Movement in the United States*, Holt, Rinehart & Winston, 1962, p. 9.

2. A somewhat fuller account of 'The Whole Town's Talking' (from which the quotations above are taken) is given in C. A. Siepmann, *Television and Education in the United States*, UNESCO, 1952, pp. 65–9. I began to speculate about its possible significance for us in an article 'Television and democracy', *Journal of Education*, 1957, pp. 106–10.

3. Council of Europe, *New Types of Out-of-School Education*, Strasbourg, 1968, pp. 30–56.

4. J. Keating, 'Collaborating for social development', a paper prepared for a private conference organized by Devon Local Education Authority and Independent Television Authority, 1970.

5. E. I. Johnson, *The Community Education Project*, a four-year report 1952–6, San Bernardino Valley College, p. 3.

6. My account draws heavily on E. I. Johnson, *Metroplex Assembly: An Experiment in Community Education*, Center for the Study of Liberal Education for Adults, Boston University, Mass, 1965.

7. O. T. Magnuson, 'Improving public debate with television and social organization', *Educational Broadcasting Review*, April 1970, pp. 35–8.

8. H. Mendelsohn, 'What to say to whom in social amelioration programming', *Educational Broadcasting Review*, December 1969, pp. 19–26.

9. E. Johnson, op. cit., 1965, p. 11.

10. E. Johnson, op. cit., 1952–6, p. 63.

11. Town Meeting, Inc. and the American Institute of Planners, *Communication to Build the Future Environment* (mimeo), 1968.

12. E. Johnson, op. cit., 1965.

13. H. Mendelsohn, op. cit.

14. E. Johnson, op. cit., 1965, pp. 32–7.

15. J. Keating, op. cit.

16. E. Johnson, op. cit., 1965, p. 6.

17. Lord Kennett, *Controlling our Environment*, Fabian Research Series no. 283, 1970, p. 10.

18. Mary Holland, *Observer*, 14 March 1971.

Chapter 12

1. 'Liverpool 8', *Listener*, 22 July 1971.

2. Marghanita Laski, *Listener*, 18 March 1971.

3. 'The Liverpool story', *Where?*, February 1971.

4. K. Jones, 'Community television', *Adult Education*, March 1965.

5. G. Woodside, *Community Interests in Video Technology*, National Educational Closed Circuit Television Bulletin no. 5.

6. *Challenge for Change* is more than the name of a publication. It is a remarkable programme of community development projects, using film and VTR as stimili, in which the National Film Board cooperates with departments and agencies of the Government of Canada. See George C. Stoney, 'The mirror machine', *Sight and Sound*, January 1972.

Index

Abingdon gas holder, 60
Agnew, Spiro, 105, 106
Aldermaston marches, 35–6
Allport, Gordon, W., 41–4
Anteroom effect, 112

BBC, 77, 136
  Charter, 14, 19, 87, 144, 172
  and ITV, 135–6, 224–5
Bank of Ideas (Norway), 178
Bayliss, Fred, 185
Beaton, Leonard, 73–4, 119–20
Belson, William, 73, 153
Benn, Anthony Wedgwood, 15,
    112, 161–3
Berelson, Bernard, 126
Biafra, 106, 119–20
Blumler, Jay, 93
Bow Group, 34
British Society for Social
    Responsibility in Science, 65–6
Broadcasting
  Britain's egalitarian policy,
    221–2
  goals enlargement, 141–6
  neutrality issue, 171–4
  proposed charter, 145, 149–50
Byers, Lord, 109–10

Campaign, 177
Cancion de la Raza, 193, 194,
    205–6
Cathy Come Home, 176
Gause for Concern, 176

Challenge for Change (Canada),
    233
'Citizen Sam', 41–4
Cockburn, Alexander, 71
Cohn-Bendit, Daniel, 71, 72
Common Market debate, 167
Communication, 116, 196
  US crisis, 197–9
  and participation, 66, 81–3
Community action, 96, 222
Community development, 80
  projects, 61, 80
  use of media, 228–32
  see also Town meetings
Community workers, 174, 206–8
Consumer movement, 35–40
Current affairs programmes,
    73–4, 146–57, 220
Cutforth, René, 133
Czechoslovakia, 51, 87, 106, 155,
    176

Day, Robin, 99, 100, 102, 119, 167
Decision-making process, 45–7,
    57–8
Democracy
  broadcasting's responsibility to,
    145, 175, 222, 240–41
  participatory and representative,
    17, 27–30, 36–40, 48–9, 56
Denmark, 96, 130–31
Department of Education and
    Science, 92–3
Dickson, David, 65, 66

Education, 39–40, 92–3, 205, 231
  adult, 80–81, 236–8
  liberal, 21–6
  participatory programmes,
    179–86, 223–4
  levels of and programme
    planning, 131, 153, 238–9
  television's role, 20, 21–6
Educational technology, 178–9,
  236
Edwards, Donald, 151
Efficiency and participation, 61–6
Eire, 191–2, 211
Elliott, Philip, 133–4
Emmett, Brian, 142–3, 144
Experts in programme planning,
  205–6, 206–7

Fools Group Theatre, 216
Forster, E. M., 28
France, 98, 191, 211
Frank, Reuven, 105, 106, 137,
  150
Fraser, Sir Robert, 19–20, 89–90,
  99–100, 116–17
Free for All, 169
Frost, David, 70, 170

Galuška, Miroslav, 156
General Election, 109–11
Germany, 166–7
Goldberg panel, 150–51
Golborne Social Rights
  Committee, 80, 96
Government, 49–50
  changes in machinery of, 63–5
  moves towards participation,
    53–61, 92
  reticence, 91–6

Heading for Change, 179, 181–3

Independent Television
  news coverage, 88
  a public-service system, 136
  and BBC, 224–5
In Place of Strife, 118
Individual versus society, 41–7
Information
  glut, 129–32, 217–18
  see also News reporting
Interviews, 102, 112, 113

Jay, Antony, 32
Johnson, Eugene, 193, 204, 206

Kahn, Hermann, 51–2
Keating, Justin, 192, 211
Kefauver hearings, 124–5
King, Cecil, 108, 128, 134–5
King, John, 169, 170

Lal, Shiraji, 65, 66
Laski, Marghanita, 227–8
Living and Growing, 179, 180–81
Local authorities, 59–60, 79–80
Local radio, 221, 225–30

McLuhan, Marshall, 67–8,
  69–70
Marquand, David, 55, 64
Metroplex Assembly, 193–7,
  209–13
Metropolitan District Plan,
  200–204
Mills, C. Wright, 44, 45
Ministry of Social Security,
  60–61, 63

National Suggestions Centre,
  177, 178
National Viewers and Listeners
  Association, 13
Neutrality in broadcasting, 171–4

'New Immigrants, The', 206–7
News at Ten, 109, 136
News reporting, 88, 89, 98,
  105–7, 135
  background needs, 149–51
  body to assess, 102–3
  educative approach, 146–57
  imbalance and distortion, 97–8,
    114, 115–16, 121–3, 146–8,
    151–2, 153
Newspapers, 25, 89, 134–5
  in participatory programming,
    203–4, 232–3
Nordensteng, Kaarle, 142
Northern Ireland, 117–18

On Site, 176–7
Open University, 182, 236
Osborne, John, 35, 46

Palmstierna, Hans, 213, 214,
  215
Participation, 41–4, 51, 55, 79–81
  Benn's plea for, 161–3
  and efficiency, 61–6
  official backing, 53–61
  in science policy, 65–6
Participatory programming,
  171–5, 209–11, 219, 240
  British precursors, 174–86
  educational, 223–4
  feasibility, 222–3, 235–41
  local radio in, 225–30
  media and agencies, 230–35
  television resources, 221–5
  USA, 187–212
  West German experiment,
    166–7
Pelikán, Jiří, 155
People and Planning, 54, 56
Pilkington Committee, 144
Pollution, 52, 166, 212–14,
  217–18

Pressure groups, 13–14, 27–30,
  35–40, 80, 94–5
  in local government, 79–80
  television time, 162–5
Programme planning, 181, 182
  definition, 205–9
  Ombudsman-type, 176–7
  for social change, 177–80
Public, 95
  ignorance, 123–4, 126–8, 130

Rachmanism, 120, 149, 176
Radice, G., 45–6, 46–7, 80
Radio, 88, 211, 225–30
Radio Merseyside, 226, 228–30
Representing the Union, 179,
  183–4, 223
Richmond, Kenneth, 68–9
Rubin, Jerry, 70
Russell Committee, 81, 238

San Bernardino Valley Project,
  193, 196
Schramm, Wilbur, 97–8, 102–3
Science policy, 65–6, 218
Scupham, John, 149–50
Sesame Street, 136, 205
Shelter, 40, 149, 176
Shulman, Milton, 18, 21–2, 74–6,
  128, 141
Skeffington Report, 54, 56, 58–9,
  60, 90
Society, individual versus, 41–7
Soviet Union, 76, 98, 103
Sparkbrook Association, 59
Speech, accents, 24
Sport, 74–6, 111–12, 141
Suffragettes, 27–8
Surveys, 73, 88–9, 111, 124–5,
  126–7, 153
  and programme planning,
    205–6, 206–7
Sweden, 52, 62, 96, 212–18

Télé Promotion Rurale, 191
Telefís Feirme, 191–2
Telephone, in participatory
 programmes, 210, 211
Television, 118–19, 121–2
 audience sophistication, 154–6
 cable, 165, 233–4
 closed-circuit, 230–31
 criticisms, 70–73, 76
 editing for impact, 107, 132–7,
  195
 as information provider, 18–20,
  87–91, 103–4, 123–4, 130–31
 as a liberal educator, 21–6
 news coverage, 73–4, 97–8,
  99–100, 105–7, 115–16, 119–20
 purpose, 13–18
 show-business values, 108–13,
  136–7
Television Act, 14, 19, 77, 87,
 136, 172
Television Viewers' Council,
 231
'Town Meeting', 194, 197, 210
Town meetings, 188–9, 193–9
Trade Unions, 162, 163–4,
 183–4

United States, 76, 98, 99, 105–7,
 151–2
 participatory programming,
  188, 193–212

Video-tape, 230, 231–2
Viewing post concept, 203

Warwick University, 62
Weeley Pop Festival, 147–8
Welsh Language Society, 27–8
Westland helicopter, 148–9
Whale, John, 115–16, 118, 146
What?, Spot, 177–8
Whole Town's Talking, The,
 189–91
Williams, Raymond, 15, 36, 49,
 112, 113
Windlesham, Lord, 120, 121
Workers' Educational
 Association, 236, 237, 239
World Cup, 74–6

*Youth and Community Work in
 the 1970s*, 54, 56–8
Yugoslavia, 51